MAKING SENSE OF
SOCIAL THEORY

MAKING SENSE OF SOCIAL THEORY

A Practical Introduction

Second Edition

Charles H. Powers

ROWMAN & LITTLEFIELD PUBLISHERS, INC.

Lanham • Boulder • New York • Toronto • Plymouth, UK

Published by Rowman & Littlefield Publishers, Inc.
A wholly owned subsidiary of The Rowman & Littlefield Publishing Group, Inc.
4501 Forbes Boulevard, Suite 200, Lanham, Maryland 20706
http://www.rowmanlittlefield.com

Estover Road, Plymouth PL6 7PY, United Kingdom

British Library Cataloguing in Publication Information Available

Library of Congress Cataloging-in-Publication Data
Powers, Charles H.
    Making sense of social theory : a practical introduction / Charles H. Powers. — 2nd ed.
    p. cm.
    Includes index.
    ISBN 978-1-4422-0118-7 (hardcover : alk. paper) — ISBN 978-1-4422-0119-4 (pbk. : alk. paper) — ISBN 978-1-4422-0120-0 (electronic)
    1. Sociology—History. 2. Sociology—Philosophy. 3. Schools of sociology. I. Title.
    HM435.P69 2010
    301.01—dc22
                                                                            2009029809

∞ ™ The paper used in this publication meets the minimum requirements of American National Standard for Information Sciences—Permanence of Paper for Printed Library Materials, ANSI/NISO Z39.48-1992.

Printed in the United States of America

To Catlin and Bonnie,
who continue to give me
as much love and understanding
as a father could hope for,
and who have grown into caring
adults I am very proud of

Contents

Preface

MAKING SENSE OF SOCIAL THEORY IS WRITTEN for people who utilize sociological knowledge in their daily work and for students. By design, it is short, clear, and manageable. For this reason, the book should be a useful resource for people who deal with organizational challenges in their work and should raise the level of discourse among students receiving their first concentrated exposure to theory in the social sciences. When used by students, *Making Sense of Social Theory* elevates mastery over and interest in material many tend to assume will be confusing and removed from real experience. People tend to finish this book with an enhanced awareness of themselves as social science professionals having something to offer, precisely because of (not in spite of) being aware of key social science discoveries expressed as theoretical axioms and principles.

Making Sense of Social Theory is divided into five parts. Part I consists of chapters explaining the role of theory in a science like sociology. Part II reviews some origins of interest in social science theory and basic lessons for constructing social science theory having real-world relevance. Part III introduces some of the most enduring social science insights pioneered by four of the founders of the sociological tradition. Part IV introduces four of the most prominent theoretical perspectives that developed once sociology gained momentum in the middle of the twentieth century. Part V recaps sociological insights and reflects on the present state and future of development of contemporary sociological theory.

Most books that try to offer a survey of social science theory attempt to be encyclopedic in coverage. Those books approach the challenge of offering a survey by covering many of the nuances in that literature. *Making Sense of Social Theory* is different, and intentionally so. This book's defining feature is that its approach to surveying the field is to consolidate many of the most fundamental insights of sociology into a coherent package, while conveying to students what it means to be a social scientist and how social science understanding has improved over time. When used by students, *Making Sense of Social Theory* provides a basic introduction to *the use* of theory in sociology as a social *science* discipline. The aim is to help readers become better sociologists (a) by cultivating an active appreciation for sociology's promise as a science; (b) by focusing self-consciously on a manageable set of useful axioms and clear, robust, and powerful explanatory principles; and (c) by acquiring a conceptual map for understanding the historical development of the discipline.

Making Sense of Social Theory is written with a different sense of mission than standard *surveys* of sociological theory. Books offering a survey typically try to maximize the range of coverage. In contrast, *Making Sense of Social Theory* highlights only the most fundamental points, expressing those points as clearly as possible in order to facilitate appreciation and application of them. Readers should finish this book with a reasonably well-integrated and coherent sense of sociological theory as a whole, and then be well equipped to understand and appreciate other theoretical works they might encounter. *Making Sense of Social Theory* puts into practice the view that elegance in science is found in simplicity. Keeping the focus on those theoretical insights that are most important, the book aims to help readers acquire a skeletal framework with its most obvious features in plain view.

Acknowledgments

I AM INDEBTED TO THE MANY SOCIOLOGICAL THEORISTS I have had the benefit of interacting with over the years. Chief among them are Jonathan Turner, Jerald Hage, Robert Dubin, Ralph Turner, Randall Collins, Harry Johnson, and Harold Garfinkel. Another kind of intellectual debt is owed to people who have helped me work out the themes and issues covered in this book. In this regard, I am indebted to many people with whom I have discussed aspects of social science theory or strategies for conveying complex ideas in understandable ways. These people include Marilyn Fernandez, Ray Maghroori, Joan Powers, Sandra Chiaramonte, Tony Waters, Karen McGovern, Donald Powers, Witold Krassowski, Suzanne Szabo, Steven Fedder, Philip "Boo" Riley, Bill Prior, Juergen Backhaus, Gerrit Meijer, Demetra Kalogrides, Mitch Allen, Bill Hunter, Everlee Jones, Edward O'Boyle, William Corsaro, Laura Nichols, Andrew Sofranko, Susan Rigdon, Nancy Brennan, Gloria Hofer, Edward Clarke, and Craig Rusch, to name just a few. My special thanks also go to the people at Rowman & Littlefield who were involved in production and marketing of this second edition of *Making Sense of Social Theory*, particularly Alan McClare, Reid Hester, Susan McEachern, Elizabeth Yellen, Janice Braunstein, and Evan Wiig. Special acknowledgments also go to Terrell Hayes, Robert Heasley, and Stephen McNamee for reviewer comments that have been a great help. But since I have had the good fortune of support and encouragement from many talented people, the faults remaining in this manuscript are solely my responsibility.

PART I

UNDERSTANDING
WHAT THEORY IS ABOUT

PART I OFFERS AN INTELLECTUAL FRAMEWORK for understanding sociology as a social science. For that reason, part I should help readers better appreciate the full importance of content presented in the remainder of the book.

Chapter 1 contains more conceptual nuances than any other chapter in the book, and the three chapters of part I alert readers about the kinds of things to look for when reading the rest of the book. Time spent trying to really understand the first three chapters will be time well spent. Part I explains the role of theory in science.

Part II complements part I by helping to illustrate that theory can and should be used in a social science in much the same way that theory is used in the other sciences. This is important to cover early rather than late in the book, so that readers will be thinking about the theory content of later chapters within the context of this book's special approach to the subject matter.

Part III and part IV cover standard theory content but follow a distinctive approach by formally stating a set of pivotal axioms and principles so that theoretical insight is more readily available for us to test or use. Part III introduces four of the giants of sociological theory, focusing on the works of Émile Durkheim, Karl Marx, Max Weber, and George Herbert Mead. Part IV offers readers a conceptual grasp of four of the theoretical frameworks that have developed in sociology: structural functionalism, conflict theory, symbolic interaction, and exchange theory. While this same list or a similar list of people and perspectives is covered in other books on sociological theory, the approach used in this book is distinctive. Part V reviews the way this book explicitly and self-consciously employs a science approach, identifying underlying assumptions and predictive insights that can be used to understand real events.

Making Sense of Social Theory focuses attention on insights that (a) have defined meaning (are unambiguous), (b) are robust (apply in a variety of different situations), and (c) are powerful (explain big differences in things that are meaningful). These three criteria describe what is most often meant by good theory in a true science. Scientists seek to work toward theoretical frameworks that are unambiguous in the sense of having common meaning to the different people using them, are sufficiently generic to have broad application, and enable us to make appreciable improvements in predictions about things that matter.

Perhaps more than any other book available on sociological theory, this one adopts a practical and nonpolemic approach to sociology as a science. The books that come closest, such as Jonathan H. Turner's excellent work *The Structure of Sociological Theory*, are different in their concern for detail. More detailed books place high value (perhaps the highest value) on the thoroughness of their coverage of theory content. The less detail-oriented strategy followed in this book places greatest value on conveying a basic understanding of what social science really means and what the fundamental connection between theory and research must be when sociology is practiced as a science.[1] People reading this book should be able to easily understand how to do theory and use theory connected to the social science research enterprise.

While explicitly about sociological theory, this book has what many readers will appreciate as a decidedly interdisciplinary flavor. There is good reason for this. Sociology did not develop in a sealed intellectual vacuum. Rather, many of the most important sociological theorists actually began in or were heavily influenced by other academic disciplines. Economics, anthropology, and psychology are foremost among those disciplines. And most of the other social science and related disciplines have been influenced in significant ways by sociology, and have adopted useful theoretical insights from sociology. These disciplines include anthropology, criminology, management, ethnic and women's studies, economics, urban and regional planning, gerontology, marketing, counseling psychology, and educational administration.

Making Sense of Social Theory invites readers to actually use theory. I have learned over the years that people have a better grasp of theory and do better science when using the science vision communicated in this book. Among other things, this means designing research in order to improve on current understanding rather than to validate what we already believe, and it means using theoretical knowledge from the social sciences when rising to challenges in our jobs and our communities.

Making Sense of Social Theory tries to (a) reduce coverage of material to insights that are held by many, (b) present insights in a reasonably clear way in order to reduce fear and frustration, and (c) devote some time to application so that readers can see the relevance of theory to the real world. This approach involves *focusing on what is most important* and requires asking readers to *apply ideas to the real world as they experience it.*

1

Becoming a Better Social Scientist

I WOULD LIKE TO BEGIN ON A PERSONAL NOTE to those readers who happen to be students taking their first theory course in a social science. Over time, my students have taught me two important lessons about teaching theory. The first lesson is that learning theory is work. Students have to read and think about the material and apply the material in order for the course to be successful. No one can do these things for you. It is incumbent on you as a reader to do those things for yourself. The second lesson I have learned is that if there is too much theory material covered at one time, or if the material is too confusing, many students will shut down before they really give themselves a chance to master the subject. This is a tragedy anytime, but especially in a social science theory course. Learning theory is a necessary step in developing an accurate and coherent understanding of any discipline. With that in mind, *Making Sense of Social Theory* is written as a first exposure to theory. It is short and clear. There is no reason this book should turn off any student who has a reasonable degree of commitment to study. Carefully reading this text should be well worth the investment of time and effort for anyone wanting a coherent introduction to sociological theory, or to theory in the social sciences more generally.

This book codifies assumptions social scientists find useful and explanatory insights social scientists keep returning to. By codifying these key ideas, *Making Sense of Social Theory* provides readers with a theory tool kit worth retaining for future reference. Although I do not attempt to cover everything one might find in more encyclopedic theory books, *Making Sense of Social Theory* explicitly identifies thirty-three different predictive social science insights formalized as axioms and principles.

Making Sense of Social Theory focuses on those insights sociologists and people working in the allied social sciences can be most confident about. These are *robust* insights, easily applied to a wide range of settings and situations. They include some of our most powerful and most enduring social science discoveries. Although care has been taken to write with some clarity and precision, the material is by nature difficult. The first chapter in particular introduces a number of distinctions that will be critical later in the book. A careful reading of the first chapter will be helpful.

Sociology as a Science

Sociology is considered a social science. Being a *science* means that there is a *commitment to following a culture of evidence in trying to develop and test progressively better understandings of, and better explanations for, what we can observe or discover about the real world.* A body of work that fails to use evidence about the real world in order to develop and test explanatory frameworks may be interesting. It may be important. It may be worthwhile. But it is not "science" in any accurate sense of the term.

The data social scientists use is often *qualitative,* allowing for carefully detailed description of a case or a small number of cases. Qualitative investigation is usually recommended when we feel we may be able to better understand social dynamics by carefully examining particular cases that are unusual in the sense that important factors or processes which are normally obscured from view can be brought into sharp and clarifying focus. (Qualitative studies thus often play a crucial role in preliminary research or in the search for new hypotheses about sociological process.)

At other times our studies are *quantitative* in the sense that the variable degree to which a comparatively large number of different cases possesses a set of traits can be measured and compared with some confidence. Quantitative data are essential when determining how widespread phenomena are, and when trying to establish how consistent and how strong patterns of relationships may be among a set of variables.

Whether quantitative or qualitative data are used, it is important to employ data carefully with a clear sense of scientific purpose. A scientist does not set out with the goal of proving that a theory is correct. Rather, the purpose of research is usually to analyze information that will enable us to more accurately distinguish between (a) kinds of phenomena or sets of events our theoretical insights help us to explain, and (b) kinds of phenomena or sets of events for which our theoretical insights seem inaccurate or incomplete. This is an important point. The entire idea behind science is to *make progress by improving our body of theoretical insights over time.* Far from assuming that existing knowledge claims are accurate, real science proceeds on the assumption that existing knowledge claims are all provisional and somewhat flawed. It is in the nature of good science that any claim to theoretical understanding invites challenges and modification. The goal is always the articulation of better, clearer, more penetrating, more revealing insight. Thus, scientists realize that science does not possess real and complete truth. Our theoretical insights merely convey the closest formulation we are currently able to devise in our effort to explain what we can observe about the world around us. That is what science is.

It is important to be aware of the special role of theory in a research science like sociology. To the extent that an academic discipline such as sociology is practiced as a real science, *theory occupies a special place* for three important reasons. First, theory is what captures what scientists currently know or suspect about the dynamics making the world work as it does. In other words, good theory captures our best present understanding. When formally stated, theory makes it clear what we think we know that extends *beyond the realm of whatever was traditionally understood as "common sense" that was shared by everyone.* Second, whether explicitly or only implicitly, good theory identifies those questions that are most important for people in a discipline to try to answer next. Third, improvement in theory, refinement of our theoretical insights so that they better comport with the world as we observe it, is the primary way progress is judged in a science. When theory is changing, we know that people are moving away from old modes of understanding toward new ones. That movement is scientific to the degree that it is governed by theoretically informed hypothesis testing and careful collection and analysis of data.

An example from the physical sciences will illustrate what we mean by science moving forward. Most people now take plate tectonics for granted, as if this understanding of geology has always been obvious. But it was anything but obvious until a few decades ago. The very thought that entire continents might be sliding around, somewhat like blocks of ice on a smooth surface, was thought of as quite ludicrous, rationally unthinkable, and childish during the first half of the twentieth century. But over time, cumulative research produced a preponderance of evidence to support the theory that plates of the earth's mantle are pushed up and out in some places (e.g., Mariana Trench) and pushed under adjacent plates in other places (e.g., Tibetan plateau). Now scientists and even the general public take the idea of plate tectonics for granted.

Plate tectonics marks an important contribution to scientific understanding. The dynamics involved (e.g., subduction) allow us to understand important changes (i.e., they have theoretical *power*). This illustrates the important point that theory is not restricted to staying with understandings that have long been "self-evident" or seem to have enjoyed confirmation by previous scholarship. It is appropriate that efforts at theory building also have a speculative dimension. In a science, theory is supposed to be out ahead of research, with research "catching up" only as fast as (a) research scientists can find better ways of testing theoretical ideas and then (b) get around to testing those ideas in a wide range of settings and under a variety of different circumstances. Thus, research does more than test theoretical ideas. Research provides data making it possible to modify and improve theoretical ideas. A primary way research does this is by establishing *boundary conditions* specifying the circumstances under which various theoretical dynamics seem to be at work.

It takes some effort to appreciate sociology and the other social science fields as sciences. To do so, it may be useful to remember that a lot of people (especially in the United States) discount the social sciences somewhat because they tend to take sociological discoveries for granted, as if those discoveries were of things that had always been known. But the truth is that before sociology, people thought almost everything about society and individual behavior was either (1) God given (e.g., what people thought of royal prerogatives in some societies), and/or (2) dictated by human nature or family genetics (e.g., the concept of criminality reflecting "bad blood").

We can take some consolation in knowing that the only reason anyone could possible say sociology (or for that matter any of the other social sciences) is just "common sense" is that many of sociology's great discoveries have proven so illuminating and so useful that they have gained widespread acceptance. Most people have therefore forgotten where the discoveries came from. Consider the concept of *self-fulfilling prophecy*. This sounds centuries old. Indeed, it sounds biblical. But sociologist Robert K. Merton is the person who coined this particular phrase.[1] As soon as Merton coined the term, it found its way immediately into common use because the concept is clear (unambiguous in its meaning), robust (can be applied in many different settings), and powerful (explains a lot). Merton also initially developed the concepts of *role model* and *focus group*, and he was just one sociologist. William H. Whyte developed the concept of *groupthink* (the propensity of people to uncritically adopt and support prevailing viewpoints and judgments), and the list could go on. Every time we recognize someone using a focus group, or employing a role model, or discussing what we can recognize as a self-fulfilling prophecy, or invoking what we understand as the concept of groupthink, we can take a moment to reflect. These are instances in which people have the insights they do because some sociologist had a revelation that was shared with the public for the common good.

Sociology has given the social sciences a lot of good theory in the form of practical assumptions and explanatory principles that are clear, robust, and powerful. All three qualities are important in scientific theory. *Clarity*, when present, makes it possible for scientists to spend more time discussing whether theoretical ideas are instructive than in arguing about what the ideas mean. *Robust* theoretical insights are ones that turn out to apply under many different sets of circumstances and conditions. Theoretical explanations can be said to be *powerful* when they capture essentials so well and help us to account for so much variation that their importance is easily detectable (even if we have only a small number of cases to look at) and their practical significance is readily apparent.

What Do Sociology's Explanatory Insights Cover?

As is the case in any field, sociological attention is closely (and properly) riveted to the study of certain kinds of phenomena. Sociology is distinctive in the attention it pays to what lies *between* people, that is, to what *links* individuals with others in the social world. Sociological study must thus necessarily extend beyond consideration of individuals in isolation. In focusing on the social world, sociologists consider different kinds of linkage among people: (a) direct interpersonal attachments, (b) shared beliefs, and (c) interconnecting linkages among people that are systemic in nature, such as manifestations of government regulation.

As practitioners of a science, sociologists aim for good descriptions of these things and then seek to explain variations between cases. We also want to know about the consequences of any differences that emerge and we seek to understand how to promote constructive change. This suggests a definition for scientific sociology based on what we try to do. *Scientific sociology can be characterized as effort to develop (1) more accurate descriptions, (2) more compelling awareness of causes, (3) more thorough understanding of consequences, and (4) more revealing theoretical insights relating to the nature of and changes in (a) direct interpersonal attachments, (b) shared beliefs, and (c) interconnections among people that are systemic in nature.*

Like every other science, sociology is based on commitment to theoretically grounded empirical research aimed at producing better descriptions of reality, more realistic explanations of variation between cases (or within cases over time), more revealing understanding of ramifications and consequences, and more useful ways to intervene in order to bring about desired change. But sociology is distinctive in its subject matter and conceptual approach. The core concern is with what connects people (that is, on what is social). This clearly distinguishes sociology from psychology. Distinction from the other social sciences is perhaps less obvious, but nevertheless real. Sociologists try to develop a whole picture of society, in contrast to more compartmentalized fields like economics or criminology. Sociologists believe that their more-encompassing conceptual approach ultimately leads to a fuller and more realistic understanding.

As a matter of more or less historical accident, sociology has on the whole been less descriptive but more concerned with developing and testing explanatory theories than has its sister discipline, anthropology. However, this does nothing to negate the fact that the scientific and theoretical goals of sociology and anthropology are viewed by many as indistinguishable. The disciplines' common scientific and theoretical goals are the better understanding of processes through which patterns of social interaction and social organization (interpersonal attachments, shared beliefs, systemic linkages) are created, shaped, maintained, and changed.

All this goes to explain one of the reasons Auguste Comte, who is thought of by most people as having been the founder of sociology, was correct in calling this discipline the "queen" science. It is arguably the most integrative of all the sciences, and certainly the most integrative of the social sciences. It is in many ways the most challenging of the sciences, dealing as it does with variables that can be difficult to conceptually disentangle, operationally measure, or isolate in a laboratory.

It is important to reiterate and always keep in mind the broad goals of sociology as a social science. Our social scientific goals are (1) more accurate description of sociological phenomena, including (a) patterns of interpersonal attachments, (b) shared beliefs, and (c) systemic interconnections. And we seek (2) better explanation of variability in those patterns, (3) more accurate anticipation of consequences resulting from those patterns, and (4) development of theoretical insights to guide policies and shape programs that will produce better outcomes, often by taking account of and changing (a) direct interpersonal attachments, (b) shared beliefs, and (c) interconnections among people that are systemic in nature. These are the goals that make sociology a genuine science.

Specific Goals of This Book

Theory goals have to be ambitious because theory drives science. Indeed, improving explanatory theory is the ultimate purpose of science as an enterprise. Science, by its nature, sets the ambitious goal of developing more informative theory so that we can better understand, anticipate, and react to events.

Making Sense of Social Theory imposes two important expectations on readers: acquiring a workable understanding of the nature of the scientific enterprise and trying to apply some of sociology's clearest, most robust, and most powerful theoretical insights. *Making Sense of Social Theory* translates a number of social science insights into thirty-three formally stated theoretical axioms and principles (twelve axioms and twenty-one principles). The distinction between axioms and principles is core to the material to be covered.

Axioms are *assumptions* scientists sometimes find it useful to make when trying to understand the nature of the world on a conceptual level. Importantly, axioms do not have to be thought of as universally true. The fact is that theorists often make assumptions they know are overstated. Nevertheless, making axiomatic assumptions can be useful.

Axiomatic assumptions provide an analytical framework for looking at phenomena we are trying to understand. Allowing ourselves to be guided for a time by one set of axiomatic assumptions makes it easier to see things we might otherwise miss. For example, although it is simply not true that people always act out of self-interest, momentarily assuming self-interest on the part of everyone in a setting provides an analytical framework, thus making it easier to be alert to particular kinds of behaviors, beliefs, and regularities that, if present, we would certainly want to take into account. We can then relax that set of axiomatic assumptions and adopt another for a period of time, employing it as an analytical aid in looking for other factors we would also like to be alert to, in the event that those factors might be present in the setting we are studying. Momentarily adopting one set of assumptions as an analytical tool for looking for certain kinds of things, and then adopting a different set of assumptions in order to look for other things, helps social scientists develop a fuller, richer, more accurate, more penetrating understanding of the world.

Even if we know an axiom is imperfect, explicitly stating an axiom can help us in our efforts to better understand a particular setting or phenomenon. Also, if we make an axiomatic assumption explicit, it is easier to design our research projects in ways that allow us more accurately to identify boundary conditions outside of which the utility of the axiom seems doubtful.

Part of developing a coherent understanding of sociological theory is learning to identify the most common axiomatic assumptions social scientists make, and cultivating the habit of keeping them explicitly in mind if they are useful. Twelve such axioms will be discussed in *Making Sense of Social Theory*.

Second, and ultimately most important, readers will complete *Making Sense of Social Theory* knowing some explanatory principles. Theoretical principles are cause-and-effect statements articulated at the level of general concepts. Well-developed theoretical principles can be used (a) to understand why outcomes are alike in some cases and different in others, (b) to generate research hypotheses we can use when testing and refining our ideas, and (c) to suggest policies and programs for improving outcomes in the settings where we live and work.

It is worth taking note of the fact that predictive principles are what distinguish theory from metatheory in science. *A metatheory is a framework for understanding that is given its contour by the orienting questions we ask, by key concepts framing our sensitivity (or our blind spots), and the axiomatic assumptions we are inclined to make.* But metatheory lacks predictive principles. Every mature theory builds on a metatheoretical framework and then adds predictive principles that have been or can be tested. Principles allow a theory to mature beyond the constraints of its metatheoretical origins.

Third, *Making Sense of Social Theory* provides readers with a skeletal outline of the history of the discipline of sociology. It does so by introducing some of the sociologists who have made seminal contributions to the development of the field and by briefly summarizing the essence of their most noteworthy contributions within the intellectual context of their times. A few of the important people discussed are Harriet Martineau, Émile Durkheim, Max Weber, Karl Marx, Herbert Mead, Robert Park, Talcott Parsons, Robert Merton, Herbert Blumer, George Homans, Kathy Charmaz, and Richard Emerson. An awareness of some of sociology's main explanatory perspectives (structural functionalism, conflict theory, symbolic interactionism, and exchange theory) will emerge from our review of the discipline's development.

Fourth, *Making Sense of Social Theory* conveys an integrated sense of the discipline of sociology as a social science by recognizing that different groups of theorists have made distinct contributions that often complement one another and rarely negate each other. Some people have the erroneous perception that accepting the validity of theoretical premises associated with one school of social scientific thought requires the wholesale rejection of all other theoretical approaches. This simply is not true. All the theoretical perspectives sociologists have contributed make important contributions to a more realistic understanding of societal dynamics and processes. Recognizing this, and being able to draw inspiration from each perspective, strengthens us as social scientists.

Fifth, readers should gain from *Making Sense of Social Theory* an awareness of sociology's past theoretical trajectory and future promise. A possible road map of future intellectual activity and direction can be projected from a few of the big questions that continue to excite sociological curiosity and interest. Some of these questions will be introduced within the context of our review of the discipline. Focusing on these questions is a tangible way people can prepare to make their own meaningful intellectual contributions in the future.

Levels of Analysis in Social Scientific Inquiry

Sociology's intellectual frameworks offer insight into what are often referred to as *micro, meso,* and *macro* levels of analysis. *Microphenomena* are those having to do with thought, decision making, and behavior in direct interpersonal relations. *Meso* level events deal with more complex organizational phenomena in businesses, schools, government agencies, nonprofit charities, and other organizations that, despite often being quite large and sometimes very complex, can nonetheless be thought of as having relatively discrete boundaries, allowing for a meaningful analytical distinction between those activities that are a part of the organization and activities engaged in by people who happen to be members of organizations but also are also driven by outside agendas owing to their other commitments. (An employee who calls the school where his children are enrolled is rarely making a call on behalf of the business that employs him. Instead, he is diverging from his work role and acting in his family role.) *Macrophenomena* concern trends in society at large and forces driving those trends.

Distinguishing between Axioms and Principles

Sociological theory seems to some people like an arcane, ivory tower topic. This is unfortunate, because sociological theory has great relevance for everything that happens in the real world. It forms a basis for understanding events and, quite often, for inspiring solutions to problems. A device this book uses to focus readers on a few of sociology's many theoretical tenets that are worth learning is to formally translate some of these theoretical tenets into axioms and principles. Axioms and principles make up much of our disciplinary tool kit, so becoming comfortable with them will make it easier to read *Making Sense of Social Theory* and capitalize on the knowledge the book provides.

Studying disciplinary history affords a good avenue for learning theory, and in this book we will cover many of the most important high points in sociology's historical development. Learning axioms and principles will be important as a way of bringing sociology's theoretical understanding to the surface so that it can be used consciously, carefully, and consistently.

One caveat is that it is important to remember that all principles in every science are provisional. That is, all they seek to offer is the closest approximation of the dynamics at work producing variability and change in the world. To practice real science is to appreciate that a more penetrating level of understanding will eventually supersede our current level of understanding. In science, we utilize empirical observation in a process of theoretically informed hypothesis testing designed to take us to a higher (although never perfect or complete) level of understanding. Refusing to budge from the points of view we start with is not a scientifically acceptable way of thinking. We stay with a set of axioms and principles only so long, to the degree and under the conditions that seem consistent with observable reality. We amend, modify, or discard axioms and principles when they are consistently and convincingly disconfirmed by tests conducted under a range of circumstances in a variety of settings.

Theory for Sociology as a Science

Theory *by definition* offers ways to explain variation in the things a discipline cares about. Sociologists care about the way people are interconnected with one another through direct attachments (face-to-face associations), through shared beliefs (widely held concepts of what is appropriate and inappropriate, or perhaps more or less acceptable versus abhorrent), and through systemic interconnections, including regulatory constraint (as in the case of the subordination of citizens to laws). Readers should finish *Making Sense of Social Theory* having a tool kit composed of axioms and principles that can be used to understand why direct attachments, shared beliefs, and systemic interconnections (a) assume different shapes in different places, (b) produce particular ramifications, and (c) can, in some instances, be relevant in yielding better social, organizational, and societal outcomes.

Some people have the mistaken idea that good theory is necessarily complex and confusing. But this is simply not true. It is equivalent to believing that a book must have a very special message if the writing is so obtuse that after reading it and rereading it, and rereading it again, you are still unsure what the author really means. Impenetrability may be interesting and in many instances genuinely artful (James Joyce), but the aim of science is different. Being obtuse is simply not a quality we intentionally seek in scientific writing. In fact, the opposite is true. *Good scientific theory is supposed to reveal things rather than obscure them.* At its best, the elegance of scientific theory is to be found in simplicity. It is, of course, true that we have to be prepared to suffer some confusion on our way to revelation. But revelation is nevertheless the ultimate objective. This book strives to identify and make clear (and ready for application) core insights for understanding interpersonal (micro), organizational (meso), and societal (macro) phenomena.

Good theorists are, almost by definition, ahead of the crowd. So expect theory to be hard. But the goal in *Making Sense of Social Theory* is always to decipher core insights and contributions in a clear way. And when we are studying long-dead theorists, people who at first glance may seem like relics of the past, our goal will be to appreciate the continued relevance of the ideas they advanced. The (twelve) axioms and (twenty-one) principles in *Making Sense of Social Theory* are written to capture and convey theoretical tenets that are robust and powerful. This book is an attempt to distill and present these theoretical insights with clarity of scientific purpose.

A World of Liberation

In any science, theory has its greatest value when it offers insight that can help us better understand how the world around us operates. The ideas examined in this book meet that standard. They are meant to be applied.

Some Vocabulary of Science

This textbook considers theory within the context of science. Knowing the meanings of some key science terms will help keep the role theory plays in science fully in view.

Axiom: An axiom is the working assumption that a given trait is common to all cases of a particular analytical type (e.g., all people, all organizations, or all societies). For example, it is sometimes assumed that all people try to maximize their own personal advantage. This axiom will be introduced more formally and more precisely in chapter 2 as the Benefit Maximization Axiom: *People tend to make benefit-maximizing decisions based on their priorities.* But the important point is this: we are making an axiomatic assumption when some quality or characteristic is presumed (for analytical purposes) to be present in all cases, and when we use that presumption to reason other ideas out.

Indicator: A measurable piece of information used to gauge some more abstract concept. For example, income measured in a country's legal currency (e.g., dollar, yuan, rupee, peso, yen, euro, dinar) is often used to gauge differences in economic class. Note that the *validity* of an indicator, in other words, the degree to which an indicator actually measures what it is supposed to measure and how good a proxy it is for what we are using it to represent, should always be open to question.

Principle: A hypothesis stated at the level of generic concepts. An example is a principle drawn from the work of Georg Simmel,[2] which will be discussed in more detail in chapter 3. The Conflict/Cohesion Principle is: *Other things being equal, cohesion within groups or other social entities increases as a function of the degree of conflict between those entities.* The wording of this principle is generic, yet clear. This makes it possible to apply the same principle to different units of analysis under a wide range of conditions. Generically worded principles also tend to be timeless in the sense that they can be applied to events in any time period across the sweep of human history. A soccer game is not a war between nation-states (though a soccer game precipitated a four-day border clash between El Salvador and Honduras in 1969). But ball games and military clashes can be viewed as having some analytical dimensions in common, and exploring these analytical similarities can be informative.

Boundary Conditions: Circumstances we can use to anticipate when a particular theoretical dynamic is likely or is unlikely to be at work.

Independent Variable: A hypothesized cause.

Dependent Variable: A hypothesized consequence.

Hypothesis: A premise that variables are systematically related to one another.

Research Hypothesis: A hypothesis stated at the level of measurable indicators, making an empirical test possible. For example, an intensification of conflict between two countries—this might be operationally measured by exchange of military gunfire or closure of border crossings as a result of hostilities—would be expected to lead to an increase in cohesion within each country; this might be operationally measured by sales of national flags. The research hypothesis is that sales of national flags tend to increase with border closures and exchanges of military gunfire across national boundaries. Thus, a research hypothesis is concrete and testable, and should be reasonable to expect as one possible manifestation of the operation of a more abstractly worded theoretical principle. No single test of one research hypothesis predicted on the basis of a principle offers definitive proof that a principle is correct. Nor can one test definitively disprove a principle. But a series of tests and retests of different research hypotheses testing the same principle under different conditions and in different settings can go a long way toward either establishing or undermining confidence in the accuracy of a theoretical principle. With repeated tests in different places at different times, performed by different researchers under different circumstances, evidence will mount, either strengthening or weakening our conviction that the principle is clear enough, robust enough, and powerful enough to be useful.

Null Hypothesis: A finding that there is no clear pattern of association when a research hypothesis is tested using a particular data set.

Microlevel Phenomena: These are events involving face-to-face interaction. For example, how arguments transform friendships is a subject of microlevel inquiry.

Mesolevel Phenomena: These are events involving organizational process. For example, decision-making authority is highly concentrated at the top of some organizations while a good deal of discretionary authority is granted to lower-ranking functionaries in other organizations. Trying to understand this variability in organizations is a subject of mesolevel inquiry.

Macrolevel Phenomena: Societal-level trends, society-wide change, and the development of distinct differences between societies. Why divorce rates are higher in some countries than others is an example of a macrolevel question. Why some governments exercise relatively strict regulation of the financial sector while other governments exercise much looser regulatory control is another example of a macrolevel question.

Science: Effort devoted to developing, testing, and refining our explanations, in search of a progressively better understanding of the way the world works.

Metatheory: A conceptual framework consisting of orienting questions pointing to certain kinds of things we should try to understand, sensitizing concepts that alert us to factors that may be particularly important to look at when asking our orienting questions, and axiomatic assumptions that help guide our analytical thinking.

Theory: Metatheory supplemented with predictive principles enhancing our ability to explain why cases differ and/or change over time.

Theoretical Robustness: Robust theoretical insights are ones that turn out to apply under many different sets of circumstances, and that help us to produce valid predictions under a wide range of conditions.

Theoretical Power: Theoretical explanations can be said to be powerful when they capture essential forces and processes, enabling us to account for so much variation that the importance of the insight is easily detectable, even if we have only a relatively small number of cases to look at.

These concepts are all components of a standard science view. Research is used to test competing theoretical ideas that might explain how the world works. This means that theoretical activity and research activity are intrinsically linked in the scientific method. Neither theoretical activity nor research activity has its full value in isolation. Good research is grounded in theory and guided by theory, in hopes of ultimately providing scientists with empirical findings that can help us in the formulation of better theory.

The Theory–Research Connection in a Multiparadigm Science

When conducting research, it is important to relate research efforts to earlier work and also to a central question of disciplinary interest. Peter Blau and Otis Dudley Duncan's test of job success offers a good illustration.[3] Before Blau and Duncan did their research, sociologists were divided in their understanding of inequality in the United States. Some sociologists firmly believed that America was a *meritocracy*, that is, a land of open opportunity where the smartest and hardest-working individuals moved ahead of everyone else. (This suggests the rich deserve what they have.) Other sociologists held with equal fervor that the United States was a society based on *ascription*, with the outcomes of each person's life tightly constrained by the circumstances of her or his birth. (This suggests the rich enjoy what they have because of accidents of birth.)

The big question Blau and Duncan addressed was, Is the United States actually a meritocracy, or is it a place where socioeconomic status is inherited rather than earned? Their work had impact because they focused on a question commanding attention, and because they were explicit in identifying this important question for their readers and conducting a reasonable test of two competing explanatory frameworks, using data that were carefully gathered for the purpose.

Blau and Duncan found that there is enough truth to both points of view (meritocracy and ascription) that each must be taken seriously by sociologists who are scientifically inclined. In this respect, work by Blau and Duncan represents a scientific ideal. They asked important questions about cause and effect, and they reached conclusions only after careful consideration of available data.

The research Blau and Duncan conducted was important because it convinced most sociologists that our understanding of the real world often needs to be informed by more than one theoretical point of view. Multiple perspectives (the use of ascription inspired by conflict theory and the use of achievement inspired by structural functionalism) do not invalidate one another so much as they inform us about the complexity of the real world where different dynamics are simultaneously at work. Blau and Duncan's research led them to draw from sociology's different theoretical perspectives rather than blindly privilege one perspective and ignore all others. Indeed, years of research following Blau and Duncan have affirmed conflict theory by helping all sociologists better appreciate obstacles to mobility, at the same time that those years of research have affirmed structural functionalism by identifying ways in which educational and other institutions have developed to provide structural avenues for individual advancement while promoting the general betterment of society.

It is good to remember that the best scientific research often poses competing possible explanations. Considering more than one explanation in the same model helps us to refine and improve our understanding instead of blindly validating our presuppositions. Time and time again, sociologists have found that improved understanding is more likely to emerge from an integrated test of two perspectives than from a single-perspective approach.

Being Sure to Appreciate the Value of Interdisciplinary Research

It is important to remember that the sociological value of research comes from the nature of the theoretical questions being explored, the rigor of the investigation, and the power of the insights yielded. Intellectual cross-fertilization has been amazingly fruitful for sociology as a discipline because sociological theories are so robust that they have often enjoyed broad circulation and strenuous testing by people in other disciplines. For example, when he conducted a qualitative conversational analysis of joking in a Native American community, anthropologist Keith Basso added in important ways to our understanding of the place of playful interaction and peer exchange when a person's conceptions of good and bad are taking root.[4] More recently, in their quantitative study of survival rates of POWs during the U.S. Civil War, economists Dora Costa and Matthew Kahn provide compelling statistical evidence of the importance of a person's location within social networks.[5] Basso's insights, and those of Cost and Kahn, are revealing and can be broadly applied in many settings. Both studies examine data sets sociologists do not typically study, and use those data sets in creative ways to test theoretical ideas that came in substantial measure from sociology. This kind of cross-fertilization is of great value to the discipline, and we should always be alert to the past value, current importance, and future promise of interdisciplinary cross-fertilization. At least in the case of sociology, the potential for useful interdisciplinary work has always been a function of the quality of theoretical development within the discipline.

Recap

This chapter dispels several myths about science. Science has less to do with memorizing inflexible formulas than it does with devising creative ways to test compelling ideas. And theory has less to do with philosophical complexity than with a culture of evidence that helps us reveal practical insights in comprehensible form. In the process of working through chapter 1, the readers have been exposed to some of the contributions of five of the most influential sociologists who have ever lived: Robert K. Merton, William H. Whyte, Georg Simmel, Peter Blau, and Otis Dudley Duncan. Merton was a conceptualizer who (among other things) brought into use the concepts of self-fulfilling prophecy, role model, and focus group. Whyte introduced the concept of groupthink. Simmel helped us recognize that solidarity among people often increases when they feel they are facing a common adversary. And Blau and Duncan conducted important research on status attainment and made a strong case that the best explanations are typically informed by insights drawn from more than one theoretical point of view. Most important, readers should now appreciate the fact that *development of clear, robust, and powerful theoretical explanation of variation or change* is the foremost goal of any science. Finally, sociology can be distinguished from other fields by its focus on interpersonal attachments, shared beliefs, and the systemic interconnections that structurally locate people in relation to others.

Quiz

Test yourself with these questions and check your answers before moving on. The answer key is at the end of the book.

1. An academic field that is devoted to using observations of the real world in trying to develop explanatory frameworks that not only describe but actually explain variability is called a _____ .
2. What distinguishes sociology from natural and life sciences is its focus on
   a. the way people are interconnected with one another in a face-to-face manner
   b. the nature of beliefs people share
   c. systemic interconnections, such as those created by government regulatory agencies
   d. all of the above
   e. none of the above

3. Ideally, scientists
   a. try to prove the presuppositions they start their research with
   b. want to move beyond current understanding and improve our ability to explain variation between cases and/or change over time
   c. reject the claim that anything about society can be better explained
4. Ideally, we aim for theory that is
   a. clear
   b. robust
   c. powerful
   d. all of the above
5. Metatheory is normally said to contain (circle all that apply)
   a. orienting questions we want to answer
   b. sensitizing concepts indicating variables we think may be important to look at
   c. axiomatic assumptions it seems useful to make
   d. predictive principles
6. Theory contains
   a. axioms but not principles
   b. principles but not axioms
   c. axioms and principles

Check your answers in the answer key at the end of the book. If you get any wrong, consider reviewing chapter 1 before continuing. It is important to be clear about these questions before moving on because they reflect the logical grounding people need to understand sociology as a social science subsequently to explore the predictive power of sociological theory.

Application Exercise

Each chapter of this book will conclude with an application exercise. These application exercises are only illustrations and should demonstrate that thinking in theoretical and scientific terms can be useful.

Robustness is an important concept. Theorists want to formulate insights that are relevant to many different kinds of cases and different kinds of situations. This is why theorists generally try to express their insights in sufficiently generic terms to be used by researchers studying a range of different phenomena and by social scientists working in organizations and running programs. The point is that good theory is more than description of a single event.

Consider the Conflict/Cohesion Principle. Develop your own assessment about the robustness of this principle. If you think it is robust, offer two widely different examples of events the principle could help explain. If you do not feel the principle is robust, state briefly why you think this principle might be hard to apply to significantly different cases.

2

Theory Is Not as Hard as It Sounds!

SOMETIMES, PEOPLE WHO STUDY SOCIOLOGY ARE QUESTIONED about it. *What is sociology, anyway? Is it useful?* Questions like these, about the value and the practicality of sociology, are easier to answer once one starts thinking in terms of axioms and principles capturing social science insights that can be practically applied to real-world situations. The terms *axiom* and *principle* seem awkward at first, but their meanings are fairly straightforward. More important, axioms and principles can convey a great deal of explanatory power, and they distill social science knowledge into a form that is easy to apply in different situations.

Introducing Axioms

William I. Thomas, who began his career as an anthropologist and then shifted to sociology, was writing almost a century ago from his base at the University of Chicago. Thomas conducted community studies in immigrant neighborhoods. In studying immigrants' adaptation to their new country, Thomas realized that whatever people *believe* to be true tends to be real in its consequences. If a person fails to apply for a job because he or she is convinced there is no chance of getting the job, then failure to get the job is assured (something Robert K. Merton would later describe as a *self-fulfilling prophecy*). Thomas looked at this in a somewhat broader light, however.

Thomas realized that all people respond to situations on the basis of their perceptions about those situations. We can refer to this phenomenon as the Definition of Situation Axiom. It is an axiom because it identifies a characteristic that is often useful to assume is true of people in general, even if it is not absolutely true in every single case. Keeping this axiom in mind reminds us to ask some vital questions, even if we are distracted by other factors during the course of investigation. This and other axioms consequently help us notice things we might otherwise miss. Our perceptions about a situation can easily be wrong, of course, but we still respond on the basis of what we think is happening.

One's definition of situation was not something people tended to think about before the birth of sociology. Before the emergence of sociology as a discipline, it was, for example, common to think of unemployed people as lazy if they were not looking for work. But thanks to the accumulation of sociological research on labor force participation, we now know a great deal that was not commonly understood a century ago. Among other things, we know that employment-seeking behavior is substantially determined by what people have come to believe is possible.

Thomas actually came to his insight about definition of situation while studying juvenile delinquents.[1] If teenagers believe they have been permanently relegated to the social margins, their perceived range of options about choosing friends or activities quickly shrinks. The places and activities where marginalized teens expect to be accepted by others (or even socially tolerated by others) are drastically constrained.

Recognition of the importance of this axiom was subsequently developed into labeling theory by Howard Becker and a number of other people associated with the Chicago school. One of the most often cited applications is found in Edwin Lemert's use of the concept of secondary deviance in his 1951 book, *Social Pathology*.[2] This application of labeling theory notes that once a person has been labeled as undesirable, it becomes much harder to stay out of trouble because many normal opportunities are closed off. *Secondary deviance* refers to socially disapproved activity those people who have been labeled as bad engage in because their normal choices have been dramatically restricted.

Risk of employment in the adult entertainment industry suggests the power of both the Definition of Situation Axiom and labeling theory. Of all the things one can say about employment in adult entertainment, the most certain is that employment in those jobs is highly correlated with economic desperation and perceived scarcity of alternatives.

Among sociologists today, there is a great deal of confidence in Thomas's Definition of Situation Axiom. Sociologists use this axiom all the time and it helps us understand much of what we encounter and observe.

Definition of Situation Axiom: **People respond to situations according to what they believe to be true about those situations, rather than what is actually true.**

Coming to a conclusion that all people are the *same* in terms of responding to situations as they perceive them was useful to Thomas as he tried to account for the fact that people react differently to what may appear to outsiders to be similar situations. If perceptions of situation are different, we should expect responses to be different as well. Why does one person laugh when he or she is made the target of a joke, while another person lashes out in anger? We all know the answer. A person's reaction depends, at least in part, on what the person thinks is going on. Is the joke *interpreted* as a sign of affection and inclusion, or is it *interpreted* as a sign of derision and disrespect? One's definition of the situation matters very much.

It should be remembered that a person's interpretation is not always clearly expressed. It may even be subconscious. For example, the perception of threat elevates heartbeat (the fight-or-flight response) even before a person has time to consciously process what she thinks is happening. But whether conscious or subconscious, whether with full or only partial awareness, whether verbalized or not, it seems clear that the way people define the situations in which they find themselves has a big impact on their reactions. Being alert to this factor offers social scientists a powerful tool for understanding human affairs.

One should stop to consider this for a moment. The definitions of situation that people in a setting have come to acquire must be carefully considered when trying to develop a sociological understanding of that setting. Nonsociologists often fail to take into account the situation as it is defined from the point of view of the people whose actions are being explained. This failure is a critical mistake. When this happens, there is a high probability that any explanation will be wrong, no matter how convincing it might sound to listeners with a sound-bite mentality. We should expect understanding to be grossly inaccurate (quite often even counterproductive, that is, less useful than no understanding at all) when it ignores the definitions of situation held by people in the setting.

Sociologists almost never make this mistake because the Definition of Situation Axiom is now part of sociology's stock knowledge. (*Stock knowledge* is a term sociologists use to refer to things people in a particular group, in this case sociologists, assume that others in the group know and appreciate.) Sociologists can generally assume that other sociologists understand what definition of situation is and are aware of its importance.

Before moving on, try to think of a case in which someone you know reacted in a way that he or she later regretted, because he or she failed to consider the definitions of situation of other people. Most sociologists find it easy to apply the Definition of Situation Axiom to real events. When we allow ourselves to be informed by the Definition of Situation Axiom, many things become clear that are otherwise hidden from view. Readers are urged to apply this axiom, and all the other axioms and principles in this book, to real cases and events. Sociological axioms and principles will then take on a richer meaning.

Another important sociologist was George Homans (1910–1989), who built a series of explanatory principles based on an assumption that people make rational choices about how to maximize benefits in light of their priorities. We can call our presumption that all people seek to maximize their own interests the Benefit Maximization Axiom.

Benefit Maximization Axiom: **People tend to make benefit-maximizing decisions based on their priorities.**

People often calculate costs and benefits when deciding what to do. The Benefit Maximization Axiom simply introduces the premise that all people are trying to maximize beneficial outcomes for themselves. When introduced as an assumption, benefit maximization can be used to deduce that people who make different choices must either face what they perceive as different circumstances or have different priorities. Then we can start asking interesting questions about, for example, why some college students but not others would accept, if offered, the same employment opportunity. Perhaps this is because circumstances differ. Students do not all receive the same amount of financial help from their parents. And tuition bills are much higher for some students than for others (depending, for example, on where one goes to school). There are also differences in priorities. Some students hunger deeply for expensive status-conferring possessions (such as trendy clothing) while others do not (at least not as much). Moving beyond axioms to account for variation between cases requires the development of explanatory principles.

Homans was a smart person and realized that the Benefit Maximization Axiom was only a beginning. He recognized that sociologists would eventually have to answer the question, why do people value what they value? Homans was unable to answer this question adequately, and he left the matter for a later generation of sociologists to address. But Homans was able to help codify our thinking about calculation, and in this respect his work provides sociologists with a useful principle introduced in the passages that follow.

Introducing Principles

Homans's work provides a particularly good illustration of sociological theory because he was conscious in his use of axioms and principles, and he was explicit in his desire to move beyond *axioms* identifying what cases have in common, by stating *principles* that are designed to predict and explain differences developing between cases (or changes emerging in a single case over time). This is clear in much of his work, but is best illustrated in his book *Social Behavior: Its Elementary Forms.* In that work, Homans makes a clear leap to a principle when he recognizes that the more desirable a person judges something to be, the more the person will sacrifice in an attempt to achieve the desired outcome.

Homans actually codified a number of other principles, broadly drawn from the work of economists (especially economists who moved over to sociology, such as Vilfredo Pareto, about whom Homans wrote his first book) and of psychologists (especially his friend and colleague, the famous behavioral psychologist B. F. Skinner). People select among alternative lines of conduct by factoring in the probability of achieving desired outcomes, along with the value associated with those outcomes, and the projected costs anticipated by choosing that course of action. These calculations are then compared with possible alternative courses of action by contrasting expected cost-benefit ratios. People weigh probabilities when, for instance, they decide whether to be content with small gains that they consider to be almost certain or to try for bigger gains that seem less certain.[3]

It is legitimate to refer to the work of George Homans as true theory because it represents an explicit attempt to explain variability in outcomes. The Principle of Rational Choice is at the center of his explanatory framework.

Principle of Rational Choice: **Other things being equal, the likelihood of following a particular course of action (1) increases as a function of (a) the value of the desired outcome and (b) the probability of success in achieving that outcome, and (2) decreases as a function of (c) the projected cost of the activity, (d) fear of ultimately being held responsible for externalized costs, and (e) availability of alternatives having attractive cost-benefit ratios.**

Although the Principle of Rational Choice may sound somewhat similar to the Benefit Maximization Axiom, principles differ from axioms in both their form and their meaning. Axioms are framed in terms of what we believe to be similar and invariable, or what we may at least find useful to assume as similar and invariable when we are trying to study and understand certain kinds of phenomena. For understanding time investment, for example, we may find it useful to assume that as a general rule people try to make benefit-maximizing decisions everywhere, in all historical time periods, in every situation. Of course, things are not really that uniform. And yet, it can sometimes be analytically useful to assume that they are. In contrast, principles are always stated in terms of hypothesized relationships among variables; for instance, other things being equal, the more someone wants something, the more he will do to try to get it. What makes one insight an axiom and another insight a principle is determined by what the theorist makes explicit through the choice of words. Axioms are explicitly worded to accentuate how cases of a particular kind (people, groups, organizations, communities, societies, etc.) are assumed, at least for analytical purposes, to be alike. In contrast, principles are worded to accentuate cause-and-effect relationships giving rise to differences.

When given a properly constructed theoretical principle, it is often possible to infer an axiomatic assumption even if the theorist has made no axiomatic assumption explicit. A person could, for example, infer the Benefit Maximization Axiom if given the Principle of Rational Choice. It is also possible to try to explicitly state principles that seem to have been implicitly suggested by someone else's analysis, but to do so requires that the analysis offer clues to causation.

Homans and others have considered elementary exchange and have arrived at a number of principles that are quite revealing. For example, Homans notes that anger often results from a shortfall between expected and actual outcomes.[4] A student who expects to receive a course grade of D but actually gets a C is rarely angry. But a student who expects a B and gets a C will typically be rather angry. This leads to the counterintuitive realization that we should sometimes expect students receiving Cs to be more angry than students receiving Ds. Using theory to arrive at counterintuitive predictions like this one demonstrates the value of trying to be explicit about theoretical insights.

Anger Principle: **Other things being equal, anger increases in magnitude (a) to the degree that actual outcomes fall short of expected outcomes and (b) opportunities forgone seem to exceed the benefits that have been actualized.**

Of course, whether a baseline expectation is even reasonable is a separate issue. But that is a different question. Thus, being explicit about axioms and principles helps us first to appreciate how far our explanation moves beyond the kind of common sense we often hear people employing in their accounts of everyday life; being explicit also helps us to be more aware of questions that remain unanswered. Why do people have the expectations that they do? We are still far from a satisfactory answer to this pivotal question.

A great feature of abstractly stated principles is that they can be generic enough to apply to many different kinds of situations. We have already considered grades. Family income may offer another illustration. Some married couples draw apart because one person believes things are getting better over time (for example, feels accomplished because there is some growth in household income), while the other person judges the improvement to be a failure because it falls short of the rate of improvement that this individual had anticipated. This can yield an interesting dynamic of anger moving in both directions in what becomes a vicious cycle. Person A is angry because improvement in the performance of person B has not matched expectations. But person B is angry because person A fails to recognize the performance improvement that person B has achieved. While there are of course many potential causes of marital disharmony, sociological research has revealed that differences in expectations are one of the things that often undermine marriages by eating away at appreciation for what one has in and with the other person.

In real life, few things are so simple that they can be entirely reduced to the dynamic captured in a single principle like the Anger Principle. Nevertheless, the Anger Principle captures some of what goes on in the real world and allows us to develop a higher level of understanding than we would otherwise have. In science, the goal is to move forward by successive approximations. First, be explicit about a principle you suspect to be generally true. Then think of specific predictions one should be able to make if the principle is fully accurate. We call this kind of prediction a *research hypothesis*. With a research hypothesis, the accent is on operational indicators being used to test theoretical premises. Making a clear link between the hypothesis being tested in a specific empirical context and the more general theoretical principle is an essential characteristic of good research. When this link is clearly made, testing a research hypothesis simultaneously tests the more general principle. However, this works only if our reasoning is sound and if our operational indicators yield valid measures of the abstract variables contained in the principle.

What Part of Sociological Work Is Sociological Theory?

In any science, people are doing theory when they are trying to better explain processes through which conditions change or different outcomes are generated. This has to involve more than describing the variation or change itself, because theory is more than a description of outcomes. There must be description, understanding, and explanation of the process through which variations develop or change comes about. Theory is the attempt to identify the dynamics producing variations or change in the real world. We have more theory work to do, to the extent to which we find ourselves unable to identify processes through which changes are generated and differences are produced.

Thoughtful effort to understand the dynamics producing change, and then to use real data to test and improve our understanding of those dynamics, is what defines any science. What makes sociology distinctive is its preoccupation with the social universe of interpersonal attachments, shared beliefs, and systemic interconnections, including but not limited to regulatory and other systemic constraints. In other respects, sociology is fundamentally like every other science. The difference is that it has the social world (the whole social world) as its subject matter. This means that good sociological theory will always offer either some explanation why social attachments, shared beliefs, and systemic linkages differ from place to place, or why they change over time. And good sociological theory will provide us with insights about the consequences that might result from different kinds of attachments, different systems of belief, and different patterns of systemic interconnections and constraints.

In science, our goal is to move beyond commonsense viewpoints representing whatever has become the conventional wisdom of the times. And we ultimately want to improve on and move beyond the views we happen to have right now. There is nothing more antithetical to the idea of science than either (a) allowing the meaning of our analysis to be obscured in unnecessarily convoluted language or (b) allowing our understanding to come to a standstill from eagerness for affirmation of prior convictions, rather than endeavoring to progress toward a more adequate understanding of the essential character of the world we observe.

Recap

In this chapter, we have looked at ideas advanced by two of the most influential sociologists who ever lived. These were George Homans (who drew in important ways from psychology and economics) and William I. Thomas (who began his professional life as an anthropologist). Each has been widely cited for more than a half century, and their prominence is underscored by the fact that both served terms as president of the American Sociological Association. Homans's work provides some of the pivotal foundation for exchange as a theoretical perspective in sociology (explored in chapter 14), and Thomas's work was known to Mead (discussed in chapter 10) and provides part of the foundation for symbolic interaction as an explanatory perspective (discussed in chapter 13).

True to the promise of this book, important ideas having explanatory power are made clear, easily accessible, and available for readers to use. These include two widely employed axioms (the Definition of Situation Axiom and the Benefit Maximization Axiom), and two useful principles (the Principle of Rational Choice and the Anger Principle). What we mean when we use the terms *axiom* and *principle* should now be clear. And the utility of being explicit about our theoretical axioms and principles should be more apparent with each passing chapter. Approached through its axioms and principles, sociological theory is really not very difficult. But it *is* versatile and useful.

Review of Axioms and Principles

Definition of Situation Axiom: People respond to situations according to what they believe to be true about those situations, rather than what is actually true.

Benefit Maximization Axiom: People tend to make benefit-maximizing decisions based on their priorities.

Principle of Rational Choice: Other things being equal, the likelihood of following a particular course of action (1) increases as a function of (a) the value of the desired outcome and (b) the probability of success in achieving that outcome, and (2) decreases as a function of (c) the projected cost of the activity, (d) fear of ultimately being held responsible for externalized costs, and (e) availability of alternatives having attractive cost-benefit ratios.

Anger Principle: Other things being equal, anger increases in magnitude (a) to the degree that actual outcomes fall short of expected outcomes and (b) opportunities forgone seem to exceed the benefits that have been actualized.

Quiz

Check your answers in the back of the book. If you get any wrong, think about reviewing chapter 2 before continuing.

1. A statement that asserts that something is more or less true in all cases is a/an
   a. axiom
   b. principle
   c. research hypothesis
2. According to the Principle of Rational Choice, when people make choices about how to spend their time, money, or reputation, they weigh
   a. the benefit they expect to receive
   b. the costs they think may be involved
   c. probabilities of success in realizing goals
   d. all of the above
3. All sciences involve a search for
   a. more accurate description
   b. more convincing analysis of causes
   c. more accuracy in anticipation of consequences
   d. all of the above
4. Which of the following should have a dependent variable and at least one independent variable stated at the level of generic concepts?
   a. an axiom
   b. a principle
   c. a research hypothesis
5. The goal of science can be most accurately described as
   a. seeking validation of theories we believe
   b. empirically testing predictions based on theory so that we can refine and improve theory over time

Application Exercise

For this application exercise, interview two people about Valentine's Day. Do your informants tend to remember Valentine's Day (February 14) as (a) an emotionally neutral day, (b) just about the best day ever, or (c) a big letdown? Briefly sum up the way your informants say they have experienced Valentine's Day. (A surprisingly large number of people find Valentine's Day to be a letdown because experiences often fall short of high expectations.)

Think about whether the experiences reported to you tend to validate the Anger Principle or call its accuracy or applicability into question. Do you think the wording of the principle can be improved on? If so, how? Write down what you think.

3

Sociological Theory
and the Scientific Method

THE SCIENCES AIM TO INCREASE OUR UNDERSTANDING of the world by improving theory. They all employ the same basic scientific method. This method can be described as having five steps. Followed in sequence, the steps in the scientific method provide a strategy for developing a better understanding of how differences are produced; this in turn makes it possible for us to develop more accurate predictions, and under the best of circumstances enables us to engineer better outcomes for organizations, for communities, and for society at large.

Steps in the Scientific Method Illustrated with Hawthorne Findings

Understanding steps in the scientific method is a key to mastering ideas presented in this book. Here, *Making Sense of Social Theory* reviews and illustrates the steps of the scientific method using an illustration from the Hawthorne Western Electric plant. The Hawthorne plant was a factory plant where Western Electric Corporation manufactured telephone equipment in an industrial zone on Chicago's western outskirts. Between 1924 and 1932, Western Electric teamed up with social science professors and partnered in conducting important research into the social dimensions of work in a manufacturing business. Several findings came out of these studies, but the most famous was the discovery of what has come to be known as the *Hawthorne Effect*. When ordinary people who are engaged in everyday behavior realize that their behavior is being studied, their behavior changes for a time. Thus, behavior observed during initial stages of research is often atypical. Fortunately for researchers, behavior tends to return to habitual patterns with the passage of some time, so observers are usually able to chronicle more typical behavior by staying in the setting for an extended period of observation. The Hawthorne Effect has proved to be a vital methodological discovery informing the way sociology's observational studies are conducted.

Many other important discoveries were made during a period of extensive social science investigation at the Hawthorne plant. One of those discoveries will be referenced here as a clear illustration of the way the scientific method can be followed as a set of steps. This example is important for debunking the way "science" is sometimes inaccurately portrayed: as the embodiment of final truth. Good scientists never claim to know everything. Instead, the views that characterize a scientific mind-set are (a) certainty that we do not know everything, (b) conviction that our understanding will improve at a faster pace if we are explicit about how we think the world might work (not how we are certain it works, but how we think it might work), and (c) persistent faith that rigorous effort to test and identify the faults and limitations in our current thinking will allow us to improve our theories over time. A scientific mind-set and the method it entails can be described as having five steps.

The first step in scientific method is to identify some variation or change that seems worth trying to understand and explain. This step in the method is crucial because it defines our focus. (Remember that in order for us to be sociological, our attention needs to be riveted on some aspect of interpersonal attachments, shared beliefs, or systemic interconnections and linkages.) It is important to understand the logic of each of the five steps of the scientific method, and to appreciate how the five steps can be closely interconnected. To illustrate the first step, we can point to sociology's special disciplinary interest in interpersonal attachments and consider one of the research questions raised at the Hawthorne plant. The research question was: Why are some interpersonal relationships (a bond between person A and person B) characterized by high levels of liking (friendship) while other interpersonal attachments are not? How can we explain this difference? That is, how can we account for the fact that some but not all work acquaintances are what the people involved would call friendships?

It is useful to stop and recognize what makes this a sociological research question. The focus is on one of the aspects of the social universe sociologists are particularly curious about: interpersonal attachments. Also recognize what makes this a scientific question. The goal is to explain differences, in this case the fact that some but not all interpersonal attachments involve strong friendship. Some work relationships involve tepid friendship. Some are emotionally neutral. And some involve antipathy of various levels of intensity. Wanting to explain variance makes this a scientific question, and the fact that the variance is about interpersonal attachments makes it a sociological question.

The second step in the scientific method is to suggest one or more theoretical premises, which can typically be translated into axioms or principles that might explain the kinds of outcomes we are trying to understand. Social science researchers at the Hawthorne plant started with an explanatory premise they felt initial confidence about. The premise they began with was that, other things being equal, friendship can be expected to grow as people interact with one another more frequently.

Some readers will recognize that the causal ordering suggested in this premise (interaction leads to liking) may be somewhat problematic. Perhaps people make opportunities to increase interaction with those they like and find ways of avoiding people they dislike. This is the kind of thorny theoretical issue that scientists are able to methodologically sort out over time with the accumulation of good data carefully collected to test those theoretical premises we are self-conscious about.

The idea that interaction leads to liking is a premise that someone might reasonably call a theoretical principle. A theoretical principle purports to explain variation in a dependent variable that is conceptualized in a generic way (liking) based on variation in one or more generically worded independent variables (frequency of interaction). The meaning is completely clear, yet stated in general terms so that it can be applied and tested in a wide range of settings. This distinguishes statements of principle from research hypotheses that are usually much more specific with regard to time, place, and setting.

The third step in the scientific method is to identify one or more research hypotheses that should be true if the stated theoretical axioms and principles are in fact accurate and do apply in the settings under study. A research hypothesis is thus a specific application of a more general theoretical premise stated at the level of generic concepts. A research hypothesis replaces generic variables with concrete measurement indicators suited to particular cases in specific settings, so that a prediction can be made and then tested by looking to see if predicted outcomes turn out to be true (confirming evidence) or false (disconfirming evidence).

To illustrate, social science researchers at the Hawthorne plant decided to look at interpersonal attachments among people who interact at work. More specifically, they identified two relatively small work groups to look at closely. Beginning with the general premise that interaction leads to liking, researchers developed the research hypothesis that the more each pair of people interacted, the deeper sense of friendship the members of the pair would report having for each other. This was a good research hypothesis. A testable prediction was made about a set of specifiable outcomes in a particular setting.

The fourth step in the scientific method is to actually test empirical research hypotheses by judging whether observable outcomes match predictions. We test research hypotheses by collecting the information we will need to confirm or disconfirm the accuracy of predictions we make. Researchers at the Haw-thorne plant tested the research hypothesis that workplace interaction between people in a work setting tends to lead to stronger feelings of friendship. This is summarized nicely by George Homans in his 1950 book, *The Human Group*.[1] The researchers expected to solidly confirm their research hypothesis. In fact, confirmation for the research hypothesis was relatively strong based on data for interpersonal attachments *among peers* of the same occupational rank. However, the relationship was reversed for interaction involving people of different ranks, such as factory workers and line supervisors. People of unequal ranks tended to try to avoid excess interaction, insulating themselves from a need for interaction by retreating to job descriptions and workplace rules. Generally, supervisors and workers liked one another more when their interaction was somewhat limited. Liking tended to diminish when people of different ranks were called on to in-teract more.

When researchers examined this relationship more carefully with data in hand, an explanation presented itself, and that explanation had to do with vul-nerability and trust. People who are supervised are always vulnerable for what they might expose in their interaction with the supervisors who evaluate them. This vulnerability tends to breed distrust. Although it is possible for trust be-tween status unequals to build over time, we can say that the more vulnerable people are, the more trust is required for friendship to develop. Even supervisors are vulnerable in such situations. Among other things, supervisors are vulner-able to a decrease in the authority they need to direct people and evaluate their performances. Supervisors also have to worry about accusations that they show favoritism to people they spend time with.

This demonstrates how following the scientific method can help us to see things that are otherwise easy to overlook. Researchers thought they had a good grasp of the phenomena under study and arrived at a principle that allowed them to anticipate different outcomes in different cases. The research hypothesis was clear and well thought out. Indicators seemed tangible and valid. Data collection was careful. But when researchers were able to test their research hypothesis, they discovered at least one way in which the starting theoretical premise was want-ing. This does not represent a failure in scientific method; quite the opposite is true. This is precisely what the scientific method is for.

The fifth and final step in the scientific method is to use the results of em-pirical research in order to rethink, and try to improve on, whatever theoretical ideas drove the initial design of the research project. As a result of this particular study, social science researchers gained much greater appreciation for the im-portance of the vulnerabilities inherent in rank or authority differences. With this one finding that was counter to the predicted outcome, sociology took a big step forward. It did so because researchers were using the scientific method ap-propriately, to improve on the frameworks we use as social scientists for looking at and trying to understand the world around us. We can realize the fifth step of the scientific method by offering new formulations that help us account for unexpected findings. One highly plausible formulation has to do with trust in the workplace.

Trust Principle: **Other things being equal, people withdraw from roles/relationships if practical, and tend to use formal and informal rules to minimize their obligations and reduce room for ambiguity if withdrawal is not practical, (1) as a direct function of perceived vulnerability in the setting and (2) as an inverse function of degree of trust in the people in that setting.**

Good empirical research often empowers further theory construction, and it is important to recognize that this is the ultimate goal of science. We want to improve on our existing base of insights. This puts theoretical work in a directive position at the beginning of the steps of the scientific method (particularly step 2) as well as at the culmination of the research process (particularly step 5). *Making Sense of Social Theory* was written in a conscious effort to invite readers to understand theory as an active part of the scientific method followed by people practicing a culture of evidence.

Illustrating the Use of a Principle

Remember that a principle is simply a hypothesis stated at the level of generic concepts. In other words, it is a cause-and-effect statement of relationship suggesting that changes in one abstractly worded variable (or set of variables), which can be manifested in a variety of forms in different settings, tends to have a predictable impact on some other abstractly worded variable. A good illustration is found in the work of Georg Simmel (pronounced "Zimmel" because the German *s* is pronounced like the English *z*), who was one of the founding figures in German sociology. Simmel advanced the theoretical principle that, other things being equal, *cohesion within groups or other social entities increases as a function of the degree of conflict between those entities.* We can call this the Conflict/Cohesion Principle. It is just one of many revealing insights that can be found in Simmel's work *Conflict and the Web of Group Affiliations.*[2] Change in one abstract variable (conflict) leads to a predictable pattern of change in another abstract variable (group cohesion). Conflict and group cohesion are abstract in the sense that they are relevant in many settings and express themselves in many different forms. Hence, Simmel could use his principle to explain differences in outcomes in many different types of cases in a wide variety of settings and circumstances.

This point about the generic character of truly powerful and abstractly worded theoretical insights can be illustrated with the principle of gravitational attraction. The principle of gravitation asserts that the level of attraction between two objects is directly proportional to the objects' combined mass and inversely proportional to their distance from each other. This principle helps us understand why apples falling from trees quickly hit the ground (a big combined mass and a short distance translate into irresistible attraction) while the moon stays in orbit around the earth (about 20 percent more combined mass, but with gravitational attraction muted by an average distance of about 250,000 miles, so that gravitational force is insufficient to counteract the moon's inertial force). While the earth's gravity is not strong enough to cause the moon to come crashing down, gravity is strong enough to drag the moon along in its orbit, thereby helping to maintain its velocity and, consequently, helping to keep it in orbit.

Principles derive their power, in part, from the fact that they are generic enough to apply to many different things. Simmel's Conflict/Cohesion Principle offers a good social science illustration of this point. It is abstract enough to allow for application to many different units of analysis, ranging all the way from team sports to nations at war.

Conflict/Cohesion Principle: **Other things being equal, cohesion within groups or other social entities increases as a function of the degree of conflict between those entities.**

The statement of abstract principles allows us the flexibility to test ideas in different ways in order to improve our understanding about the realities of the empirical world. Working from his Conflict/Cohesion Principle, Simmel would have been comfortable predicting (in other words, making the *research hypothesis*) that there will be an increase in the number of national flags displayed on the streets during a period when foreign hostilities are increasing. But he would also have been comfortable making a prediction that at the University of California, Berkeley, college sweater sales will increase more before a Stanford–Berkeley game than before a Berkeley game against the University of Washington. Why? Because Berkeley and Stanford have a long-standing cross-bay rivalry. Alabama–Auburn, Army–Navy, and Texas–Texas A & M provide other examples of often-heated rivalries in college sports today.

Caveats to Make When Testing Principles

There are five caveats to make when testing principles. The first is that principles can and should be tested in many different settings, to assess their robustness and power, one of many crucial points in Guillermina Jasso's notable efforts to put sociological theory on a stronger footing (e.g., 2008).[3] Testing in different settings is part of the scientific process. Science is best understood as a communal effort. A lot of research is conducted on the same idea by a variety of people under a range of settings in order to see just how pervasive and consistent a particular dynamic really is. The fact that we can see Simmel's principle at work in many different settings suggests that his insight is robust, meaning it can be applied to different kinds of sociological units, in different places, operating under different circumstances, and even in different time periods. And his principle is also powerful, in the sense that it allows us to make predictions about substantial variation in things that are truly significant, not simply about small variations of no clear consequence.

A second caveat to remember when testing principles is that other professionals reviewing our research have a right to expect that we have been careful in defining concepts (defining concepts clearly, with a minimum of overlap among definitions of different concepts), and in constructing measurement indicators that really are *valid* indicators of the more generic variables identified as important in our formally stated theoretical principles. Measurement validity is essential in good science. Always ask: Are we doing a good job in measuring the variables named in the principles as stated? Will others immediately see that the operational measures used for research hypotheses are valid? The indicators we use when testing research hypotheses have to be valid measures in order for conclusions about our theoretical principles to be sound.

A third caveat is that the world often works in a nonlinear way that can be described only through research that is sensitive enough to detect threshold effects and feedback loops. To use an example from the medical world, antibiotics can fight disease, but small doses of antibiotics may not reach the threshold necessary to kill all of a certain harmful bacteria a person has in his or her system. If antibiotics are administered below the necessary threshold, the person will still be sick, but may now have a more antibiotic-resistant strain of the disease.

Thresholds matter. To use a more sociological illustration, a police officer may let a driver going five miles over the speed limit pass by without remark, but will give an expensive speeding ticket to someone going seven miles an hour over the speed limit. In the real world, thresholds matter.

Feedback mechanisms also matter, and are central to the theoretical contributions of sociologist Vilfredo Pareto, explored in his book *The Transformation of Democracy* (originally published in 1921 but translated into English and released in 1984).[4] In looking for sociological factors influencing the business cycle, Pareto noted that long periods of prosperity are associated with a change in shared beliefs. Search for immediate gratification becomes common and is often promoted as a social value. This has many consequences, including encouraging accumulation of consumer debt. Small increases in unemployment do little to change values encouraging a play-now-and-pay-later attitude. But with significant spikes in unemployment, norms can change rapidly and dramatically. One clear indication of shift in beliefs occurs when frugality, which comes to be viewed as an unattractive quality during long periods of growth and prosperity, suddenly starts being viewed by the majority of people as an attractive and commendable attribute. As the American economy worsened in 2008 and 2009, savings rates actually went up while discretionary consumption went down. Sociologists understand that the world often operates in ways that are not fully expressible in simple linear terms, requiring that we try to take thresholds and feedback loops into account.

A fourth point to remember about testing principles is that each principle comes with an *other things being equal* caveat. Whether that caveat is explicitly stated or not, all theoretical principles should be thought of as beginning with this caveat. We always have to consider the possibility that other dynamics can be at work (whether we are aware of them or not) and might overshadow what we are looking for. We cannot always anticipate or control for all other relevant factors. When we can anticipate and measure other factors that might influence the dependent variable, we try to include them as control variables in our models. Inclusion of control variables allows for a more reliable test of research hypotheses and allows us to speak with more confidence in reporting on evidence for a research hypothesis.

A final caveat is that part of the scientific outlook is that our theories are imperfect. In fact, research is exciting for scientists specifically because it helps us improve our theories, often by making us more aware of the limitations on the accuracy of theory in its current state. The goal of science is always to search for *better* understanding, which means moving beyond theoretical omissions and shortcomings of the past and present. This is exactly what researchers at the Hawthorne plant did when they tested the premise that high levels of workplace interaction produce high levels of liking among people in the same work setting. Researchers gained appreciation for how dramatically the consequences of interaction can vary depending on levels of trust among those people who are interacting; these variations are often influenced by differences in level of authority.

Getting a Thoughtful Start

It is usually true that research turning out to be significant begins with a good question. Coming up with a good question is a feat of intellect and inspiration. It requires conceptual work to think out what the pivotally important issues really are. The pivotal issues in sociology (and for that matter, the other social sciences as well) generally revolve around the creation, the validation, the maintenance, the transformation, or the demise of interpersonal attachments, shared beliefs, or systemic interconnections of various kinds.

The social science concepts that command most interest are the ones that help us recognize differences among attachments, shared beliefs, and systemic interconnections. While a complete list of terms would be very long indeed, a "partial short list" of concepts many social scientists find useful would probably include these terms among others: social isolation, social distance, self, status, role, identity, socialization, social control, class, market, opportunity cost, externalized cost, network, vested interest, reference group, power, authority, chain of command, norm, value, vertical integration, regulation, and institutionalization.

The Ethics of Theory-Driven Research

Many would find "research ethics" to be an unusual topic for discussion in a book on theory. But a recurring theme of *Making Sense of Social Theory* is that for sociological theory to be more than philosophy or the history of ideas, but to be scaffolding for scientific progress, it must be understood in terms of its relationship to and value in research enterprise. Consequently, working on theory necessarily implicates research and therefore carries a research ethics dimension.

There are important ethical provisions to keep in mind whenever we are conducting social research. We sociologists are ethics bound to protect the anonymity of our informants and research subjects. We make sure that private information remains confidential. And sociology's code of ethics prohibits research we can reasonably anticipate could hurt people. This means we avoid intentionally placing anyone (including ourselves) in compromising or potentially dangerous situations. And we try to anticipate and avoid doing things that could reasonably be expected to harm or embarrass our subjects.

We also have ethics obligations to science itself. These include honest description of our research activities and honest reporting of facts uncovered, including *inconvenient facts* that fail to accord with what we expect or want to find.

Over the years, there have been some ethical lapses by people conducting sociological research, but thankfully, these have been comparatively few in number. Ethics are important to sociologists, and the American Sociological Association has a detailed and demanding code of ethics.

The ethics of theory-driven research are grounded in a spirit of open inquiry and a culture of evidence. Whatever our views as social scientists may be, we always need to subject our own beliefs to strenuous test. We do this by articulating principles that allow us to make a variety of predictions that can be assessed through honest examination of the world around us. This outlook is at the root of German sociologist Max Weber's call for *value-free* sociology.[5] We will return to Weber repeatedly in this book because he is one of the most important figures in the development of sociology. Among other things, we remember Weber (pronounced "Veber" because the German *w* is pronounced like the English *v*) for his insistence that, as researchers, we acknowledge and call attention to *inconvenient facts* that fail to accord with our personal beliefs.

Some people misunderstand what Weber meant by value-free sociology. He did not mean we should ignore what we believe is important when studying society. He did mean, however, that even though it is appropriate to let our passions influence what we choose to study, we should never allow our passions to blind us to the point that they dictate what we "find." A scientific orientation suggests that we should hope to conclude research by better understanding (which is to say, understanding differently than we did at first) those things we are passionate about. Wanting to conclude our work by validating what we originally thought, and wanting that too strongly, can lead a person off the path on which a scientific culture of evidence is based, and onto a path of self-deception or deception of others.

Being Mindful: The Postmodernist and Ethnomethodological Challenges

Making Sense of Social Theory is consciously written as a social *science* treatise. It both advocates for and reviews sociology as a search for testable principles that can guide us in our efforts to make a better world. This approach is predicated on assumptions common to all sciences, including the social sciences: (a) there are understandable dynamics at work in this world, (b) we can improve our understanding of those dynamics over time by following the scientific method, and (c) following the scientific method means, among other things, putting some version of our best available understanding into words so that we can subject it to ongoing testing and improvement over time.

The basic premises of scientific sociology have been questioned by people who wonder whether it is possible for sociology to get progressively closer to the truth. People who express skepticism about social science do make good points, and it is wise to be mindful of them. The most common contemporary expression of skepticism about science claims is found in postmodernist thought, captured in works such as Jean-François Lyotard's book *The Postmodern Condition*, which is deeply suspicious of science claims about knowledge and progress.[6]

Postmodernists recognize that the ways in which people frame their discussions often impart a viewpoint, thus privileging certain ways of understanding a set of events over other ways of understanding the same events. Put more pointedly, viewpoints can be presented in ways that are laden with implicit meaning and tinged with hidden bias, often diverting attention away from harsh realities that should be revealed. Many postmodernists therefore see the common knowledge of the day as little more than an ideological cover for long-standing forms of oppression. They point out that well-hidden bias is harmful to society to the degree ideology becomes thickly interwoven with daily life and culture. This usually happens when bias has been programmed into texts and permeates them thoroughly. Keeping this in mind, many postmodernists worry, not without reason, that today's truths—including social science truths—may in fact be fictions that go unquestioned and are reinforced in our daily routines.

Postmodernists combat what they see as false knowledge claims and hidden biases by trying to *deconstruct* texts for the purpose of discovering the subtle and not-so-subtle meanings that are conveyed in them. The postmodernist goal is to reveal and debunk false knowledge claims that are found in layers of mutually reinforcing mistruths that serve special interests. They want to expose biases that slip uncritically into public discourse.

The postmodernist critique is that much of what people come to view as truth actually amounts to fiction created by our use of oral language and written text. This analytical framework, which encourages caution about knowledge claims, including those grounded in science, is quite helpful when trying to proceed carefully with a scientific eye toward explanation.

The postmodernists have a particular fear that knowledge claims grounded in science are hard to counteract because science carries a special kind of legitimacy in our society. But although this sounds like an outright rejection of any science approach, it actually suggests a point of convergence where social scientists can embrace substantial parts of the postmodernist position and can incorporate it into a conventional social science worldview. This convergence is possible for two reasons. First, postmodernist deconstruction rests squarely on the premise that some of the things that are now understood (post-deconstruction insight and awareness) are more accurate than other things that were formerly believed (pre-deconstruction bias and myopia). To the extent that postmodernists accept that it is possible for some accounts to be more accurate than others, and to the extent that postmodernism entails a belief that more-accurate accounts are preferable to less-accurate accounts, postmodernists and scientists share a common objective and a common concern for validity in research.

Second, the postmodernist recognition that social fictions can be created and sustained raises standard science-style research questions. How are social fictions fabricated and perpetuated? And when and how are such fictions, once established, then uncovered, revealed, and overturned? These are good social *science* questions reflecting postmodernist concerns and sensibilities.

Most social scientists are able to appreciate and accept the validity of these postmodernist words of caution. Sociologists need to participate in uncovering socially constructed fictions as a common type of shared belief. And once those socially constructed fictions are uncovered, social scientists need to participate in debunking them. These are necessarily social science issues and not merely postmodernist concerns.

There are, of course, all kinds of missteps and errors that can occur during any single research project. But given a long time horizon, discoveries are made and mistakes are corrected in science. Science as a cumulative process abhors falsehood just as nature abhors a vacuum. The propagation of social fiction as truth is antithetical to the very idea of science, just as the use of social fiction to demean and exploit people or hold them back is antagonistic to the humanistic concerns at the base of most social science.

A theoretical perspective in sociology that some view as a forerunner of post-modernism is ethnomethodology. Ethnomethodology was pioneered at the University of California, Los Angeles, by Harold Garfinkel, who argued that people can function only by fooling themselves and others into believing that there is a commonly understood social reality.[7] This makes it possible for social life to continue, in essence, by people conspiring with one another to maintain a collective fiction of shared reality. Garfinkel maintained that we do this by using certain people (ethno) techniques (methods, hence the term *ethnomethodology*).

The ethnomethodological approach can be illustrated by common use of the phrase *you know*. In everyday interaction, people use this phrase to help move interaction along by mutually validating without stopping to confirm that others really do have the same meanings in mind. If we agree not to test our assumption that there is a shared body of meanings, we can proceed to do things as if we do share a common body of meanings, even if there is only an illusion of common shared meaning.

Garfinkel found that when people fail to actively sustain an appearance of common understanding, interaction grinds to a halt. If you don't believe this, you might consider a simple mental experiment. Imagine what would happen if the next time someone says *you know* to you, you respond by asking them to explain. In essence, your reaction would challenge the existence of shared meaning. Reactions like this are generally not responded to as if they are friendly, helpful, or constructive. They are, instead, generally responded to as if they are unfriendly and oppositional or even hostile. Garfinkel and the ethnomethodologists he inspired understand how fragile the illusion of shared reality is, and also how important it is for at least the illusion of shared meaning to be actively maintained if social interaction is to continue as usual.

A useful technique for determining how people manage to affirm and sustain a sufficient sense of shared reality to allow interaction to continue is to perform a *breaching experiment*. In this sort of experiment, one calls commonality of understanding into question and then carefully records what gets done to repair the breach. Repair work takes the form of reaffirming that there is a commonly held sense of shared reality. At one point, some of Garfinkel's students went home for a holiday and treated their parents like strangers (which was not without its ethical implications), challenging the shared assumptions of familiarity and intimacy. Everyone but Garfinkel was surprised how sharp the parental reaction was. When breaching events first occur, the natural response is to provide the person who calls the assumption of shared meaning into question with a second chance to reaffirm the original presupposition of shared meaning. That is, the person is usually given (in fact, quickly given) an opportunity to recant for having said or done something incredibly stupid, idiotic, and uncool. Normal interaction usually breaks down if the person fails to rapidly get in line with the prior picture of shared meaning.

Ethnomethodological work has gradually come to emphasize *conversational analysis* as a strategy for discovering how people sustain the presumptions of shared meaning that are a precondition to stability in everyday social life.[8] In this respect, the research techniques used by ethnomethodologists are rather similar to techniques used by postmodernists, although postmodernists normally focus on global outlooks that are perpetuated within a whole society, while ethnomethodologists more often point their gaze at the strategies individual people use in their interpersonal attachments in order to sustain sufficient sense of shared meaning to allow a given face-to-face interaction to continue.

Recap

This chapter concludes part I of the book. At this point, readers should have a clear idea what science really means and see how theory work can be thought of in terms of its connection to making testable predictions, research into the accuracy of predictions, and subsequent improvements in our explanatory theoretical frameworks. This may require debunking some old ideas about science. Science does not claim to possess ultimate and final truth. If it had ultimate truth there would be no reason to continue the quest to improve our knowledge and understanding.

Social sciences deal with the most difficult subject matter to understand because of the ambiguities and complexities involved. This is why Comte referred to sociology as the queen of all the scientific disciplines. We can't touch what lies between people or put the social connections between people under a microscope where it can be easily seen. Yet, what lies between people, the social, is real in its consequences and calls out for our careful study. Studying the social world is intellectually challenging, and this is why sociological theory is so interesting for those who allow themselves to practice theory as it is being explained in this book.

Some Terms to Know

Hawthorne Effect: When ordinary people who are engaged in everyday behavior realize that their behavior is being studied, their behavior changes for a time.

Measurement Validity: The extent to which an indicator actually measures what it is purported to measure.

Other Things Being Equal: The caveat that many dynamics are at work in the real world, many of which our principles fail to take into account.

Inconvenient Facts: Facts that fail to accord with what we want or expect to find.

Deconstruction: Careful examination of material (often written text, but sometimes conversation) to *reveal points* that are subtly communicated (often in hidden ways that escape easy detection), privileged, and affirmed.

Conversational Analysis: Careful examination of communication (usually oral, but often written) in order to discover how people use words in order to do the work of achieving certain outcomes.

Review of Principles

Trust Principle: Other things being equal, people withdraw from roles/relationships if practical, and tend to use formal and informal rules to minimize their obligations and reduce room for ambiguity if withdrawal is not practical, (1) as a direct function of perceived vulnerability in the setting and (2) as an inverse function of degree of trust in the people in that setting.

Conflict/Cohesion Principle: Other things being equal, cohesion within groups or other social entities increases as a function of the degree of conflict between those entities.

Quiz

Check your answers in the back of the book. If you get any wrong, consider reviewing chapter 3 before continuing.

1. List the steps in the scientific method as they are enumerated in this book.
2. Write out Simmel's Conflict/Cohesion Principle to see if you remember it correctly.
3. The *other things being equal* caveat suggests that
   a. an indicator does a good job of representing what a researcher says it measures
   b. other factors, not indicated in our principle, might be having an impact on the outcome
   c. a particular theoretical axiom or principle helps us to explain variation in outcomes in many different kinds of situations
4. What does Weber's concept of value-free research caution against?
   a. doing research on things we have strong opinions about
   b. doing research on subjects that are in the political arena
   c. designing research in order to find what we want to find

5. What group of theorists focuses its efforts on trying to "deconstruct" texts in order to uncover meanings that are subtly implied, privileged, and affirmed?
   a. all sociologists
   b. postmodernists
   c. ethnomethodologists

Application Exercise

Briefly describe an organization where you have worked or volunteered in the past, and what you did in that organization. Then think of the kinds of events causing trust to be gained or lost in that workplace. Based on what you have experienced yourself or have heard from others, what kinds of events seem to you to be particularly important for shaping (either increasing or diminishing) trust in a work setting?

Briefly discuss whether it seems to you that the matter of trust is important to consider when trying to understand workplace dynamics. How important would you say it is?

PART II

THINKING ABOUT THE ROOTS, METHODS, AND USES OF SOCIOLOGICAL THEORY

Having completed part I of this book, readers should understand what axioms and principles are and how social scientists can use them. But there is a difference between a textbook understanding of something abstract like theory, and an appreciation for how it can be applied. Most theory books are written with the idea that a reader will be able to answer questions about theory. But *Making Sense of Social Theory* should leave readers thinking more like theorists in an active science, using theory and constructing theory. Part II of the book is written with the intention of going farther along the road using theory as a scientist would rather than approaching it as a historian of social thought would.

Deriving the value this book has to offer requires that we try to think about theoretical explanations with concrete empirical application, keeping the practical utility of those applications in mind. The chapters in part II examine relevance of theory from the vantage point of someone being called on to actually take ownership of theory and use it, rather than simply learn it. The material is pertinent and useful.

There are three chapters in part II. The first of these, chapter 4, emphasizes the point that from its beginnings, sociology has been a relevant discipline dealing with things that matter, often doing so as part of a theory-driven research enterprise. This chapter establishes the point that sociology, from its inception, has involved scientific study of society aimed at understanding forces at work in the social world.

Chapter 5 covers some basic lessons of theory construction. Covering these lessons early is intended to convey an important message. Theory construction is an activity for everyone interested in better understanding dynamics at work in the social world.

Chapter 6 illustrates the role of theory in the progressive improvement in social science understanding of the world we live and work in. The central point of chapter 6 is that social science thought does not stand still. Our understanding is constantly moving forward, with theory embodying our most robust and powerful insights and pointing out the frontier of uncertain terrain where what understandings we are confident about meet the limits of their utility.

Each of the social sciences has a fascinating history, and the great insights of sociology can best be introduced in the context of the discipline's historical evolution (as we will do in parts III and IV of this book). But the ideas to be introduced in the later chapters have their real value if applied by readers to contemporary events and challenges. The chapters in part II will be important for helping readers to decide how to approach the theoretical ideas presented throughout the book. Always remember that good social science theory should be understandable. Difficult is OK, but being incomprehensible, or even unnecessarily convoluted, is not OK in good science. In addition, for theory to be useful for sociologists, it has to help us to understand the subject matter of sociology: the causes and consequences of variations in interpersonal attachments, shared beliefs, and systemic interconnections.

Finally, doing theory work should ultimately have us trying to move beyond the work of earlier theorists. This means trying to apply old ideas to new situations or in different settings; variously affirming the applicability of old ideas or suggesting alterations in them or additions to them as appropriate. Science advances through these efforts, great and small, at theory construction (chapter 5). Theory construction is something like the work of a potter, shaping and reshaping wet clay in an effort to move closer to the real essence we are trying to capture. Chapter 6 attempts to illustrate just how fruitful some of our past efforts have been. Then, in parts III and IV, we will more systematically examine some axioms and principles that lie at the heart of, and define the explanatory power of, some of sociology's analytical frameworks.

4

The Historical Context
for a Science of Society

E ARLY SOCIOLOGY WAS BOTH A EUROPEAN and an American creation. Understanding the different historical contexts in which sociology emerged in western Europe and North America explains a great deal about what the discipline was to become.

The Scientific Revolution in Seventeenth-Century Europe

There have been many worldwide bursts of scientific activity. One that took place in Europe in the seventeenth century is often referred to as *the* scientific revolution because it was the first to be broadly based on a clearly articulated way of thinking about and conducting scientific inquiry. The scientific method, as described in chapter 3, was considered a revolutionary way of thought in the seventeenth century. Galileo, remember, was persecuted by the Catholic Church for his use of the telescope to make observations he could use in testing the conventional wisdom of his time, that the universe revolved around the earth (placing mankind at the center of all God's creation). Along with that of Galileo, we remember names of people like Francis Bacon and Copernicus because they helped set in motion a revolutionary (that is, *world-changing*) commitment to careful, objective, and sometimes systematic, cause-and-effect investigation of the physical and biological worlds. The objective of these scientists was to better understand how the world works, with the thought that greater understanding of dynamics at work in the world would ultimately help people make the world a better place. Early successes in fields such as astronomy and anatomy encouraged later scientific study in fields such as chemistry and geology. Scientific method is thus an important part of our common cultural heritage as human beings. The scientific revolution forever changed the lives of every single person living on this planet.

Importantly, the scientific method of the seventeenth century provided a philosophical foundation for the Enlightenment period that swept Europe in the eighteenth century. Enlightenment thought touted rational analysis and decision making over habit and tradition. At its core, the view of the Enlightenment is that conditions can improve, and moreover, that the true nature of human beings is defined by a curiosity to experiment, a desire to understand, and a wish to make a more perfect world. Encouraged by the scientific advances of the previous century, Enlightenment social thought abandoned some long-held traditional ideas. These included maxims such as (a) sick people bring affliction on themselves as heavenly retribution for bad behavior, or (b) have sickness cast on them by the evil eye of devilish people.

The Enlightenment also fostered ideas that traditional trade arrangements and production systems could and should be improved on. The economist Adam Smith comes from this tradition. Other Enlightenment thinkers began writing about human beings' having "natural rights" that should entitle them to basic respect, even in the face of royal prerogative or despotic rule. Works by Jean-Jacques Rousseau, Charles Montesquieu, and Thomas Paine exemplify Enlightenment social outlooks in this tradition. The Age of Reason, which the early eighteenth-century Enlightenment heralded, called for action in the name of progress.

By the late eighteenth and early nineteenth centuries, the scientific approach had been so successful that some people began to call for scientific study of the social universe, analogous to the physical and biological sciences. Thus, people of scientific bent were no longer content to restrict themselves to the application of scientific method in studies of things they could easily touch, such as rocks, trees, and kidneys. Some began calling for the creation of social science. They were optimistic that society (economy, religion, sports, politics, law, popular culture) could be better understood through careful social scientific theorizing and through data collection designed specifically for the purpose of challenging, testing, and reformulating our ideas about social dynamics at work in the world.

At that time, European society was in the midst of convulsive change. The French and American revolutions were manifestations of the upheaval. Feudalism was coming to an end and people clamored for more economic freedom and opportunity. Aristocratic privilege based solely on family status was being questioned, and in many places a person's social standing was finally starting to be influenced by personal achievement and not just by family standing.

There was even a new and revolutionary idea that community decisions should be arrived at through a system allowing for open discussion of public policy, and for a wider range of decisions to be made by democratically elected representatives of the people. These ideas were not revolutionary in the sense that they necessarily required bloody social convulsion, but they were most definitely revolutionary in the sense that they suggested the necessity for a far-reaching restructuring of society; that is, certainly in an Enlightenment sense, the true meaning of *revolution*. Change is revolutionary to the degree that it involves fundamental restructuring of the society. Restructuring society need not involve shedding any blood at all. And it has often been the case that the bloodiest episodes in human history have resulted in no meaningful structural change at all.

The French Revolution of 1789 is a particularly important historical precursor to the development of sociology. It occurred just a few years after the American Revolution, and it embodied the ideals of liberty, equality, and fraternity (*liberté, égalité, et fraternité*). But the French Revolution took place in an older society in which the rich enjoyed more lavish lifestyles than did the rich in America. In France, the members of a relatively large and decadent elite bled a vast and destitute peasantry living in squalor. Those peasants had no frontier to escape to and the society therefore lacked the kind of safety valve the sparsely settled American frontier offered to the fledgling United States in the late eighteenth century.

Extremes of wealth in combination with an absence of a safety valve resulted in a combustible situation. With the benefit of hindsight we can understand why the situation quickly turned into what is sometimes referred to as the *Reign of Terror* after the onset of the French Revolution. Thousands of nobles and their allies were marched off for public execution by guillotine. This method of execution brought a relatively quick—and, it was thought, even humane—end to life by cleanly chopping off the head of the accused, but it also made for a bloody spectacle. Because the guillotine severs all the veins and arteries running to and from the brain, execution by this method results in a high volume of blood spurting. As the practice of lining up several people at a time for execution was not uncommon at the height of the French Revolution, use of the guillotine quite literally filled the gutters of some streets with veritable rivers of blood.

Because of its association with mob rule that could turn violent, democracy came to be feared by some of the same people who longed for it. Many British and French intellectuals of the time came to fear the thought of mob rule's turning violent and leading to prolonged periods of uncontrollable and unpredictable social chaos.

Meanwhile, the technical achievements and commercial fruits of the age of science were beginning to make themselves felt in visible ways. The case of the steam engine is particularly instructive. Experimental steam engines were being developed in the 1760s. In 1774 James Watt and Matthew Boulton began commercial production, with the first steam engines used to increase productivity by pumping water out of low-lying tunnels in coal mines. Enhanced in later decades by improvements in boiler technology, steam engines powered an industrial revolution in the early nineteenth century; they did this by freeing factories from reliance on waterwheels to drive equipment and by making bulk transport possible over long distances via railroads and steamships.

With the factory system beginning in earnest, manufacturing expanded rapidly and started a chain reaction in many places, but especially in Britain. The transformation there was far reaching. Textile factories needed wool and cotton, as well as workers. Big landowners in England and Scotland pushed subsistence-oriented tenant farmers off the land, in what peasant agriculturalists would bitterly remember as *the clearances.* Landowners, after all, needed to make room for more sheep, in order to produce more wool, needed to feed more looms, in order to generate more of the profits making mill owners wealthy and filling government tax coffers with revenue. Meanwhile, displaced farmers streamed into cities, where they tried to find low-paying jobs in the factories. Businesses were extremely profitable and production expanded rapidly. This translated into reduced prices for manufactured goods, which fueled demand for even more textiles, leading landowners to push even more peasants off the land.

These were bleak times for working people. Karl Marx, writing in England, predicted bloody revolution all over western Europe. Many members of the English middle class were afraid that England might replicate the French Reign of Terror. And the French middle class, with fresh and painful memories of the Reign of Terror, feared that something comparable might happen again in France. At this point, a decided intellectual shift was taking place as a few people in Europe began to direct their scientific culture of evidence to the study of human communities. There was an element of embryonic sociology in this that would set the stage for dramatic improvements in public health. For example, the first successful vaccination (which was for smallpox) was brought to England from India in 1783. And at the beginning of the nineteenth century, the discovery that cholera was a waterborne disease made it possible for cities to dramatically reduce death rates by discharging sewage into rivers far downstream from intakes for drinking water, as explained in Steven Johnson's book *The Ghost Map.*[1]

All these science-based improvements resulted in exponential population growth. Perhaps three hundred million people lived on Earth at the time of Christ. Approximately six hundred million were alive at the time of Columbus. This means it took a millennium and a half for the world's population to double. There were around nine hundred million people when the first vaccination was developed—a 50 percent population increase in a little under three hundred years. Then, steady improvements in public sanitation lowered the infant mortality rate. With more babies surviving into adulthood and having children themselves, rapid population growth was under way. The impact is evident in the numbers. While only one billion people were alive on the earth by 1830, there were two billion by 1930, three billion by 1960, four billion by

1976, five billion by 1988, and six billion by 1999, and we now find the world's population to be roughly in the vicinity of seven billion souls. At the same time that dramatic worldwide population growth was occurring, cities grew more rapidly than the countryside, and railroads opened isolated rural areas to commercial development. In terms of the ideas the discipline of sociology focuses on (the nature of interpersonal attachments, the character of shared beliefs, and systemic interconnections among people), the pace of change really began to accelerate in the mid-nineteenth century concurrently with exponential population growth and urbanization. There was a growing need for a science of society, and Auguste Comte was the person who most clearly articulated that need.

European Sociology at Its Beginning: A Response to the Fire Alarm of Social Chaos

Locating the moment of sociology's conception in mid-nineteenth-century European history clarifies an important point. It allows us to appreciate what some of the prevailing concerns were as the discipline was taking shape in western Europe at a particular point in time. The world was changing with unprecedented speed. That change was tumultuous. It was frightening for many people. Sociology was born in a context where there was a strongly felt need to understand the impact change might have on societal stability. In a very real way, the birth of European sociology marked a new phase of the Enlightenment. People wanted to have a more penetrating understanding of society in order to anticipate the consequences of change, and they wanted this for the expressed purpose of trying to help engineer a better life for people. In social science, there was hope for a better future, and this hope was starting to take hold by the 1830s, just as the world's population hit one billion people and just as Auguste Comte began to attract followers with his call for establishing a science of society to be called *sociology*.

It is easy to appreciate what Comte and his followers were hoping for. Remember that this was only a generation after the French Revolution. Many French intellectuals dreamed of a society engineered for peace, prosperity, and sociopolitical harmony. They felt a more utopian society could be intentionally engineered through the use of social scientific principles. Although these principles had yet to be developed, Comte and his followers were optimistic that they could be. They understood that the line between civility and chaos could grow thin, and having had a recent taste of chaos, most of them knew that they did not want the barrier between civility and chaos to be breached again. But they were convinced sociology would help them achieve economic progress and institutional development hand in hand with social stability, which is what most of them wanted.

Founder Effects: An Important Lesson

As was already noted, one of the people who dreamed of a great new era of social progress guided by scientifically tested sociological principles was the individual who conceived of sociology as a science and gave the discipline its name. He was Auguste Comte (1798–1857) of France. Comte started a tradition that really took shape in the work of Harriet Martineau and Émile Durkheim (see chapter 7) and largely defined what sociology was to become.

Comte died well over a century ago, yet his vision continues to inform us. This is in part because of the power of his ideas. It also reflects the fact that people widely recognized him as the first real sociologist, and many people accepted his definition of what the discipline should be. As part of his science vision, he advocated empirical testing of principles in hopes of uncovering useful insights that would enable us to restructure society in our effort to make a better world. Comte's vision took root and has had lasting impact on the discipline. This illustrates the importance of founder effects and suggests a revealing axiom.

Founder Effects Axiom: **Those interests and concerns of earlier figures that became active parts of institutional memory or are deeply embedded in institutional practice shape the activities of others for a long time to come.**

The point of this axiom is that the initial ideas of a founder, as well as those of other people who have been pivotal figures with the passage of time, may have lasting consequences. This is true even if the identities of those people are largely or entirely forgotten. This lingering residue does tend to fade somewhat over time, and the period immediately after control passes from a founder to the next leadership generation tends to be a particularly telling moment of transition, determining what aspects of a founder's legacy are likely to be retained. But while founding legacies are not uniformly strong and enduring, the Founder Effects Axiom is useful for reminding us of an important regularity. Early voices often tend to resonate into the future, with echoes of those early voices locked into institutional history in ways that have reverberating consequences. This has certainly been the case in sociology (this will be emphasized in chapter 7 on Émile Durkheim, chapter 8 on Karl Marx, chapter 9 on Max Weber, and chapter 10 on George Herbert Mead).

Why are founder effects more pervasive and longer lasting in some organizations than in others? That is a question about variability in outcomes, and we would need to develop a principle in order to address the question. For now, it will suffice to say that sociologists have learned that founder effects are often very real. Explaining variability in the strength of founder effects is one of the many tasks that will fall to the next generation of sociologists. (I am hopeful that the rising generation of sociologists will include many who are influenced by ideas presented in this book.)

A Different Kind of Chaos: Urban and
Ethnic Transition in the United States

Given late eighteenth- and early nineteenth-century history, it is understandable that the educated classes in Europe during the middle and late nineteenth century tended to fear the potential of class warfare and political revolution. But people in the United States were responding to a different set of societal concerns arising in the context of American historical experience. Technological change (development of railroads, harnessing of electricity, etc.) ushered in the era of big business, which was unlike anything the world had known before. Production was moving from subsistence agriculture on independent farmsteads to mass production for a consumer market. In the process, the United States was moving from an overwhelmingly rural country (in the mid-1800s) to an overwhelmingly urban country (by the mid-1900s). At the same time, there were unprecedented waves of migration to the United States from all over Europe. Looked at independently, each of these three changes (industrialization, urbanization, and immigration of people speaking many languages and bringing with them a wide diversity of customs) had enormous transforming effects on the United States. And all three changes happened at more or less the same time. So while early European sociologists knew what social change could mean at its worst and feared it, early American sociologists were far less inclined to be fearful of change. They were often bewildered by the speed of change and the increasing heterogeneity of America's social tapestry, but it is important to note that bewilderment is not the same as fear. Bewilderment at the magnitude and momentum of social change in the United States was characterized by at least as much a sense of promise and opportunity as a sense of discouragement and fear. This placed early sociology in the United States on a trajectory that separated it in substantial ways from sociology in Europe.

Many of America's early sociologists were great observers of everyday life and ethnographers of organizations and of communities. They were more conscious of themselves as collecting data than as constructing theory, though many of their data collection efforts certainly produced impressive theoretical insights.

The Beginning of Urban and Organizational Ethnography

Although ethnographic techniques were first used at about the same time by early sociologists and anthropologists, anthropologists initially restricted the use of ethnographic techniques to small hunting-and-gathering bands and concentrated their attention on food gathering and spiritual or religious observances. The use of ethnographic techniques to study larger communities, especially urban neighborhoods, and to investigate the more complex and varied range of community-based phenomena that urban neighborhoods produce, began in sociology around 1900. In contrast, it was not until the 1970s that urban ethnography assumed a relatively high profile in sociology's sister discipline of anthropology.

The pioneers in sociology's urban ethnographic efforts were Robert Park and his colleagues in sociology at the University of Chicago, W. E. B. Du Bois and his colleagues in sociology at Atlanta University, and Robert and Helen Merrell Lynd, working in Muncie, Indiana (discussed in chapter 12). Urban ethnography came to be emblematic of sociological research, and more of this work was done in Chicago than in any other city. As the nineteenth century drew to a close, Chicago was a magnet for people from all around the world. This made it the perfect field laboratory for sociological investigation.

Sociology's urban ethnographers were intrigued by the fact that cities were constantly being re-created by successive waves of arrivals from the countryside or from other countries. What emerged was a clear pattern of neighborhood succession as one group of people replaced another. Chicago sociologists observing this as an ongoing process chronicled a regular cycle of community disorganization and reorganization over time.

Comprehensive studies of ethnic neighborhoods began just after 1900. Two of the best illustrations of this work are Thomas and Znaniecki's two-volume 1918 work, *The Polish Peasant in Europe and America*,[2] and Louis Wirth's 1928 study of the divide between German and eastern European Jewish neighborhoods, *The Ghetto*.[3] Sociology's growing ranks of urban ethnographies detailed the structure of communities and the lives of people in them. A recurrent theme in sociology's urban ethnographies was that when large numbers of people find themselves uprooted and moving to a new land, they reshape and reformulate their identities. This did not mean abandoning old identities, but it did entail redefining and reshaping old identities, modifying their meaning to make them useful in a new time and place, at the same time that they reconstruct a modified version of the communities and cultures they left behind. Reconstruction of this kind produces a creatively adaptive hybrid. People retain habits that are useful for helping them face the barriers and difficulties they confront in their new environment, but also discard those old practices and beliefs that, on balance, seem detrimental or maladaptive in the new environment.

A key insight of sociology's urban ethnographies is that adaptation of old forms is often quite functional. One illustration can be found in social groups drawing together migrants from a single region to enjoy music and update old friends on life events. These groups often take on functions as employment agencies and as savings and loan organizations.

In ethnic communities, we also see especially heavy stress placed on institutions that comfort people by helping to affirm identities that people do not want to give up but that receive little validation in the new setting. Bakeries, for example, can have more importance to people struggling with identity in a hostile environment than they do in places of origin, where one's identity is taken for granted and secure. The point is that where identities from the past are concerned, making sure everyone sees the identity being expressed (dyeing beer green and even dyeing the Chicago River green on Saint Patrick's Day) may paradoxically signal that people are trying to hold on to an identity having more emotional salience in memory than daily relevance impacting everyday decisions.

Sociology's urban ethnographers have always been intrigued by the fact that people, even those without many resources, adapt old beliefs and practices to fit new conditions and to affirm their own distinctive identities, even as their ways of thinking and acting begin to diverge greatly from those of their ancestors.[4] This pivotal insight can be captured in the form of an axiom.

Selective Retention Axiom: **We selectively retain old beliefs and practices and we actively redefine old identities and commitments in ways that optimally balance our sense of belonging with our ability to successfully adjust to changing conditions.**

Here we see a clear expression of pragmatism in the intellectual outlook dominating early sociology in the United States. The community patterns that Chicago sociologists noticed being institutionalized in immigrant neighborhoods were those that filled a need. In this respect, those immigrants who claim to be most traditional are, in some instances, actually the most active change agents, modifying old patterns of association for new purposes and mobilizing ethnic affinity for distinctly modern political combat on contemporary issues. Cleaving to group identity often helps people, particularly if they find the social climate to be inhospitable and when aspirations are great but other resources are scarce.

The Pain of the Country and the Lure of the City

Sociology's early urban ethnographies almost always seemed to focus on the efforts of migrating groups to form communities. Sometimes, those groups were immigrants coming from a particular country, as in the case of Thomas and Znaniecki's *The Polish Peasant in Europe and America.* Sometimes they were internal migrants siphoned from one geographic area into another. This was the case in W. E. B. Du Bois's study *The Philadelphia Negro.*[5] Du Bois is an important figure in American history. He was the first African American to receive a PhD in any field from any American university (sociology—Harvard University). He went on to conduct pioneering research (in Philadelphia and in Atlanta) exposing many aspects of the American condition that had been overlooked or ignored. He was a major contributor to the development of urban ethnographic techniques in sociology, and in the process he made important contributions to the civil rights movement in the years leading up to the rise of Dr. Martin Luther King.

Some of the urban ethnographers focused on migrants of a particular demographic group, usually unattached young males. This was the case with Nels "Bo" Anderson's study *The Hobo*.[6] Rootless young men were of special interest to readers, and Anderson's study of them helped bring legitimacy and acclaim to sociology in the United States. In the early 1900s, few people went to college, and many young men (and some young women) from poor families left home with nothing in their pockets but hope. At that time, there were waves of economic refugees displaced by a declining farm economy. (The use of tractors in the countryside and internal combustion engines and electric motors in urban areas decimated the grain market by doing away with the need to feed draft animals. Insect infestations decimated the South's cotton industry at about the same time, around 1920.) Northern cities were magnets, attracting young men who had no promise of advancement where they were and came to the city in search of jobs and excitement.

The urban ethnographies of migrants in Chicago gave rise to a new understanding about the causes of migration. Despite outward appearances, interviews made it clear that few people leave their homes only because of poverty or persecution. There must also be some enticement: the pull of opportunities for better jobs, a wider range of educational opportunities, better public services, easier access to health care, more excitement, or higher culture. Conversely, few people leave their homes only because these pull factors make a distant destination seem enticing. Most people must also be pushed by economic hardship or persecution of some sort.

Thus, we have the famous *push-pull* principle of migration: the momentum for migration increases as a positive function of (a) the pull of opportunities or excitement, and (b) the push of poverty or persecution. But this principle of migration can easily be recognized as a simple corollary to the Principle of Rational Choice, which has already been discussed. People generally make calculations based on a range of anticipated costs and benefits, but only after also considering the relative probabilities of different outcomes actually developing and after weighing what seem to be available alternatives.

Social Problems and Sociological Theory

There is often a seedy side to sociology's urban ethnographies. The influx of rootless young men changes neighborhoods in ways a lot of people do not like. Substance abuse, prostitution, fighting, gambling, and burglary are all more common in the grimy rooming-house neighborhoods where rootless people typically congregate. University of Chicago sociologists were right there to report on the ways neighborhoods were being transformed. Sociologists differed from other observers by noting that much of the transformation being chronicled had to do with (positive) reorganization rather than (negative) disorganization. For example, Nels Anderson's work described the day-labor system of the skid row community close to the downtown area, and the barber colleges along Halsted Street that held out hope of entry-level employment training. And for single young men with no money and no prospects, there were safe dance halls where an uprooted young man could enjoy fleeting moments of contact with women for a dime a dance.[7]

Alcohol use was a widespread problem. But the urban ethnographies that sociologists wrote tended to offer an understanding of drug culture rooted in an appreciation of the basic humanity of substance abusers.[8] Early sociological research on substance abuse led to the development of intervention and reha-bilitation programs that had some success in dealing with otherwise intractable issues. Sociology has made a fundamentally constructive difference, promoting systems of social encouragement and support as the single most important part of any successful battle against substance abuse.

Early sociology at the University of Chicago was interwoven with social work. Jane Addams, founder and operator of Hull House and later a winner of a Nobel Prize, was associated with the sociology program at the University of Chicago. Even at that early stage, sociology programs were practicing community-based learning and advocating purposeful education to empower students to help build a better society and not just engage in intellectual navel-gazing.

Neighborhoods in Transition

An accompanying discovery made by sociology's urban ethnographers is that neighborhoods can change rapidly in what the Chicago sociologists called a *neighborhood succession process.* As in-migration accelerates, marginal neighbor-hoods can fill up and spill over with new people, fueling intergroup antagonism and conflict. More affluent, better-educated people sometimes leave deteriorat-ing neighborhoods (*white flight* being an example), and sometimes move into deteriorating neighborhoods in search of bargain-price housing stock and good location (*gentrification*). A spillover of people from one community into another usually starts slowly. But when a tipping point of about 30 percent is reached, locals see that the old neighborhood is going to change whether they like it or not. At that point, neighborhood transition typically accelerates, as everyone who is inclined and able to move seeks to do so. (In neighborhoods in transi-tion, movement usually slows by the time an 85 percent turnover in population is reached, for by that time everyone who remains either wants to stay or lacks viable options for leaving.)

When neighborhood transition involves gentrification, the impact can be quite destabilizing for the poor. Young, upwardly mobile people can move into a dilapidated old neighborhood with enough cash to displace everyone else. Long ago, Chicago sociologists realized that community dynamics are constrained by the commercial geography of the city. When Robert Park, Ernest Burgess, and Roderick McKenzie wrote *The City* in 1925, the pattern of ethnic succession was clear and a concentric-zone model of the urban ecology of Chicago had become apparent. Business services were concentrated in the downtown center. Factories were clustered close enough to downtown to benefit from transit hubs, but far enough away to be able to have access to more space and yet pay lower rents. Transients and organized criminal activity were heavily concentrated in a densely populated but geographically thin sandwich of land between downtown and the factories. Ethnic neighborhoods of factory workers were interspersed with or located just beyond the factories. And somewhat more prosperous people lived farther away to escape the grimy coal dust that coated everything in U.S. cities prior to the widespread conversion to cleaner-burning natural gas around 1960.[9]

What makes the urban ethnographic tradition of early sociology in the United States so important within the context of this book is that it illustrates the fundamental social science premise that careful study can change our thinking and improve our understanding. For example, government has the potential to change urban ecology by influencing where and how needs are met and tastes are satisfied. But often the impacts of government intervention are unforeseen. When the City of Chicago closed down its highly concentrated and centrally located vice district, where gambling and prostitution were visible, political leaders were surprised by the results. However, if they had asked a sociologist, they might not have been so surprised. Illicit commerce did not disappear. It simply moved into smaller and less-obvious locations sprinkled all around the city and into neighboring towns. Similarly, when alcohol was made illegal during prohibition, Al Capone (who by crossing one street moved from Chicago to the neighboring suburb of Cicero) and other bootleggers opened a widely dispersed string of speakeasies that everyone knew about and that were popular as public entertainment centers for adults from all social strata. In part because of government action, Chicago went from having what seemed like a lot of vice because it was located in one place and therefore was visible, to having what in actuality was much more vice, but dispersed throughout the city and disguised so as to blend in and not be too apparent. We can compare this phenomenon to water balloons: when squeezed, they tend to change their outer shape somewhat and the water gravitates to places where the pressure is not quite as persistent and intense.

Sociologists on the street identified new trends and saw unintended consequences right from the start. This is a big reason why sociologists sometimes seem to be out of the mainstream, politically speaking. Part of our job is to recognize trends as they are beginning and to sound an early warning of more serious consequences to come. Unfortunately, this tends to make sociologists unpopular with people who would rather shoot the messenger than address the problem. Nevertheless, an important part of our job really is to do what we can to make sure festering realities are understood before they mushroom out of control. As a practical matter, this means that sociological research frequently gives voice to the voiceless.

The Role of Big Business

The role of big business was critical in shaping the twentieth-century society that North American sociologists were trying to study. Railroads were particularly important. They interconnected the industrial parts of the economies of Canada, Mexico, and the United States. Railroads often provided both the means and the reason for relocating large numbers of people. A good case in point is the vibrant Mexican American community on the west side of Chicago, which started as a small community of railroad workers who had come to Chicago (the rail hub of the United States) from Durango, Mexico, in search of opportunity at a point when railroads around Chicago were hiring more workers.

The rise of big business in the United States was also associated with the formation of highly bureaucratic and vertically integrated industrial manufacturing firms. This provided American sociologists with tangible cases for understanding how and why different patterns of social organization emerge under different conditions. It was, therefore, not long before sociology's strong tradition of ethnographic research on communities also developed into a strong tradition of ethnographic research on organizations.

Recap

When commitment to scientific sociology began to take hold in Europe, especially in France, historical experience led most people to want progress without chaos. Chaos can ravage a society, often bringing indiscriminate harm to people. Comte wanted nothing to do with that. In fact, he hoped sociologists would learn enough to help society avoid that fate. This attitude inspired a commitment to applying sociology's theoretical insights to problems of social integration and to movements for political change. European-inspired interest in these topics continues to characterize the discipline.

The interests of early sociologists in North America tended to have a somewhat different focus. Because of prevailing historical experience, North American sociologists were preoccupied with observing and trying to understand (a) the community transformations taking place as people were ripped from the countryside and found themselves transported into cities by the winds of fate, and (b) the organizational innovations that were occurring with the rise of industrial capitalism on a large scale. By the early 1900s, sociology's urban ethnographies were leaving a lasting legacy with their studies of communities and organizations undergoing change. Their focus was on naturalistic observation of real people in their community settings, on taking the pulse of popular opinion, and in celebrating the way ordinary people live. In the process, researchers learned that communities are constantly changing. Even if a community suffers through a period of decline, people there are always adapting old social arrangements and inventing new ones, giving rise to new organizational and community forms in the process. Describing these changes has been one of sociology's primary research goals, and understanding these changes has been one of sociology's primary theoretical reasons for existence.

Review of Axioms

Founder Effects Axiom: Those interests and concerns of earlier figures that became active parts of institutional memory or are deeply embedded in institutional practice shape the activities of others for a long time to come.

Selective Retention Axiom: We selectively retain old beliefs and practices and we actively redefine old identities and commitments in ways that optimally balance our sense of belonging with our ability to successfully adjust to changing conditions.

Quiz

Check your answers in the back of the book. If you get any wrong, consider reviewing chapter 4 before continuing.

1. When sociology started in France, what chaos was it intended to avert a repetition of?
2. Match the authors with the topics.
   a. Nels Anderson
   b. Alfred Lindesmith
   c. W. I. Thomas and Florian Znaniecki

   i. Polish immigrants to the United States
   ii. hobo life
   iii. drug addiction
3. What does the Selective Retention Axiom tell us?

Application Exercise

Take a bus ride or a walk through a neighborhood you do not often venture into. This should be in a neighborhood and at a time of day with enough street traffic that you can see something and also exercise appropriate regard for safety if it is a place with which you are unfamiliar. Observe some things that seem different from what you are accustomed to. Ask yourself what you think these observations mean. Then write down an observation you would like to think about more.

5

Being Conscious about
Theory Construction

THERE IS AN UNFORTUNATE TENDENCY for people to think that theory construction must be like rocket science: something that should be attempted only
by someone who has completed a high level of advanced training and has already
reached the pinnacle of her or his professional accomplishment. If this were
the case, theory construction would be an activity always reserved for later. But
when people fail to work on theory construction at the same time that they engage in research, they handicap their own efforts. Engaging in theory construction is a part of what a social scientist needs to do in order to achieve as much
understanding as possible from every inquiry.[1] The idea that theory construction
is something to be left for the culmination of a research project or the culmination of a career is incorrect in every possible way and is in fact is unconstructive
and antiscientific.

Theory Construction as Both the Beginning
and the End of Good Scientific Work

Chapter 3 identifies five steps in the scientific method. When done well, the first,
second, and fifth steps of the scientific method are theory construction activities:
the first step conceptualizes the topic in order to articulate a good research question; the second step clearly articulates the axiom(s) or predictive principle(s)
to be tested; and the fifth step improves our body of principles or better speci-
fies the boundary conditions under which our axioms and principles seem to
apply. If the first and second steps in the scientific method are performed well
in the spirit of theory construction, they give meaningful direction to the third

step (identifying research hypotheses) and fourth step of the scientific method (collecting data appropriate to the research hypotheses and then testing those hypotheses). Clearly, research is not divorced form theory construction. Indeed, theory construction activity is needed to properly anchor good research at both the beginning and the end of the process.

By its nature, scientific inquiry involves iterative work. Scientists rarely produce a first draft and then pronounce their work done. Although sudden, wondrously serendipitous developments have been known to occur on occasion, completely spontaneous leaps forward in science most often happen in science fiction movies. Sparks of genius representing great leaps forward in science, such as recognition of the double helix in genetics, occur when people who have been deeply immersed in data that fail to match theoretical predictions are challenged to find a creative new way to look at available information somewhat differently in order to resolve some of the theory–data inconsistency.

It is also the case that most important theoretical revelations accompanying scientific discovery appear after a lot of people have contributed different bits of information and insight over many years. Science is both a cumulative and a cooperative enterprise. People credited with breakthroughs are almost always building on the work of a great many people who have gone before them.

What we usually mean when we say a scientist makes a breakthrough is that she or he is in the right place at the right time to arrive at a new and better way to understand some puzzle about the world around us. Scientists' contributions most often come in the form of theory construction work. That is, scientific breakthroughs usually involve reformulating research questions in fresh new ways, reconceptualizing variables, or modifying axioms and/or principles in ways that help resolve theory–data inconsistency. As regards the social sciences as a whole, a great many people spend a good deal of time taking a very large number of very small steps to get closer to grappling with some inconsistency between theory and data, and then one person or a few people contribute to a paradigm shift that gives us a new way of understanding the world, such that our theories come into closer alignment with the data we have.[2] In fact, big scientific breakthroughs sometimes happen in more than one place at approximately the same time, confirming the view that the scientific community as a whole lays the groundwork for breakthroughs to be made.

This kind of theory construction activity defines scientific progress. It involves an articulation of new insight that comes after a lot of repeated effort utilizing the innate human capacity for recognizing patterns of association and for testing those patterns of association in different contexts or under different conditions, so that we can sort out causal connections from spurious noise.

This is worth repeating in research terms. In theory construction, we sometimes adjust our focus by altering our research question. We sometimes modify our conceptual rubrics and analytical frameworks by changing our minds about the key variables to be looked at or by changing the way we define key variables. We always aim to modify and improve the body of axioms and principles.

A Case for Formal Theory Construction

The previous section of this chapter tries to establish the point that theory construction activity goes on throughout any well-executed scientific project. Theory construction includes all our efforts to initially conceptualize and then continually reformulate and improve our understanding of the topic being studied. The lesson of the first section of the chapter, then, is that theory construction (although often implicit and subliminal) is integral to almost all social science investigation. In this second section of the chapter, we offer a second lesson. Our theory construction efforts have more promise if we make them explicit and conscious rather than implicit and subliminal.

It is important to note that being explicit and conscious in theory construction work does not require many pages of writing. For theory construction to get off to a good start, however, it is important (a) to specify a research question (which requires at least one sentence at first), (b) to identify a few key variables and provide brief definitions as appropriate, (c) to stipulate any axiomatic assumptions that you know you will want to build into your study of the subject (should you be using axioms, this will require one sentence for each axiom, as a start), and (d) to articulate the testable principle (or principles) at the heart of your inquiry (this requires only one sentence per principle to start with, and it is common to focus on a single key principle in the initial stage of theory construction). Notice what this entails for writing activity connected with formal theory construction. The first effort at formal theory construction involves only two pages of writing. It is true that two pages of writing create only a skeletal structure, but a thoughtfully crafted skeletal structure of this kind can give a useful definition and convey the intellectual purpose of a project. As projects move forward, much more writing may be required. But initially formalizing the key elements of one's theoretical framework takes only two pages when the initial attempt is restricted to a skeletal structure. Effort of this kind creates what can be a useful working draft of the theory for a research project, and the draft endures until more explanation and elaboration are required. Other things being equal, a project that starts by taking these steps explicitly and consciously has more promise than a project that leaves initial theory construction implicit, unspecified, or vague.[3]

At this point, it may be useful to anticipate what happens later in a research project. After initial theory construction, a researcher must decide what kind of evidence will be relevant and will help her or him to conclude the project by addressing the research question in a convincing and informative way. Often, one starts with an interesting research setting or source of data, and then articulates the research question by making explicit a question of fundamental sociological interest that can be explored in the setting being looked at or with the data that are available. Starting with an interesting research setting or source of data before posing a question can be workable, but only if a question of fundamental disciplinary interest is articulated early and then kept clearly in mind so that the question (not access to the setting or convenience of the data set) drives the inquiry from that point forward.

A lesson many people have trouble remembering is that data-gathering decisions made early in the research enterprise ultimately determine what hypotheses will be actually be testable, and how adequate those tests are likely to be after data have been gathered. In order to conclude data collection with data we can use as intended, it is important to articulate a research question that is of fundamental sociological interest and to approach that question with a theory-driven research hypothesis that is testable in the setting or with the data the researcher has access to.

What we mean here by "formal theory construction" involves writing out the research question, identifying and defining key variables, specifying any axiomatic assumptions that will be heavily relied on, and articulating testable principle(s) in their generic form. For theory construction to be formal, these items need to be written out clearly and in an unambiguously interpretable way. Unambiguous interpretability is essential to good science because science involves replication in different settings, and research cannot be replicated in different settings if it is unclear what is being assumed and what is being tested. This is why the best research is guided in advance by conscious theoretical work defining what is worth looking for, and why. Conscious theoretical work done in advance should be explicitly written in the form of a guiding research question and axioms and principles, with key concepts defined as clearly as possible. When we force ourselves to be explicit in advance about the fundamental research question, the axiomatic assumptions guiding our analysis, the principle(s) we want to test, and the key variables and their meanings, we can continuously reflect in the midst of an ongoing research project, and do so in a constructively self-critical way. This involves asking questions that are necessary to good science: Is the research design focused on a fundamentally important theoretical question? Is our approach to the question posed in the right way? Is our understanding of the research question as informed as it might be, given the state of social science knowledge available to us?

It is by investing time in formal theory construction that a person studying social phenomena can best reflect, and search for wording that gets progressively closer to capturing factors and processes the researcher hopes to test for. Formal theory construction also makes it possible to communicate our current thinking with others, and to receive more constructive (clear and pointed) feedback from others. Writing key theoretical premises out in explicit terms, in advance of data collection efforts, is central to good scientific work.[4]

The heart of *Making Sense of Social Theory* is found in its translation of important theoretical precepts into axioms and principles that can be widely applied to real-world phenomena. The soul of *Making Sense of Social Theory* is found in the lesson that every person engaged in any social scientific inquiry can do better scientific work by paying conscious attention to formal theory construction. This means admitting to assumptions and offering predictive insights.

There is a risk in formal theory construction. The risk is that explicitness can expose errors. However, no scientist assumes he or she has everything completely right, so we are in good company when we clearly state what we think may be happening, even if we later turn out to be wrong. And being explicit about assumptions and predictive premises dramatically speeds up the process of correcting old mistakes and progressing.

By way of example, we can revisit the four axioms and four principles already presented in earlier chapters. These axioms and principles illustrate an approach to theory construction that is wedded to scientific method and that is both easy and useful to follow.

Axioms

Definition of Situation Axiom: People respond to situations according to what they believe to be true about those situations, rather than what is actually true.

Benefit Maximization Axiom: People tend to make benefit-maximizing decisions based on their priorities.

Founder Effects Axiom: Those interests and concerns of founding figures that become active parts of institutional memory or are deeply embedded in institutional practice shape the activities of others for a long time to come.

Selective Retention Axiom: We selectively retain old beliefs and practices and we actively redefine old identities and commitments in ways that optimally balance our sense of belonging with our ability to successfully adjust to changing conditions.

Principles

Principle of Rational Choice: Other things being equal, the likelihood of following a particular course of action (1) increases as a function of (a) the value of the desired outcome and (b) the probability of success in achieving that outcome, and (2) decreases as a function of (c) the projected cost of the activity, (d) fear of ultimately being held responsible for externalized costs, and (e) availability of alternatives having attractive cost-benefit ratios.

Anger Principle: Other things being equal, anger increases in magnitude (a) to the degree that actual outcomes fall short of expected outcomes and (b) opportunities forgone seem to exceed the benefits that have been actualized.

Trust Principle: Other things being equal, people withdraw from roles/relationships if practical, and tend to use formal and informal rules to minimize their obligations and reduce room for ambiguity if withdrawal is not practical, (1) as a direct function of perceived vulnerability in the setting and (2) as an inverse function of degree of trust in the people in that setting.

Conflict/Cohesion Principle: Other things being equal, cohesion within groups or other social entities increases as a function of the degree of conflict between those entities.

The Paradox of Formalization

Articulating axioms and principles has many advantages. One noteworthy point is that this approach to theory construction places emphasis on the big lessons. These eight statements offer a lot of insight.

And yet, there is a wonderfully inviting paradox in formal theory construction around the use of axioms and principles. At the same time that formal statement of axioms and principles makes it easier to both celebrate and use theoretical knowledge we think we can rely on, those very axioms and principles make the limitations of our understanding public. This is perhaps nowhere more apparent than with the Principle of Rational Choice, which leaves so many important questions unanswered. For example, if rational decision making is assumed, how do we explain why different people assign different values to the same thing? And if we admit that not all decision making is rational, thus making the Principle of Rational Choice start to look like a definition of rationality rather than as useful a principle as it appears on first reading, how do we account for the fact that some decisions are arrived at through a more rational process than other decisions? But far from being a criticism, this is the strength of formal theory construction in science. Explicitly stated axioms and principles keep us more focused on what we think we know and simultaneously make us more aware of the obvious limits of what we think we know. In this way, formal theory construction points toward the next generation of research questions by making the limits of our insights more apparent.

Exegesis in Theory Construction

A third theory construction lesson is that we are engaged in theory construction activity whenever we selectively borrow and/or interpret the ideas of others, and then incorporate what we have borrowed or interpreted into our own framework of understanding. Sociologists who are cognizant of all the ways their initial theoretical analysis borrows from earlier social scientists may be hesitant to see their initial work as theory construction activity of their own. But giving credit to others is not the same as denying ownership for a great deal of creative intellectual activity. Much of this creative activity of theorists falls under the umbrella of *exegesis*. Scholarship necessarily involves borrowing selectively (using part of rather than all of the work of those we borrow from) and also generally involves creative interpretion of what is borrowed. As researchers, we selectively decide what we think is important to use and how to use it when looking at a particular phenomenon or addressing a particular question. This is theory construction activity.

Exegesis is the act of determining what we think someone else meant, particularly as it relates to our own social scientific interests and inquiries. When we are diligently engaged in the effort of interpreting how another person viewed the world and how we might modify those ideas in arriving at our own theoretical approach to the study of phenomena, we are engaged in exegesis. This often involves borrowing from others in ways that shape how we define our research question and that influence the variables we look at and how we choose to define those variables; it also affects our selection of axiomatic assumptions and influences the form and content of the working principle(s) we seek to test. Looked at in this way, interpretive exegesis is clearly our own theory construction activity, even though it is influenced by and owes some intellectual debt to our reading of the works of others.

In science, we want to test whatever ideas might allow us to improve our explanatory frameworks. It is often the case that, having read and been informed by someone else's work, we can notice items an earlier author may not have been concerned with. The point, once again, is that interpretive exegesis is a form of theory construction. We look for theoretical insights wherever we can be inspired to find them. Once a theoretical insight is articulated, the preeminent scientific concerns are the clarity, validity, robustness, and power of the idea. The question of whether we accurately understand the original intent of those people we are intellectually indebted to is first and foremost a concern about the history of ideas. But how well our interpretation comports with empirical reality (not what earlier theorists believed, but reality itself) is the more important social science concern. The primary social science question is always the same. Does the idea enhance our ability to explain variation or change in sociological phenomena?

Theory Construction as an Iterative Process

A fourth theory construction lesson is that theory construction never stops as long as a project is under way. As any research process unfolds, it is likely that the researcher's ideas will change. Axioms may be reformulated. Definitions of concepts are frequently refined over the course of a research process. Often, principles are modified to reflect what the researcher is observing in the empirical data. Any researcher reformulating ideas in the middle of the research process, after having formalized a research question and other basic components of the theoretical framework at the outset of a project, is in fact engaged in theory construction as an *iterative process*. It is important to keep reviewing ideas again and again, searching for better wording that gets closer to what we can understand to be the underlying realities revealed in the data we are able to uncover. The lesson here is clear. To do scientific research well a researcher needs to be engaged and constantly alert to what may be better ways of explaining variation or change. Theory construction is not something to be left until the end. Nor is it something to be done at the start of a project and then forgotten, never to be returned to. Theory construction is *not to be conceived of as a "been there, done that"* activity.

Researchers normally try to conclude their work with at least a slightly better (and therefore necessarily different) understanding than the one with which they began. To nonscientists, failing to find what the researcher expected might sound like a dismally unhappy failure. But most scientists have exactly the opposite point of view. An exciting project is one that leads you to realize that your original understanding was flawed, and that your new understanding (while always imperfect in a science) is better than the understanding you started with. Success! Should you conclude with an understanding that clearly diverges from prevailing wisdom in the discipline, you can declare extreme success! This is precisely how a scientific contribution is defined.

Although this sounds like a simple enough point, the implication is quite significant. Consider the standard scenario for a project that begins with a good effort at formal theory construction. You begin a project with what can reasonably be termed a relatively sound disciplinary understanding regarding a question that commands broad disciplinary interest. You end the project being able to suggest an improvement over the understanding you started with. The implication is that you are making a contribution to the scholarly discourse in your discipline by moving beyond conventional wisdom.

In this scenario (where you pose a question of broad disciplinary importance and test a clear disciplinary understanding relating to that question), it is easy for a researcher to appreciate and then express the way in which the conclusion of the research contributes by moving disciplinary understanding forward toward more robust, powerful, revealing explanation. Advancing the frontier of understanding beyond the point where a discipline had been is what scholars live for and judge themselves on! Investing some effort in formal theory construction does not ensure success in this respect, but it certainly clarifies the path to success and makes a successful outcome more likely.

Remembering What Makes Sociological Topics Sociological

A fifth theory construction lesson is that important work is explicit about how it addresses disciplinary fundamentals. Never forget that the phenomena sociologists and most other social scientists are particularly interested in have to do with what exists between people: interpersonal attachments, shared beliefs, and systemic links and interconnections. What makes research sociological is that it explains variability or change in these things, and/or uses variability or change in these things as a basis for explanation of other things that are important for people to know about. Part of our theory construction work is to make sure that we clarify for ourselves how we are explaining variation or change in at least one of these factors, and/or using at least one of these factors as a basis for accounting for variation in something that has relevance in our society. A somewhat longer list of concepts that have proven to be of real value to sociologists is presented in chapter 3. Those concepts are useful to think of in the context of remembering what makes a topic sociological. While constituting only a partial short list of concepts, these are among the concepts that are often thought about by people in the midst of social science theory construction activity. They include social isolation, social distance, self, status, role, identity, socialization, social control, class, market, opportunity costs, externalization of costs, network, vested interest, reference group, power, authority, chain of command, norm, value, vertical integration, regulation, and institutionalization. These are among the concepts that help arm us, analytically speaking, for thinking about the causes and consequences of different patterns of interpersonal attachments, shared beliefs, and systemic linkages and interconnections.

Asking a Good Question

A sixth theory construction lesson is that it is important to begin with an important question. Finding the right question (important enough to motivate disciplinary interest and clear and tangible enough to support well-directed inquiry) is half the task when planning a research project. If a research question is clear and engages an issue of compelling interest in the discipline, the work should almost certainly be of interest to other social scientists. Even student pilot projects generate appreciable professional interest when targeted at a research question engaging one of a discipline's enduring concerns.

But what would good questions be? Here are some examples. This is not an exhaustive list, of course. Nevertheless, any version or aspect of any of these general questions generates broad sociological interest. A project relating to some specific dimension of any of these areas (and of course other areas as well, as these are just examples) would find a ready audience among other social scientists eager to hear of your results. All these questions are likely to be important in the future. Each defines a frontier of social science needing further exploration.

1. What are the social processes and mechanisms influencing how the benefits of society are distributed?
2. What special interests or collective groups manage to gain and exercise control over organizational or institutional power, what are the processes through which that control is gained and exercised, and for what purposes is this power exercised?
3. Why do different organizations vary in structural characteristics and cultural attributes? How do organizational structure and culture change?
4. What feedback mechanisms operate in different social, organizational, and community domains? How do they work? What dynamics influence the effectiveness of feedback mechanisms?
5. What do different people come to value most, and why?
6. When and how are sense of *self* and sense of *identity* activated and energized as important factors influencing behavior? In what ways do they influence the flow of interaction and unfolding events? When or how are they modified or deactivated?
7. How are expectations of different kinds transmitted to people, reinforced among people, or transformed?

These questions each have a number of features common to good questions in a science. Each of these questions is worded in a generic way, and yet means something that is unambiguously clear. Thus, it is easy to consider each one of these generally worded questions as it would be relevant in many different settings. A person having something to say about one question in one setting would be intellectually engaged with other people looking at different settings but inquiring into a similar question.

Each of these questions identifies an area of inquiry where social scientists have already learned a great deal yet still have more to learn. Each question could be explored in any one of a number of different ways and in different settings. And all this work actually needs to be done in the interest of establishing boundary conditions and assessing the robustness and power of our theoretical principles. Finally, each of these questions could be narrowed for study in a particular setting without compromising the sense that an important social science concern is being addressed.

Consider an example. What do different people come to value most, and why? Many social scientists are interested in this question, but they approach it from different perspectives: (a) some social scientists interested in this question are intrigued by prisons; (b) some are interested in college students' motivation; (c) some are concerned with what happens in corporations; (d) some focus on army units; and (e) some examine decisions children make on playgrounds. The list could go on but five (a through e) is quite sufficient to make the point. If there are five researchers each interested in a different type of social setting (prisons, colleges, corporations, army units, and playgrounds), and they are conducting research on a similar question but in different types of settings, they should each be interested in reading the work of the others. In other words, for scientists engaged in theoretically driven research, the judgment that someone else does relevant work is more likely to mean that the theoretical question is similar than to mean that that the research setting is similar.

Having research motivated by the same fundamentally important question, and having different researchers explore that fundamentally important question through the lenses of different settings and data sets, is how science makes progress because real scientific progress, theoretical progress, is marked by resolution of fundamental questions having broad relevance. It is through awareness of a fundamentally important question that one piece of research is connected to other work and has a reasonable chance of having impact on the discipline. Formulating the right question is a key to doing good science.

Ockham's Razor and the Elegance of Simplicity

Our seventh lesson on theory construction is what is commonly referred to among scientists as *Ockham's razor*. Science is not a game of trivial pursuits. Scientists are sober and serious about arriving at theoretical principles that are clear, robust, and powerful. Clarity means that the meaning of the theoretical premise is fathomable. Sometimes we have to struggle to keep this in mind, particularly when engaged in interpretive exegesis on the complicated (and occasionally even convoluted) work of sociological theorists.

What is scientifically pertinent is that our theory construction work reflects our best effort to reveal processes accounting for variation or change in the social world. In this effort, people of a scientific disposition generally tend to look for the clearest and most succinct ways to express their insights. The goal of science could even be described as achieving the elegance of simplicity, an idea often attributed to William of Ockham (1284–1347).

Ockham's name is spelled a number of different ways, owing to the fact that the spelling of names was yet not standardized during his lifetime. But while the spelling of his name has appeared in differing forms over the years, the meaning of his lasting contribution to science has not been the subject of any disagreement at all. Ockham's "razor" is a criterion for privileging one theory over another. When two different theoretical interpretations seem equally successful in accounting for variation or change, the preferable explanation is the one that is most simple, has the clearest meaning, and receives the greatest amount of transparent validation by what we are able to observe in the everyday world. In science, complexity and confusion are not considered good qualities in themselves, unless there is reason to believe that their presence will ultimately lead to significantly enhanced predictive power. While there are certainly exceptions, and very good ones, elegance through simplicity is usually a good mantra in theory construction. Ockham's razor is consequently a good tool to have in a toolbox of useful ideas.

Modeling as a Tool in Formal Theory Construction

The eighth lesson of theory construction is that modeling is simple and interesting, helps us avoid mistakes, and provides an easy way of engaging in iterative theory construction efforts to maximum effect.

Science is disciplined study aimed at progressive improvement in our ability to explain differences between cases or change within cases. Social scientists can easily lose sight of this because so much that passes for social science writing is more polemic or philosophical than scientific. But most good social scientists do have ideas about causal process, and diagramming is always a good technique for clarifying theoretical explanations.

When working in a scientific theory construction mode, we need to focus on whatever explanation we see being offered when we read the works of others, and/or whatever explanation we want to offer on our own. When we are trying to isolate, clarify, and refine possible explanations for variation or change, we are engaged in theory construction activity. The explanatory character of a theoretical explanation is visualized whenever we diagram a causal model. While there can be variations in style, most models show what are hypothesized to be causal connections (represented by arrows) between four kinds of variables: dependent variables, independent variables, intervening variables, and control variables. A dependent variable (outcome, consequence) is normally placed on the right-hand side of the model, with independent and control variables on the left, intervening variables in the middle, and all arrows moving in the direction of the dependent variable.

It is important to realize that the reason we designate something as a particular kind of variable (control variables versus independent variables versus intervening variables versus dependent variables) has nothing whatsoever to do with the innate features of the variables themselves. The distinction between dependent, intervening, independent, and control variables is a function of the way the variables are employed by us in the theoretical explanation we advance. When researcher A tries to explain variation in y using x as an independent variable, all we know is that researcher A hypothesizes that x is a partial cause of y. Y is a dependent variable only at those moments when someone wants to treat it as a dependent variable to be explained. If researcher B uses that same variable y as a possible cause for explaining variation or change in another variable, then what is used by researcher A as a dependent variable is being used by researcher B as an independent variable. This is completely acceptable. As a general rule, the scientific process works better and moves ahead faster when competing ideas are tested.

Sometimes in constructing our theories, we posit that some additional factor(s) may be influenced by the independent variable and may in turn suggest a mechanism through which the independent variable influences the dependent variable. For example, a greater financial well-being of a family (often operationally measured by yearly income) seems to increase the likelihood that children from that family will be successful as adults (often operationally measured by occupational prestige). But this is not uniformly true. One mechanism that seems to influence the degree to which parental material well-being translates into the eventual adult success of children from that family is the variability of children's acquisition of human capital (often operationally measured by years of education completed). Of course, it is not necessary to be from a family with money to get a good education. Nor does having family money guarantee someone a good education. But family money generally helps students get a better education. And while it is not absolutely necessary to acquire a good education in order to find a prestigious job, having a good education certainly helps in the job search. Having an idea how education relates to other variables is important to our understanding of causal process. It helps us in our ability to predict variability in outcomes. And the role we think something plays in the causal process becomes more clear if we diagram a model.

Control variables refer to factors that might reasonably be thought of as alternative causes that one particular researcher is not primarily interested in focusing on, but which other people might reasonably think could have impact. In this case, discrimination could be a good example, possibly using gender as an operational indicator. There is no mention of discrimination in the previous passages, yet it certainly might have a good deal to do with differences in adult success. Identifying control variables helps researchers arrive at better assessments of the robustness and power of the causal dynamic suggested by the independent variable.

When we are explicit about our explanatory model it is usually easy to visually diagram what we are thinking about. A visual diagram can tell us a lot and help in the iterative improvement process. Why are some people's odds of being successful better than other people's? What predictions can we make for the future? And what model can we offer to diagram the process we think may account for the variable outcomes we observe?

At any stage of inquiry, but particularly in the early stage of initial theory construction, diagramming the explanatory model one has in mind is a productive

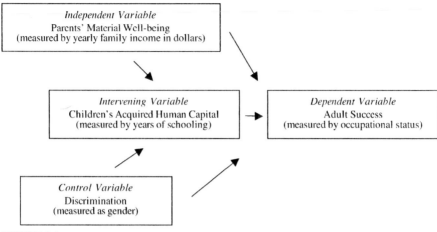

FIGURE 5.1
Modeling

activity. It is also easy and quick, so it is hard to imagine why someone would hesitate to diagram a model. It is useful to do because researchers usually change their models around in the initial stages of inquiry. Having a model diagrammed speeds up this review and revision process. Factors initially thought to be important can drop out of the analysis, or factors originally overlooked can be added. Variables are often redefined and given new meaning or even new names. And sometimes the causal order of factors is changed. Having a model to look at helps in the process of review, reflection, and improvement necessary to producing good work.

In this case, generic names for variables are given more accent than are operational indicators. When scholars are in the theory construction mode, their focus should generally be, as much as is practical, on the generic version of variables, and on capturing underlying dynamics in general terms. Concern with exactly what we choose to use as empirical indicators (income in dollars, gender, etc.) can then be treated as a separate question. Do our data really measure what we want to measure and what we are saying we intend to measure? If we think that yearly family income in dollars will generally be a reasonably good (valid and reliable) measure of parents' material well-being, but that simply noting one's gender may not be as good an indicator of discrimination suffered, then the problem to address is a research methods (measurement) issue. We can keep hunting for a better way to operationally define and measure all variables, but especially those where we feel measurement may be a bit indirect.

There can, of course, be as many independent, intervening, and control variables as a researcher wants to place in a model. However, keeping the number of variables small is sometimes a good theory construction practice. Focus on the dynamics that seem most important, rather than naming everything anyone might see as somehow related. Some reasons for this will become clear in the pages that follow.

Positive and Negative Values for the Same Variable

A ninth lesson in theory construction concerns the specification of our variables. Sometimes people mistake one variable for two when diagramming models. This is a common error that can be avoided by thinking clearly about what a variable actually is. If there is a variable, different values must be possible. And many variables can be conceived of as having both positive and negative values as well as high and low values in the positive range. Consider happiness and unhappiness. To say that one marriage is happy and another is unhappy may be best thought of as a contrast between the two marriages on a single variable. To say that one social unit of a particular kind (in this example, a marriage) is high or positive on a particular variable (in this case, happiness), while another unit of the same kind (another marriage) is low or negative in this regard (fraught with unhappiness) can be viewed as making a comparison of two cases (two marriages) if the two cases are thought of as having different scores (high or positive, and low or negative) on the same variable (happiness). Thus, one marriage is happier than the other.

A model showing happiness as one variable and unhappiness as another variable would be poorly specified. The reason for contrasting the two marriages in the first place is to find out why they are different in terms of the variable degree to which one thing (happiness) characterizes the two. That is, we want to know why some marriages are happier than others. It is, of course, possible that a researcher discussing happiness and unhappiness means two distinct things rather than differences of magnitude of the same thing. In that case, the theory construction challenge is to develop labels and definitions that will make the difference between meanings of variables distinct for readers.

Similarly, gender is typically introduced into diagrammatic models as one variable (gender) having different values (female/male). To introduce two variables (male and female) runs counter to the logic of analysis used in the social sciences. In general, errors in theory construction are more often made in introducing too many variables rather than two few.

Beware of Tautologies

The tenth of our lessons about theory construction is to always exercise care in defining variables so as to avoid the danger of tautologies. A *tautology* is a statement of causal relationship between two variables that are labeled or defined or measured in such a way as to overlap, so that they are not distinctly different. For example, when sociologists contrast one organization with another, they sometimes do so in terms of degree of hierarchical structure, or chain of command. At other times they do so in terms of bureaucratization. But bureaucratization is often defined in terms of a number of different characteristics, one of which is the possession of a hierarchical chain of command. This means it would be a tautology to say that hierarchy leads to bureaucracy or that bureaucracy leads to hierarchy, because the two factors are partially the same simply by definition. They may not be exactly the same, but their meanings certainly overlap. In fact, they overlap so much that "degree of hierarchical organization" and "bureaucracy" are, in some significant degree, different terms for the same thing. Having fallen arches does not cause a person to be flat-footed; having fallen arches is, simply by definition, part of what it means to be flat-footed. Similarly, the fact that an organization has hierarchy cannot be said to lead to bureaucracy because hierarchy is a definitional characteristic of bureaucracy. In order to develop a useful explanatory model, it is important that the variables in the model be quite distinct from one another, both in the ways they are defined and in the indicators used for their measurement. Otherwise, our findings would be true by definition and therefore rather meaningless.

Correlation Does Not Establish Causation

The eleventh lesson of theory construction is that correlation does not mean causation. The goal of scientific theory is to extend our ability to explain variation between cases and/or change within cases. This means our goal is to explain causation, but causal relationships can be difficult to identify.

An important cautionary note is that correlation does not establish causation. It is quite common that we encounter spurious association: a correlation between variables that can be better explained by the connection of each variable to some third factor that we may not even be aware of. One example is the statistical correlation between the number of Catholics in a state (as a proportion of the state's population) and the number of abortions performed (per 100,000 people). It is actually the fact that states with higher concentrations of Catholics also tend to be the states in which abortions are more frequently performed. This means that there is a positive correlation between number of Catholics and prevalence of abortion; as a general rule, the more Catholics there are as a percentage of the population, the greater the number of abortions that are performed. But is there a causal connection? The answer is no. The two variables being correlated in this instance are in fact correlated with each other, but the correlation is spurious (incidental to association with their common association with a third factor) rather than causal (one thing leading to another). The correlation between concentration of Catholics and prevalence of abortion results from the fact that both variables are independently related to access to medical services, and this is a function of availability of medical personnel. For a variety of historical reasons, Catholics tended to settle in areas that now have high concentrations of medical schools and train a lot of doctors. Where there are more doctors, more medical procedures of all kinds are performed. Concentration of Catholics is uncorrelated to prevalence of abortion once the number of doctors (per 100,000 people) is controlled for. It is always important to consider the fact that when two variables are correlated, the correlation may be spurious. Correlation does not imply causality.

Another cautionary note comes in the form of time sequencing. Causes must come before consequences. When reflecting on the logic of a model, one should always review time sequence. Do variables thought of as causes appear in the model before variables thought of as consequences? Here, the objective of theory construction is to capture the theoretical analysis properly.

Boundary Conditions in Theory Construction

A twelfth theory construction lesson is that nonfindings, where data collection does not yield strong evidence for the existence of a relationship, often lead to the discovery of boundary conditions. For example, parents often avoid benefit-maximizing behavior with regard to their children, and there are religious and ethical proscriptions against taking advantage of people in certain ways under particular sets of conditions (see, for example, chapter 9). In other words, although we know that benefit maximization does occur, we also know that its applicability is limited by conditions that need to be defined. Identifying boundary conditions is a common outcome of social science research, and an important part of our theory construction work. This is among the reasons that it is useful to have a large number of people conducting research into the same basic question but in a wide range of settings and using a wide variety of data sets.[5]

Recap

Theory construction activity should be a part of every investigative social science project. Theory construction starts with the conscious theoretical work done at the outset of a project. Formal theory construction involves explicitly writing out a guiding research question and axioms and principles, along with key concepts defined as clearly as possible. Theory construction is iterative, meaning the research question, conceptual definitions and axioms, and predictive principle(s) used should be frequently reviewed, reflected on, and rewritten for improvement over time. Formal and iterative theory construction makes it easier (1) to recognize the significance of the ideas being tested, and (2) to appreciate the importance of the theoretical contribution being made.

Some Terms to Know

Tautology: A statement of causal relationship between two variables that are labeled, defined, or measured in such a way as to overlap, so that they are not distinctly different. To say that something causes itself is a fallacy of reasoning.

Spurious Correlation: An appearance of association between two variables resulting from the fact that each variable is independently associated with some other variable. A spurious correlation consequently has nothing to do with causality.

Quiz

Check your answers in the back of the book. If you get any wrong, consider reviewing chapter 5 before continuing.

1. What makes formal theory construction formal?
2. What should be formalized when engaging in formal theory construction?

Application Exercise

Select one of the research questions presented in this chapter, modifying it if you care to, or write your own research question. Then briefly describe the kind of data set one might use or the kind of setting one might investigate in order to potentially add to our understanding of this research question.

6

Economics Was Not Enough

C HAPTER 4 CONSIDERS THE SOCIAL CLIMATE IN EUROPE and in the United States as a way of understanding the empirical concerns of the first generation of sociologists. Chapter 5 arms readers with useful theory construction lessons sociologists learned as they began exploring those empirical concerns and trying to develop social science theory they could use. Chapter 6 approaches the historical roots of sociology by looking at theoretical concerns that necessitated the development of a new discipline moving beyond the discipline of economics from which sociology had emerged. From a theoretical point of view, economics was simply not enough. The theoretical framework that evolved within economics simply did not take into account many of the key factors that astute observers felt were essential to understand. Even many prominent economists saw the need for a shift in scientific analysis. Marx's life came to an end before the organization of sociology as a discipline, so Marx always referred to himself as an economist. But Weber, Pareto, and several other early economists moved to sociology as they tried to develop more comprehensive theories for understanding economic change within a broader context of societal change.

While this chapter could easily have followed chapter 4 in terms of content, it also makes an excellent follow-up to chapter 5, by demonstrating the art and illustrating the value of writing out theoretical principles as chapter 5 advocates. Chapter 6 illustrates the explanatory insight that can come from formalizing principles when considering big questions that are pertinent to the lives and experiences of many people. Big questions we now ask include: What are the inexorable social and cultural consequences of globalization? Why did the Soviet system, with all its riches and potential, collapse? How can we make sense of the fact that so many people became financially overextended during the adjustable-rate mortgage crisis? Why are so many corporations and government agencies—corporations and agencies that once were relatively self-sufficient (that is, performing more tasks internally rather than contracting out)—now contracting out more than ever before? Social scientists now have reasonably good (at least, first approximation) answers to all these contemporary questions, simply by looking to five principles (presented in this chapter) that were articulated in economics and sociology at the time the two disciplines were differentiating form each other (from about 1840 to 1940). Although two of the principles are borrowed from economics, those two principles cannot be used to answer the questions just posed without also introducing the three companion principles developed as sociology tried to evolve beyond conventional economics to forge a more robust and powerful framework for socioeconomic understanding.

The Intellectual Backdrop of Early Sociology

Sociology is a comparatively young discipline. There was not a sociology class taught in the United States until 1875; William Graham Sumner taught it at Yale University. There was not a university teacher with the title of professor of sociology anywhere in the world before 1891, when Émile Durkheim, in France, was appointed professor of sociology and education. There was not a freestanding department of sociology anywhere in the world until 1892, when one was established at the University of Chicago. But sociology did not just spring forth out of nothing; it was forged by an amalgamation of people who were working on the margins of several disciplines and who were united by their interest in a common set of issues.

The intellectual parentage of sociology is to be found in economics more than in any other single discipline. Sociology has borrowed substantially from economics. In particular, exchange theory (to be examined in more detail in chapter 14) self-consciously emerged out of and has moved forward from mainstream economics. Sociology has also bequeathed a great deal back to economics, although sometimes without receiving much credit. In fact, much of what sociologists have learned about meso-(organizational-)level phenomena and macro-(societal-)level phenomena has been in response to inadequacies of conventional economics.

Conventional economics is tremendously important. Where it works, sociologists use it. But when it does not tell us enough, sociological axioms and principles make up some of the shortfall. The process of arriving at principles explaining causes and consequences of economic change demonstrates the practical use of formal theory construction techniques to consolidate and communicate predictive insight *while working on improvement of our predictive insights over time*. Beginning with chapter 7, *Making Sense of Social Theory* will make use of some of the theory construction techniques discussed in chapter 5 and illustrated in this chapter to explicate key insights in the works of some of sociology's seminal figures and theoretical perspectives.

Key insights on evolution, supply and demand, and shifts in popular culture can be traced to the time when sociology was an embryonic discipline just beginning to differentiate itself from economics and the other social sciences. It was also during that period that the stage was set for trying to explain why market mechanisms are used to organize economic activity in some time periods and some realms of economic activity but not others. Articulating succinct predictive insights in clear terms as theoretical principles, we can appreciate the progress that was made around the questions that initially distinguished sociology from economics.

Markets Are Part of Sociology's Subject Matter

There is nothing quite so central to sociology's intellectual history, and yet nothing so frequently overlooked in treatments of sociology's intellectual history, as the subject of economic markets. First, markets are one of the main ways human interaction is organized. This fact alone makes an understanding of markets central to sociology. If sociologists were to ignore markets, we would be denying our own reason for existence as a discipline, which is to better understand how patterns of social organization and shared meaning are shaped and have consequence, because markets are a ubiquitous form of social organization. Wherever one looks, one sees some kinds of activity that are conducted within market mechanisms or applying quasi-market rules. Second, while economics concerns itself primarily with market operations as one basic design for organizing the activities of different people together in coherent ways, sociology is more encompassing and deals in equal measure with (a) markets; (b) hierarchies, such as government agencies or corporations; and (c) networks, such as friendship cliques, information chains, and strategic alliances among businesses. Markets, hierarchies, and networks are fundamentally different structural forms. Third, sociology has the crucial task of helping us understand which forms of organization will predominate over what spheres of activity. Fourth, while economics has a lot to say about the structure and operation of markets, and political science has a lot to say about the structure and operation of hierarchies, sociology is important in understanding all three notions (markets, hierarchies, and networks).

For sociologists interested in the organization of economic activity, three pivotal questions are: When will market organization (where everyone is considered a potential trade partner on equal footing in the marketplace) prevail over hierarchy and network? When will hierarchical organization (such as government control) supplant market and network organization? And when will network organization (such as insider alliances) hold sway over market and hierarchical forms of organization? But answering these questions is only part of sociology's special charge pertaining to the study of economic phenomena. Sociology also takes account of ways that information can be distorted and choice can be limited, invalidating assumptions on which conventional economic thinking is based. Conventional economic theory developed out of models about perfect markets. But it is the all-too-real market imperfections that sociology helps us to understand.

What Are Markets as a Form of Organization?

Economics is itself a comparatively new discipline. By far the most important figure in the history of economics as an academic discipline is Adam Smith, whose most famous work, *The Wealth of Nations*, was first published in 1776. Smith described markets and advocated the expansion of markets as a form of organization. In this respect, he advocated a kind of social revolution, for free markets would allow people to escape the constraints of tradition and habit.

We are now so familiar with the word *market* that we sometimes fail to think about the fact that markets are a distinct form of social organization that was much less widespread two hundred years ago, when most human beings were subsistence agriculturalists who never strayed far from the place they were born, seldom deviated much from the traditions they inherited from their parents, and rarely broke from the constraining commitments of the neighborhoods where they led their lives. It is absolutely critical in the conceptual maturation of a sociologist to appreciate the fact that *a market is a form of social organization* and therefore is squarely in the central domain of sociological inquiry. Markets are not alien territory to sociologists. As a form of social organization, markets cry out for understanding. And social science appreciation of market phenomena is richer and more revealing thanks to all that sociologists have added and continue to add to conventional economic wisdom.

A sociologist needs to know what a market is and how it differs from other forms of organization, because markets are one of the most prevalent forms of social organization. Indeed, part of being a good sociologist is recognizing why it is that markets actually perform better than other forms of organization under certain sets of circumstances and less well under other sets of circumstances.

What is a market? What distinguishes markets as a characteristic form of social organization? To satisfy Smith's conceptualization, a perfect market must have four characteristics: (1) people must be engaged in exchange that can be at least loosely conceptualized as having buyers and sellers, or traders engaging in discrete transactions (that is, who you trade with today is not determined by who you traded with last week); (2) there must be freedom of choice so that each buyer/

seller/trader can decide whom, if anyone, it makes the most rational sense to trade with at a given point in time; (3) there should be *transparency*, or ready availability of complete and accurate information, so that potential exchange partners can make informed decisions; and (4) barriers to entry to the market in order to buy/sell/trade must be minimal so that a steady stream of new consumers/producers/traders can come and go at will from the arena where transactions take place.

Many of Smith's views are reflected in the Principle of Rational Choice, expressed earlier in this book. Most people are familiar with the process as Smith described it. The *invisible hand of the market* following laws of supply and demand allows people to select among the best available options. Smith thought this would produce good results for almost everyone over the long run. He was a passionate advocate of markets at a time, the end of the eighteenth century, when envisioning market organization of the whole economy was a rather new and radical idea. Vestiges of feudal obligations and commitments and the hold of old traditions continued to severely limit what people thought of doing or were allowed to do. In this sense, Smith was a revolutionary. He wanted to see a speedy end to vestiges of feudalism, and he wanted to see society reorganized on market principles that would allow people the freedom to defy encumbrances of feudal tradition. For Smith, the entire society would be better off if people were able to discover their real talents and move about in search of places to put those talents to use with greatest potential impact. This had a strongly religious overtone, and Smith thought that misapplication of talent was shameful as well as wasteful. He understood a market as a mechanism that enables talent and resources to go where they are most needed. In this sense, true markets constitute an assault on traditional ties and established commitments.[1]

Within a few years of the publication of *The Wealth of Nations*, the British economist David Ricardo helped explain more clearly why everyone can, in theory, be better off if markets are operating smoothly. Ricardo's explanation was based on the concept of *comparative advantage*. If talented people who can do many things very well have an incentive to focus their effort on what others cannot do (rather than spending most of their time doing things anyone can do), the whole world will be better off. Ricardo also thought about national economies in terms of comparative advantage. His view was that some countries might have advantages in manufacturing and others in agriculture, and that free trade and open markets would allow each type of country to grow richer by developing its own natural advantages and importing everything else. Advocates of globalization are still saying essentially the same thing. Market theory sounds as if it makes a lot of sense, at least if markets are perfect and have all the qualities Smith and Ricardo talked about.

A *very* important point to remember, however, is that markets are human creations and are never perfect. Markets will not always generate the rosy consequences Smith and Ricardo envisioned. We sociologists have a lot to say about this, and when we do speak out, we are contributing to a better understanding of the economy.[2] In this respect, a good deal of sociological work is closely related to institutional economics. Institutionalists in both sociology and economics pay careful attention to the ways in which capitalism in any country is influenced by particular developments in legal code and administrative and regulatory arrangements.

Institutional Economics and Institutional Sociology

An outstanding example of the importance of institutional development can be seen in the concept of *limited liability* protection. Since about 1860 in Britain and the United States, corporations have been legally understood as separate persons. This means that *if* a corporation is found to be responsible for doing something wrong, the corporation can be sued for no more than the corporation itself. A shareholder's investment consequently defines the limit of what the shareholder risks to lose. Until about 1860, before the limited liability laws were passed, shareholders had to be more cautious because they could be held personally responsible for the actions of the company. If the company went into debt, investors might have to repay that debt even if this required spending one's own savings. But not so after passage of the limited liability laws.

The widespread institutionalization of limited liability laws around 1860 marked a sea change in the business environment, and reviewing the Principle of Rational Choice will certainly indicate why. In deciding whether to purchase stock in a company, a potential investor will consider possible costs and risks as well as potential gains. Limited liability laws placed a cap on risks, and this made investment more attractive.

Writing in the 1770s, Adam Smith took a stand against the concept of limited liability laws. He argued that limited liability would make it easier for owners to relinquish daily administration to paid managers, and would ultimately result in a pattern of less cautious (more risky) and less responsible (more dangerous) business activity. But those who wanted limited liability maintained that limiting risk would spur business growth by encouraging more investment, as well as more risk taking and innovation.

Both Adam Smith and his opponents on this point turned out to be right. The institutionalization of limited liability laws helped fuel a century and a half of mind-boggling business growth, but at the same time, the limited liability laws seem to (a) have contributed to the rise of management as an occupational category distinct from ownership and (b) have arguably been responsible for a great deal of quite risky corporate activity. Whatever one's judgment about the cumulative costs and benefits associated with the institutionalization of limited liability laws, awareness of those laws clearly adds a powerful element to our explanation of events—it explains so much that its importance is easy to detect.

People who question the logic of limited liability laws frequently use Bhopal, India, as a tangible case study. A terrible accident occurred in 1984 at a pesticide plant in Bhopal, resulting in the accidental release of a large quantity of toxic gas into the air. Over two thousand people died almost immediately. Thousands more died in the coming months, and many survivors suffered lasting health problems. Who pays? Under British and U.S. law and the laws of many other countries, liability is limited to the value of the corporation. This situation can become quite complicated if the offending corporation is, for example, heavily in debt and/or is a legally independent subsidiary of a larger and richer parent company. The legal and ethical issues are quite clear, and with them, the relevance of particular institutional developments is equally clear.

Since Bhopal, and with growing fears of the possibility of the ecological disaster that could follow from careless corporate activity, more people are beginning to discuss whether it might be time to modify limited liability laws. When raised, this is a hotly contested question because any change would have far-reaching economic consequences. For a theorist, the kinds of institutional developments that occur, their timing, and the process through which they come about are all interesting questions.

A Moment for Reflection

It is worth stopping to remember that market-oriented and corporation-dominated capitalism are human-made rather than God-given forms of organization. There are other organizational forms on which economies can be based. The former (and failed) Soviet Union, for example, had a *command and control* economy based on *hierarchy*, with centralized government planning and decision making. Communist economies ran for decades, guided by the hierarchical command and control of a government that determined what needed to be produced, who needed to produce it, and who would be allowed to consume what was produced. This type of economy stood in marked contrast with the invisible hand of the market at work and incentives enticing people to do what is in most demand. The Communist economies did run; they just did not run very well.

As social scientists we ask a great many questions. (1) How are the economies of different societies organized? This calls for us to describe systems. (2) How well do these different systems work? This requires that we pay attention to process. (3) What are the outcomes of different kinds of organizational design? This calls for us to consider consequences. (4) How does change come about and why does it take so long? This also requires that we pay attention to process. (5) How can we improve policy? This suggests that we should consider the implications our principles might have for social engineering.

All these questions are sociological questions, as much as or even more than economic ones. At their root, they force us to recognize that there are different ways of organizing interaction among a plethora of people. This requires that we set our sights on understanding why one form (markets, or hierarchies, or networks) prevails at a given place and time and over a given range of activity.[3] But in order to address these sweeping questions about the way an economy and society are organized, it will be useful to first consider three robust principles having to do with underlying economic dynamics and societal dynamics.

Early British Sociology

Adam Smith's work signaled a serious beginning of social scientific study of the economy. Intellectually emboldened by Smith (in Scotland), and empowered by Comte (in France) with his optimism about the prospects for social science, Harriet Martineau and others in Britain took up the task of engaging in pioneering sociological research, as described in the last chapter. Eighteen years younger than Martineau was another great English sociologist, Herbert Spencer (1820–1902). Although Spencer did not have a university position (indeed, he had been sickly as a boy and was almost entirely homeschooled), he was a great intellect with an enormous public following. For example, Spencer's concept of *survival of the fittest* was useful to Charles Darwin as Darwin formulated and refined his theory of evolution.[4]

Principle of Evolution: **Other things being equal, the rate at which social units differentiate from one another is (1) a direct function of their isolation and (2) an inverse function of their size.**

Darwin's principle of evolution, heavily influenced by Spencer's thinking, has a number of sociological applications. We know, for example, that when organizations are divided into different units that remain somewhat separate from one another, such as academic departments in a university, those units sometimes develop their own distinct cultures. The same can be said of prison culture, forged in isolation from the "free world" outside the prison walls, and of the prison subcultures of different gangs within prisons, or different school cliques that enforce a kind of social isolation separating themselves from other students.

In addition to being useful for the study of small groups, like prison gangs, the Principle of Evolution is crucial for our understanding long-term change in human civilization. Globalization of trade and electronic communication each reduce isolation, and by doing so they work to overcome isolation and cultural distinctiveness.

Drawing from Smith, Spencer recognized markets as the mechanism that would make people break down the doors of isolation by placing different people and practices in direct competition with one another. In theory, the most desirable and efficient practices would be copied far and wide, and people would come to recognize that many of their idiosyncratic practices were only marginally successful experiments that should be replaced by more successful ways of dealing with challenges. Some readers will applaud this view. Others will be repelled by it. But whether cultural pluralism is better or worse than homogenization is not the issue in this chapter. The issue is the premise that market dynamics, by bringing people into closer contact, have made the world more homogeneous rather than more heterogeneous. Some people regard this as a counterintuitive finding, but the Principle of Evolution explains why this is the case.

Throughout Spencer's sociology, there is a clear recognition of markets as an organizational form worth studying. Whatever the limits of utilitarian economics and the various intellectual frameworks it helps inspire, the notion that incentives influence supply is an important insight that should be in our repertoire of predictive principles.

Principle of Supply and Demand: **Other things being equal, the level of incentive potential suppliers have to provide something and consumers have to find substitutes (1) are positive functions of demand and price, and are (2) inverse functions of supply and aggregate elasticity.**

Smith and other economists working in the utilitarian economics tradition recognized that price is subject to fluctuation, partly as a function of supply and demand. When people are free to make exchange decisions, how much consumers will be called on to pay for something is a positive function of how many people want it and how badly they want it. At the same time, price is a negative function of how much is available from suppliers right now. But as price changes, so do incentives for new suppliers to begin supplying, for old suppliers to increase supply, and for current and future consumers and users to find suitable alternatives. Consequently, price tends toward equilibrium in the sense that a price change will generally trigger reactions that, at least in some degree, offset forces propelling continued changes in the same direction by increasing supply or suppressing demand.

While the Principle of Supply and Demand is broad in its applications, it leaves the interesting questions unanswered. For example, consider the idea of *perverse incentives* that encourage people to engage in behavior you do not want many people adopting. For example, airlines that charge people hefty sums for checked luggage, without charging a commensurate sum for carry-on luggage, encourage people to board planes with larger and heavier carry-ons. This may not be what airlines actually want to encourage, at least in the long run. *Perverse incentive systems* are those encouraging things you do not want. Another example can be found in workplaces where employees may have to make serious self-sacrifices for paltry performance bonuses. When this is the case, the rational choice may be to do as little as possible and be satisfied with base pay, while offloading as many responsibilities as possible to those few people who try to earn meager incentives that can be earned only through extraordinary performance. The temptation to off-load responsibility to others may be equally common in environments with great job security (the civil service and schools where teachers have tenure, for example) and in environments offering little job security (where the more rational decision may be to look for a more secure job and hope for higher pay and better benefits).

Economists Switching to Sociology

German economist Karl Marx and German economist-turned-sociologist Max Weber were two of the key founders of the sociological tradition (for details on their work, see chapters 8 and 9). But many other economists were also pioneers of the intellectual frontier between sociology and economics. Two of these, Thorstein Veblen in the United States and Vilfredo Pareto in Switzerland, made monumental contributions to the development of sociology.

In his famous 1899 book, *The Theory of the Leisure Class*, Veblen observes that people sometimes use market resources to elevate their social standing through *conspicuous consumption*. That is, people seek to appear to others as smart, hardworking, and having good taste, not just by demonstrating those qualities directly, but by living in big houses, wearing the right clothes, eating trendy food, and going on long vacations to faraway places.[5] Conspicuous consumption is a powerful idea in itself. But if we look beyond the surface we find that Veblen's concept speaks to an important point of divergence between economics and sociology as disciplines. Veblen introduced conspicuous consumption as evidence that *people are driven primarily by a desire to acquire status*, rather than by calculations about material gain per se. For example, many businesspeople are driven to make more money not because they need the money or even want the money for itself, but because accumulating more money is a measure of stature and success in the circles in which they travel. Being able to purchase objects and afford new experiences becomes a signal of personal worth. The Principle of Rational Choice still applies, but not in the narrow sense in which economists normally use it.

In the individual decisions people make day in and day out, the benefits people are usually trying to maximize are not those that are easily measured in terms of immediate financial gain. Only Mr. Scrooge consistently acts, one decision at a time, to maximize financial position. And of course, Mr. Scrooge is a fictional character.

If one accepts the premise that desire for status is what really drives rational choice calculations, sociology becomes indispensable for proper economic analysis: it is sociology, more than economics, that addresses the question of status. This, then, brings us to new insight on an old question. Why on earth do people want what they want and value what they value? The answer, Veblen argued, is because those are the things/qualities/traits people associate with acceptance and social status. If Veblen was right, sociology subsumes economics in this crucial respect. Simply stated, standard utilitarian economics presents far more questions than it answers. But if we think of the ultimate end of rational calculation as acceptance or status seeking, many of those questions are answered and the world as we observe it begins to make more sense.

Sociology and the Business Cycle

Over the years, many famous economists have embraced sociology because they believe that economics, as it is commonly practiced, leaves out too many pieces of the puzzle. Perhaps the most important of these economists was Vilfredo Pareto, who among other things used sociology to explain the timing and severity of movements in the business cycle. His ideas are perhaps most succinctly captured in a collection of papers published in 1921, *The Transformation of Democracy*, which explores recurring patterns of socioeconomic and political history. He writes that people get swept up in speculative bubbles during periods of rapid and sustained economic growth. They see everyone else making easy profits, with little apparent risk. As that happens, people begin to want more for themselves. Caution is thrown to the wind and people begin acting imprudently, paying insufficient attention to possible costs and exposure to risk. But importantly, Pareto refers to people in the plural rather than the singular. He is not talking about rational decisions made one at a time, but about crowd psychology, and the social pressure people place on those around them to do what everyone else is doing.

Of course, Pareto did not think everyone would be swept up in equal degree by the spirit of the times. But the beliefs that are widely shared in a society at any given time do make a difference in what individuals think, and also in the social pressures that individuals are made to feel by those they come into contact with. Some periods are characterized by higher levels of desire for pursuit of pleasure and immediate gratification, and by reduced levels of caution, lower savings rates, and more cavalier attitudes about risk. Those social trends encourage speculative investment and consumer exuberance. This accelerates short-term economic growth, but undermines the prospects for longer-term economic well-being at the societal level.

When the cumulative consequences of exuberant consumer spending and speculative investment (which Pareto talked about as manifestations of desire for self-gratification and unchecked individualism) begin to accumulate and manifest themselves, an economic downturn is inevitable. Bad economic times make people act more cautiously, show a higher propensity to save, begin to ridicule comfort and pleasure seeking, and demonstrate aversion to risk when making decisions. These behaviors relate to social science, and it is noteworthy that it was Pareto who discussed them: one of the most famous economists of all time, he is remembered by many as the father of mathematical economics as well as a great business consultant. And yet he left economics for sociology because he was convinced that the key to understanding what happens in the economy is in developing, as Pareto attempted to do, broad social science principles explaining shifts in public sentiment and mood that might impact the economy.[6]

Principle of Cyclical Change in Beliefs: **Other things being equal, (a) the more social constraint there is, then the more slowly that innovation and problem solving occur, which generates pressure for greater tolerance of individuality, but (b) the more tolerance there is of individual action, then the greater the number of new problems people create, which generates greater insistence on conformity.**

Although the Principle of Cyclical Change in Beliefs is not the most robust and powerful of sociology's principles, it does help us understand major movements in the business cycle. This principle also captures something important about Pareto's way of thinking about society. Like most of the other major European social scientists of his time, Pareto was interested in explaining differences in and mutual effects among (1) economic conditions, (2) widely held beliefs, and (3) common organizational forms and administrative strategies. Marx and Weber were also interested in these topics. What distinguishes Pareto from Marx and Weber is the way these three economists-turned-sociologists understood interconnections among these three factors. Marx always considered himself an economist first, and for good reason. He died before sociology really emerged as an independent discipline, but in addition, he viewed economic conditions as having primacy and ultimately determining everything else. This makes Marx an *economic determinist* (see chapter 8). Weber, for his part, viewed values as having primacy (see *The Protestant Ethic and the Spirit of Capitalism*). This makes Weber more of a *cultural determinist* (see chapter 9). In contrast, Pareto viewed society as being composed of interdependent analytical components, so that change in any one has repercussions for all the others, making him more of what we might call a *general systems theorist*.

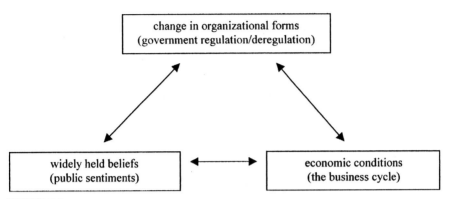

FIGURE 6.1
Pareto's Mutual Determinism

Pareto was remarkably perceptive in using his sociological theory to anticipate in his final work the difficulties of the Great Depression. So it should be no surprise that his insights tell us something about current economic events including the mortgage and credit card situation that was gaining crisis proportions by 2007. After long periods of economic hardship, savings accumulate because shared beliefs encourage the exercising of great self-restraint. However, people eventually grow tired of the social constraint, and beliefs begin to change and self-restraint increasingly comes under question and ridicule. But as trends toward liberalization gain more momentum, there is a tendency to *overshoot*. That is, the trend carries so far in one direction that negative consequences begin to accumulate.

Trends are rarely reversed until significant negative consequences have accumulated. The more confining rules are and the longer the period over which confining rules are strictly enforced, the greater the number of people who will come to favor a relaxation of the rules; this relaxation launches a long-term trend toward innovation. But a social climate fostering innovation also fosters hedonistic and speculative behavior of all kinds. The longer this trend toward relaxed and sporadically enforced rules continues, the greater the number of people who will be harmed and/or will perceive themselves to be harmed because of a lack of rules or enforcement. This change in public sentiment launches a long-term trend toward greater social constraint that restricts freedom and discourages experimentation of all kinds.

Markets versus Hierarchies versus Networks

Sociologists necessarily concern themselves with markets as an important mode of organization. But as made clear earlier in this chapter, there are other important forms of organization. These include hierarchies, as pointed out by Oliver

Williamson (co-recipient of the 2009 Nobel Prize in Economics) in his conceptually important 1975 book, *Markets and Hierarchies*,[7] and networks, as explored
in the Manuel Castells's 1996 book, *The Rise of the Network Society*.[8]

An illustration may help. Market organization implies that the partners with
whom one cooperates are easily changed. If I don't like the brand of yogurt sold at
the store where I normally shop, I can easily visit one of the other grocery stores in
my neighborhood. No law or social custom or alliance restricts where I shop. For
me, deciding where to shop and what to buy is a market decision. Where can I get
what I want at the best price and most convenient location? My situation is very
different from that of my father when he was my age. My father did the grocery
shopping and a friendship tie dictated where he shopped. Like so many small-town
people, or in his case a small-town migrant to a big city, he did not allow himself
the freedom of a market decision about where to shop—a deep bond of friendship
dictated his decision. We shopped at the small store of John Vaenoski (whom a
lot of people knew simply as "Johnny the butcher"). Mr. Vaenoski offered far less
variety in his little store than was available at local supermarkets. And prices were
higher because small stores do not enjoy economies of scale. But for us, where to
shop was a matter of long-term friendship and deep personal commitment. Where
to shop was not a decision involving any economic calculation. It was not a market
matter. The economics were irrelevant. We ate what Mr. Vaenoski carried in his
store, and we paid the prices he posted without thinking about it, even though we
knew without checking that our grocery dollar would buy more food in a bigger
store. Although this is not everyone's experience, it is the common experience of
a lot of people who live in small towns or in the city neighborhood sociologists
have come to regard as the urban villages Herbert Gans identifies in his 1962 book,
The Urban Villagers.[9] For some people, shopping behavior reflects simple market
decisions. But for others, shopping activity is determined by friendship bonds and
other social commitments. Sociologists have contributed greatly to understanding
how economic activity of all kinds is organized.

Sometimes hierarchy also looks like a market. When I taught at Talladega College in Alabama, there was state liquor control. This meant there was only one
legal place in the town I lived in to buy wine or beer. My choices were to buy
alcohol at that state-controlled liquor store or not buy any at all (which of course
was a good choice and viable option). That was hierarchy at work. It was by no
means a true market even though the establishment where alcohol was found
was called a store and it sold beer and wine. Alabama's system was not necessarily a bad one. But whatever it was, the sale of alcohol was not organized on true
market principles. Had it been, privately owned liquor stores would have opened
and there would have been much more choice, more convenience, and probably
lower prices, all stemming from competition.

The broad implications of a topic like state liquor control may be clearer if
we think about corporate decisions. Ford has the resources to produce all the

car batteries it needs for the cars it sells. But Ford can purchase batteries more cheaply than it can manufacture them. Weighing all the short- and long-term costs involved, what should Ford do? This is a crucial sociological question because it goes directly to the heart of the question of alternative modes of social organization. Is it best to follow a market mode of organization and save money by purchasing batteries at the lowest price available on the spot *market*? Or would it be better to adopt *hierarchy* as the mode of organization and produce batteries inside the company? Or might a third strategy, the *network* strategy, be preferable? A network strategy would suggest the advisability of a strategic alliance, with Ford establishing an enduring relationship with an outside vendor. The concept of a strategic alliance is a good one. The supplier has the promise of a long-term (or at least an intermediate-term) commitment. In return, a supplier promises to meet needs on time with high-quality material, and often promises to innovate or retool when called on to do so.

In an important 1937 paper, economist Ronald Coase explains that risk presented by uncertainty is a critical factor when one is selecting among alternative modes of organization.[10] If one battery is not at the right place at the right time, a car must be pushed into a parking lot instead of driven onto a showroom floor. And if the undelivered part is a transmission gear rather than a battery, an entire production line will grind to a halt. This illustrates that the relative risk and potential costs associated with different uncertainties must be figured into business calculations. If what seem to be cost-effective market solutions significantly increase exposure to risk, then it makes sense to bring operations inside the organization and try to be organizationally more self-contained and self-sufficient. This strategy of bringing operations inside the organization and trying to be organizationally as self-sufficient as possible is what is meant by *vertical integration.* Vertical integration has different branches of an organization providing inputs or performing services for other branches, rather than buying the components and purchasing services that might be available at a lower price in the spot market.

The lesson is a critical one. Uncertainty tends to make otherwise unattractive hierarchical or bureaucratic organizational solutions look better than they would otherwise appear, and tends to make otherwise attractive market solutions for organizing activity less attractive than they would otherwise appear. This insight won Coase the Nobel Prize in Economics, but it is at least as important in sociological analysis as it is in economic analysis, as sociologists have historically treated form of organization as something that is potentially variable and must be explained.

Uncertainty Principle of Hierarchy: **Other things being equal, the rationality of a market solution in comparison with a hierarchical solution to an organizational challenge is (1) a positive function of the cost effectiveness of the market** solution and (2) an inverse function of risks of uncertainty that come with the market solution.

Many factors need to be considered when one is weighing risk. Labor unrest and quality of component parts are two of the factors most people instinctively recognize as important, although there are many others. Sociological analyses often deal with risk factors.

The implications of improved technology also weigh heavily in sociological analysis. It can be noted that most improvements in transportation and communication technology favor markets over hierarchical organization, as do improvements in manufacturing precision and equipment reliability. This helps explain why manufacturers in the United States procure so many components from overseas, and why there is high turnover in suppliers in many industries. However, technological advancement and the scientific knowledge explosion tend to force organizations in some sectors of the economy to maintain a steady stream of innovation in order to remain competitive. When customization and innovation are required, sustained network partnerships tend to be superior to either markets or hierarchies: network partnerships provide more flexibility than hierarchies, yet generate more sustained commitment than markets. Networking thus tends to optimize the balance between (a) the need for long-term commitments justifying the cost of innovation and (b) the need for flexibility required to be successful at innovation.

Innovation/Complexity Principle of Networking: **Other things being equal, the tendency to adopt network/strategic alliance solutions to organizational challenges is a positive function of (a) the complexity of activity and (b) the necessity to maintain ongoing creativity and innovation in order to remain competitive.**

The way sociologists first borrowed from and then built on the utilitarian economics tradition sharpens our conceptual understanding of contemporary challenges and adds to our tool kit of explanatory insights.

Recap

If we examine sociological insights marking the intellectual frontier along which sociology initially distinguished itself from economics, using formal theory construction techniques, we are able to account for three critical factors about society: (1) relative tendencies toward increased heterogeneity (when social units and subpopulations are small, isolated, and autonomous) versus increased homogeneity (when social units are large, interaction is frequent, and autonomy is limited); (2) major cyclical shifts in normative restraint as an aspect of popular culture, having broad social and economic implications; and (3) the observed propensity of different enterprises to utilize market, hierarchical or bureaucratic, and network or strategic alliance forms of organization under different conditions. This marks a huge social scientific accomplishment. Had sociology not made any other contribution as a discipline, it would have lived up to Comte's expectation of being the queen science. But sociology's differentiation from economics only represents the beginning of our disciplinary effort at making theoretical and scientific progress. In the chapters that follow, we will introduce other axioms and principles to a compendium that adds to sociology's robust, powerful, and ever-increasing body of theory.

Some Terms to Know

Transparency: The ready availability of complete and accurate information.

Conspicuous Consumption: Seeking to enhance one's own prestige by spending money in ways that send visible signals that suggest that an individual should be regarded as a person of merit.

Overshoot: The tendency for the momentum of social trends to continue in the same direction until mounting problems make additional movement in that direction untenable, and reversal of the trend inevitable.

Review of Principles

Principle of Evolution: Other things being equal, the rate at which social units differentiate from one another is (1) a direct function of their isolation and (2) an inverse function of their size.

Principle of Supply and Demand: Other things being equal, the level of incentive potential suppliers have to provide something and consumers have to find substitutes (1) are positive functions of demand and price, and are (2) inverse functions of supply and aggregate elasticity.

Principle of Cyclical Change in Beliefs: Other things being equal, (a) the more social constraint there is, then the more slowly that innovation and problem solving occur, which generates pressure for greater tolerance of individuality, but (b) the more tolerance there is of individual action, then the greater the number of new problems people create, which generates greater insistence on conformity.

Uncertainty Principle of Hierarchy: Other things being equal, the rationality of a market solution in comparison with a hierarchical solution to an organizational challenge, is (1) a positive function of the cost effectiveness of the market solution and (2) an inverse function of risks of uncertainty that come with the market solution.

Innovation/Complexity Principle of Networking: Other things being equal, the tendency to adopt network/strategic alliance solutions to organizational challenges is a positive function of (a) the complexity of activity and (b) the necessity to maintain ongoing creativity and innovation in order to remain competitive.

Quiz

Check your answers in the back of the book. If you get any wrong, consider reviewing chapter 6 before continuing.

1. What are the characteristics of a perfect market?
2. What is the Principle of Evolution and what does it suggest about globalization?
3. When is hierarchy preferable to market organization?

Application Exercise

Think of a college you are familiar with. Consider each of the following, if they are present on campus: a bookstore, a cafeteria, a janitorial service. Selecting one of the three, try to find out if the people who do the work are employees of the college (receiving paychecks from the college itself) or are employees of a contractor, managerial service, or corporate chain. Then write down some of the factors a college might have weighed in deciding whether to (a) own and run this operation or (b) contract with an independent business to run this particular operation.

Think about one or two reasons why workers might prefer to be employees of the college or might prefer to be employees of a contractor.

PART III

SOCIOLOGY'S MOST PROMINENT FOUNDING FIGURES: DURKHEIM, MARX, WEBER, AND MEAD

HAVING COMPLETED PARTS I AND II OF THIS BOOK, readers should understand how to approach sociological theory as something that is highly useful. Insights can be made tangible by presenting them as axioms and principles with clear meaning, ready for application in the real world. In part III we turn to what sociologists have come to appreciate as the enduring contributions of four founders of the discipline: Émile Durkheim, Karl Marx, Max Weber, and George Herbert Mead. Each of these theorists has had a profound and lasting influence on the development of sociological thought. More than anyone else, these four are considered the central authors of sociology's most important works. More than anyone else, they gave sociology its defining character. They set the discipline's intellectual foundation in place. Their legacy is both powerful and enduring.

In part III, we will examine some of the great sociological ideas generated by the founders of our discipline at the end of the nineteenth century and the beginning of the twentieth century. We will begin by examining the work of Émile Durkheim because his, more than that of any of the other early sociological theorists, was specifically framed as an effort to develop sociology as a true science self-consciously adopting the scientific method. Émile Durkheim (1858–1917) of France was also the first person anywhere in the world to hold the title of professor of sociology. (Actually, he initially held a joint appointment as a professor of sociology and education.) Durkheim's work forms much of the heart of sociology's intellectual foundation. For these reasons, what people both inside and outside the discipline later came to think of as sociology has been defined in substantial measure by Durkheim's efforts (see chapter 7).

A distinctive part of sociology's foundation was emerging at about the same time in Germany, as a number of people began to think of the economics of Karl Marx (1818–1883) as another possible way of theorizing more broadly about society. It should be kept in mind that Marx's life overlapped with Durkheim's even though Marx was born forty years before Durkheim. *The Communist Manifesto*, written by Karl Marx and Friedrich Engels in 1848, a few years before Durkheim's birth, was a study of the economic and political system evolving during the period of rapid industrialization in western Europe. Marx drew attention to the importance of the economic system and the patterns of class interests that every economic system seems to create. Marx recognized that persistent strains of conflict often follow along the fault lines created by differences in the intrinsic interests of different economic classes. Marx's ideas about industrial capitalism were maturing at the same time that the young Durkheim was beginning to think seriously about Comte's call for the development of a science of society.

Although Marx actually saw himself as an economist rather than a sociologist, the theory at the heart of Marx's work can easily be understood as sociological, and many sociologists quickly appropriated it. And while Marx held the decidedly unscientific belief that he already knew perfectly well how society worked, a testable explanatory theory is readily detectable in Marx's writing. That explanatory theory continues to inform sociological thinking and will be our focus in chapter 8.

Max Weber (1864–1920) approached the study of the social world in a way that was quite different from either Durkheim or Marx. In contrast to Durkheim's tendency to use recent statistical data when possible, Weber's research efforts tended to involve historical case studies covering very long periods of time in specific geographic areas, and to look for similarities or differences between the statistical patterns observable when comparing different places. ("Recent" for Durkheim was late nineteenth century and early twentieth century.) This methodological difference manifests itself in different styles of theorizing. Weber's approach to research (using historical documents in order to analyze long-term economic transformation) has more in common with the research approach used by Marx, but the explanatory framework Weber used could hardly be more different from that employed by Marx. Weber was impressed by the degree to which shared values could unify a society even when class divisions were pronounced. And Weber rejected Marx's position that the nature of the economy ultimately determines everything else about a society. For example, Weber believed the impact of religious doctrine on the flow of historical events to be quite significant. We continue to appreciate both Marx and Weber because they generated a repertoire of penetrating insights about the way historical events unfolded over time. Their contemporaries recognized these contributions as important because Marx and Weber each raised questions that were too big for economics as an isolated discipline to answer.

Meanwhile, in the United States sociology was emerging in close association with psychology. At the time, American sociologists and psychologists were all focusing on the concept of *self*. But the sets of questions sociologists and psychologists were raising about the self tended to be different. Sociologists viewed the self both as a window on and as a reflection of group phenomena. What goes on among people in group settings, American sociologists argued, produces individual differences in self-concept. And, American sociologists argued, self-concept has the importance it does in substantial measure because of its impact on individual behavior within groups. Sociologists were asking questions like these: How is a person's sense of self and of identity forged through experience? And what consequences do self and identity have for group process? These sociologists, centered around the unassuming person of George Herbert Mead (1863–1931) at the University of Chicago, were laying the foundations for our understanding of individual adjustment to the wider social world. At the same time and in the same place, sociology's urban ethnographers were adding to our understanding of processes of change within communities (see chapter 4).

Taken together, Émile Durkheim, Karl Marx, Max Weber, and George Herbert Mead provided sociology with an enduring intellectual legacy of robust and powerful theoretical ideas that we continue to draw on. These four men were genuine intellectual giants who continue to inform our efforts to explain patterns of difference and change in the social world. Their direct legacy is the subject of part III of this book.

7

Émile Durkheim on
Scientific Study of Social Facts

M ANY PEOPLE PLACE DURKHEIM at the top of the pantheon of sociology's founders. He translated Comte's vision of scientific sociology into a compelling
theoretical perspective and helped formulate a research methodology specifically
designed with sociology's subject matter in mind.

Remembering Comte

Auguste Comte (1798–1857) was raised in France in the aftermath of the French
Revolution. The experience of the Reign of Terror left many people in France
fearful of revolutionary social disorder. Comte was one of them, and he advocated the scientific study of society as a way of solving social ills and avoiding
societal disintegration. Comte coined the term *sociology* to represent this new
field of scientific study. He explained that sociology would be the most challenging of sciences—the queen science—partly because the complexity of the
social world exceeds the complexity of the physical and biological worlds, where
things are more tangible, and partly because sociology concerns itself with the
subject matter of all fields of social organization rather than any single segment
of the tapestry of the social world (businesses, the criminal justice system, civic
organizations, religious congregations, and so forth).

Comte feared the possibility of chaotic social disintegration, but he hoped
that the discovery of social scientific principles would allow social planners to
engineer a peaceful and prosperous society.[1] Although Comte failed to generate

any predictive principles himself, we still remember him for recognizing that sociology could be a science.

Comte played a crucial role in placing the problem of order (social stability) at the forefront of sociological concerns. Comte believed that the kind of social order that bestows benefits of peace and prosperity could not and should not be taken for granted. He thought sociology would eventually make a vital contribution to humankind by arming leaders with well-tested sociological principles to be used in shaping the more peaceful, more prosperous, and more civilized world he hoped for. Comte's vision, of course, puts a burden on every sociology student. It is the burden of honing skills and becoming more constructively engaged as citizens, applying sociological insights wisely to help make a better planet. Sociology's national honor society, Alpha Kappa Delta, explicitly embodies Comte's vision by encouraging careful use of sound social science research practices for the purpose of informing richer sociological understanding ultimately resulting in better solutions to society's challenges. Comte's vision lives on in AKD, and this is a tangible indication of the lasting impact of Comte's vision of sociology as an important and distinct field of scientific inquiry.

Harriet Martineau Hears Comte's Call for a Science of Society

Harriet Martineau (England, 1802–1876) was one of the people who accepted Comte's call to develop a science of society. She translated much of Comte's work into English and also conceived of a way sociologists might actually conduct the scientific study of society. Martineau did this by using government data to tabulate aggregate statistics on subjects such as suicide. Part of her genius was in recognizing that suicide rates (and aggregate statistics on a number of other phenomena) could serve as indicators of society's well-being and could therefore be used in empirical research about the society as a whole (not just the individual people in it). Martineau's dedication to statistical measurement is widely recognized as having helped make contemporary social science possible.

Martineau's focus on suicide was a particular stroke of genius. She recognized that suicide rate would be a telling indicator about the broad condition of a society undergoing rapid urbanization and industrialization, and an especially telling indicator on those matters pertaining to social order that were of such concern to Comte.

Martineau conducted sociology's first important empirical research when she discovered that suicide was indeed becoming somewhat more common with industrialization. Her work placed scientific sociology squarely on an empirical rather than a more purely speculative or philosophical footing. In this sense, she was clearly different from her contemporaries. She did more than talk about the desirability of studying society scientifically. She actually began to study society scientifically. In doing so, she set the stage for Émile Durkheim's groundbreaking contributions and really defined the future shape of sociology as a social scientific discipline.

A Focus on Social Facts

Following Comte and Martineau, Émile Durkheim looked at the world in terms of *social facts,* or patterns of belief and behavior that can be said to be true of groups rather than individuals. Social facts are often deeply instilled in people through socialization and enforced by the coercive power of social pressure. If we look at classrooms, for example, we can see remarkable similarities in the way people behave. And why? Many of the patterns of behavior we emit are first programmed through socialization and then enforced by the groups to which we belong. In a sense, it is not the individual who has decided how to act, but the group, which then imposes its will on the individual through the exercise of social pressure.

The concept of social fact and awareness of the coercive power of groups are central to understanding Durkheim. Consider your choice of clothing today: your *choice* of what to wear and even your *choice* of whether to wear anything at all. How real are these choices?

Durkheim recognized that the social groupings we are part of impose certain decisions with the coercive force of social pressure. We must do certain things and we must avoid doing others because the consequences of disregarding group norms are more than most people can bear. Regarding many of the matters about which there is some uniformity in beliefs or behavior, the negative reactions of other people toward nonconformists are simply much more than the average person wants to withstand.[2] There are, of course, certain times when particular rules are relaxed. But the time, length, and scope of rules relaxed during the time-out periods are themselves almost always socially determined by group convention. To decide on one's own that rules no longer apply is a striking act of deviance.

What Durkheim points out, and what is certainly true and easy to appreciate, is that if a norm is deeply held and imbued with a lot of importance by the group, the group is quite capable of making defiance of the norm *very* uncomfortable and *very* costly and thoroughly stigmatizing. That is, as Erving Goffman emphasizes in his 1961 book, *Asylums,* the reputation of a person can be tainted in ways that are hard to overcome after one or two deviations from socially approved behavior.[3]

Often, we don't even recognize the coercive force the wider society exerts on us. This is because people so fully internalize norms that the average person automatically complies with most norms without stopping to think about them.

But should we deviate, the weight of social compulsion can be burdensome indeed.

Durkheim on Systemic Interconnections and Regulatory Constraint

Being intrigued by social facts, Durkheim began his career as a sociologist by trying to describe and explain variations among different kinds of societies. And as a sociologist he was of course interested in variations relating to social attachments and shared beliefs. But Durkheim also recognized the sociological importance of understanding variation in the complex systemic interconnections that largely determine the positions people occupy in relation to one another. All these concerns are evident in Durkheim's first great book, *The Division of Labor in Society* (1893).[4] In it, he notes that the urbanizing societies of western Europe were structurally changing in ways that had far-reaching consequences.

Durkheim's analysis in *The Division of Labor in Society* develops a macrolevel analysis. It does this by treating the law as a body of social facts, or patterns of belief and behavior telling us something meaningful about the social whole that is being examined (in this case, French society) and not merely about the individuals making up that society. Durkheim notes, for example, that the relationships among victims of crimes and perpetrators of those crimes tend to change when a society undergoes industrialization. Prior to industrialization, legal codes seemed to have been dominated by a tone of moral outrage about transgression. Thus, preindustrial societies tended to define justice as a mechanism for expressing moral outrage and extracting society's revenge on behalf of the victims who had been wronged. But as industrialization proceeds, Durkheim notes, law changes in a predictable way. The tone of moral outrage subsides and is supplanted by more of a sense of mutual tragedy that unfortunate things happen in a complex world. Emphasis is placed on seeking justice through restitution to at least partially compensate a person for a loss.

In every society, the legal system (if taken as a whole) seems designed to extract some blend of revenge and restitution. Durkheim recognized the proportional mix in each society as a *social fact*; he understood that this mix varies from society to society, and he tried to explain why.

As societies industrialize, beliefs change and people's experiences become more varied. This translates into what Durkheim terms *enfeeblement of collective conscience* consisting of the values and beliefs shared by most members of a society. That is to say that with industrialization, as people's experiences become more varied, agreement dissipates with regard to what is right and wrong, appropriate and inappropriate, acceptable and unacceptable. Although collective thirst for revenge against moral transgression does not disappear completely, there is shrinkage in the number of acts that demand serious punishment as an expres-

TABLE 7.1
Changes in the Pathways through Which Societal Integration Is Achieved

Structural/Cultural Feature	Type of Society	
	Preindustrial	*Industrial*
Collective Conscience	Strong	Enfeebled
Division of Labor	Meager	Extensive
Legal Institutions	Sever tenuous ties	Repair tenuous ties
Occupational Subgroups	Relatively rare	Increasingly common

sion of the society's moral outrage because the sense of shared societal agreement about what constitutes a genuine outrage dissipates.

As specialized division of labor spreads, the body of civil law grows in proportion to the body of criminal law. Durkheim recognized something significant in this change. While preindustrial societies are generally integrated around shared beliefs about what is right and wrong (collective conscience), industrial societies come to be integrated around mutual interdependence (division of labor) and newly institutionalized arrangements to regulate our dealings with others (such as taking someone to court and following legal rules when you have a serious disagreement, rather than getting together with your clan members to take the law into your own hands). Durkheim also talks about occupational subgroup formation as a third source of integration that gains importance as societies industrialize.

The *researcher* in Durkheim worked to *describe* social facts in industrializing countries in contrast with preindustrial ones, and he did this by identifying characteristics of legal codes. But the *theorist* in Durkheim wanted to explain *variation* between cases and change over time. Those are two different activities. What excited sociologists most about *The Division of Labor in Society* was the functionalist mode of theoretical analysis that Durkheim began to advance as an explanation for what he found. The most basic summary of Durkheim's explanatory theory would be to say that, in society as in physiology, *form follows function*.

Form Follows Function: Early Structural Functionalism

Why would a legal system change during industrialization? Durkheim's answer to this question includes all the major ingredients of his sociology. For societies to continue to cohere, they must be integrated in some way. Most people in preindustrial societies are semisubsistence agriculturalists. In terms of economic interdependence, there is little by way of systemic interconnections that integrates the whole society. So, Durkheim noted, where preindustrial societies are well integrated it tends to be through a system of shared beliefs, or collective conscience, which is fostered by similarity of lifestyle and myths of common origin. Strong collective conscience involves uniformity of beliefs about what constitutes good and bad and right and wrong. Strong collective conscience discourages questioning, and fosters a sense of moral outrage when people violate the rules everyone takes for granted. Vengeance as a form of justice mirrors a level of integration rooted in collective conscience, and it sustains that collective conscience by reaffirming common definitions of right and wrong. Punishment as a moral statement invigorates agreement about right and wrong if such agreement exists. It does so by reminding people that they have collectively defined some acts as being very, very bad. So where economic self-sufficiency prevails, enlivening the collective conscience through occasional expression of moral outrage helps hold society together.

The use of symbols of affinity is something else that Durkheim recognized enlivens collective conscience. It does so by affirming group memberships and by reminding people that those group memberships stand for something in particular. This was the subject of Durkheim's 1912 book, *The Elementary Forms of Religious Life*.[5] Sociologists like William Goode maintained this interest, stressing the importance of hero stories that celebrate not only group membership, but also particular qualities the group most values.[6] Durkheim makes the point that it might be more accurate to think of heroic imagery and unifying symbols as creating the substance of group feeling than talking about heroes and symbols and things created by the group. He says this for impact, but it does convey an important point.

With industrialization comes heterogeneity of lifestyles and the enfeeblement of collective conscience. That is, when people lose some of their similarity of life experience, they also tend to drift away from singular definitions of appropriateness and inappropriateness. But what then holds a society together? Under these circumstances, Durkheim notes the importance of mutual interdependence once the age of self-sufficient farming is past. The division of labor, in Durkheim's view, is a structural form that satisfies the functional need for system integration in industrializing societies. Increased division of labor also necessitates the development of new institutional forms to stabilize and regulate social attachments of different kinds. Civil law and court systems provide a mechanism for resolving disputes without disrupting the kinds of attachments that are necessary to maintain in order for society to function. One aspect of this transformation is that legal forms based on restitution largely supplant those based on retribution, because complex relations grind to a halt at moments when large numbers of people are gripped with a sense of moral outrage preventing them from conducting normal commercial, cultural, political, and social activity. It is functional, therefore, for legal codes to change, putting legal emphasis on arbitration and restitution rather than on prohibitive restriction and revenge. In other words, Durkheim treats legal changes as social facts, and as empirical indicators of structural change serving to hold industrializing society together at what would otherwise be a time of diminished societal integration resulting from enfeeblement of shared collective conscience.

This led Durkheim to conclude that *form does follow function.* Things are done a certain way (form, structure) because it helps society work better (to achieve more operational success, better functional performance, and greater integration, for example). Indeed, trying to extract vengeance where the collective conscience is enfeebled tends to turn people off. In the absence of a strong collective conscience, vengeance simply looks like cruelty.

Durkheim on Suicide and on Integration as a Societal Function

Émile Durkheim viewed himself as a social scientist. He wanted to develop explanations (theory) that he could empirically test (research). His most famous effort to do so was his 1897 book, *Suicide.*[7] Durkheim saw this subject as an opportunity to develop a strong research tradition in sociology, building on Martineau's work and in an effort to bring Comte's vision of scientific sociology to life.

Durkheim published *Suicide* utilizing government statistics to test a variety of hypotheses about suicide as a social fact, that is, about changes in and differences between suicide rates. Durkheim found that measures of social bonding or integration (for example, the number of people being uprooted in the urbanization process and the number of people practicing different kinds of religions) were highly correlated with suicide rates. But what is much more important from the vantage point of theory is that Durkheim gave us a series of powerful insights that amount to a versatile explanatory principle that we can term Durkheim's Principle of Social Control.

Principle of Social Control: **Other things being equal, the degree of social control a group or community exerts over its members (1) increases as a positive function of group/community integration (how interconnected members' activities are and how tightly bound members are by a common set of beliefs), and (2) diminishes to the degree that members have offsetting ties to other groups or communities.**

In part, Durkheim's insights derive from a typology he developed to distinguish among different sorts of suicide. This typology has had a lasting impact on sociology because it clearly embodies our disciplinary commitment to the study of both (a) direct (personal) and indirect (systemic) attachments and (b) shared beliefs. Durkheim notes that too little of either kind of integrative connection within a group (either too little attachment, which he called *egoism,* related to egoistic suicide, or lack of clarity in shared beliefs, which he termed *anomie,* related to anomic suicide) can lead to high suicide rates. Interestingly, these two types of suicide are recognizably different. Lack of attachment to others is analytically quite different from lack of normative clarity associated with enfeeblement of collective conscience. This discovery by Durkheim bore little resemblance to the commonsense ideas of his time, that changes in suicide rate are explainable primarily in terms of collective trauma (such as economic collapse or war). It was a new sociological discovery. The French book-reading public immediately recognized that sociology was able to offer rare insight, and sociology has remained a popular and respected field of study in France ever since.

Durkheim went still further. He realized that just as too little group integration is associated with high suicide rates, a group that is tightly integrated can also push members toward suicide as a way of avoiding serious embarrassment within the group (he refers to this phenomenon as *fatalistic suicide*) or in a sacrificial act trying to defend the group against hostile outsiders (which he refers to as *altruistic suicide*).

It is noteworthy that Durkheim's essays on suicide place special emphasis on anomie and anomic suicide. Why? There are two reasons. First, like Comte, Durkheim was deeply concerned, one might even say to the point of preoccupation, with the risk of societal disintegration. Second, the source of disintegration that seemed to Durkheim to loom as the largest threat during a time of industrialization was enfeeblement of collective conscience. Hence, his special concern with anomic suicide, which rises with a weakening in shared beliefs.

After the publication of *Suicide* in 1897, Durkheim turned his attention to guiding young researchers inspired by his sociological approach to understand-

Level of Integration

	(a) *too low*	(b) *too high*
(1) *shared beliefs*	Anomic suicide (shared beliefs too ambiguous)	Fatalistic suicide (weight of rules too heavy)
(2) *social attachments*	Egoistic suicide (attachments too weak)	Altruistic suicide (attachments too strong)

Sources of Integration (left axis label)

FIGURE 7.1
Types of Suicide in Durkheim

ing the world. In the years leading up to World War I, Durkheim's young research colleagues put out a steady stream of good work, much of it published in Durkheim's journal *Année sociologique.*

The Beginning of Sociology's Special Relationship with Anthropology

Durkheim always kept integration in the center of his sociological analyses. His last great work, *Elementary Forms of Religious Life* (1912), explores the use of rituals and symbols of communion (often involving totems) in cementing feelings of common group membership and in instilling people with shared understandings about evaluative standards and behavioral expectations. Celebrating heroes, participating in rituals, and engaging in communion activities all help to solidify feelings of group membership and remind members of the human qualities and social standards that the group holds most dear.

In a quirk of intellectual history, *Elementary Forms of Religious Life* was to mark a milestone in anthropological thinking. The most influential British social anthropologists of the day, Bronislaw Malinowski and A. R. Radcliffe-Brown, read Durkheim's structural functionalist theory emphasizing that form follows function. They began applying Durkheim's structural functional mode of analysis to what seemed to be exotic social patterns found in different cultures. And they arrived at new insight by asking how different social structural patterns and cultural arrangements might have developed in order to perform special functions for society. Following the lead Malinowski blazed in his 1922 book, *Argonauts of the Western Pacific,* anthropologists spent decades employing the structural functionalist approach developed by Durkheim.[8] With the passage of time, Durkheim's insightful discussions in *The Elementary Forms of Religious Life* also provided much of the intellectual foundation for structuralism in anthropology.

The Basic Structural Functionalist Model

To say that form follows function means that cultural patterns and organizational forms develop to meet needs. This dynamic can be easily illustrated. After 1980, a lot of school districts in the United States either began to provide or else dramatically expanded the availability of before- and after-school care for children. Structural functionalists would have an easy time offering an explanation. As the number of single-parent households increased, and also as the number of dual-career households increased, there was growing need for before- and after-school care. Providing before-school and after-school care at the schools themselves proved to be a practical way of meeting the need. At that time, had the United States had a pattern of larger families with stronger extended family ties and less geographic mobility, most people would have had extended-family alternatives to after-school care, and schools would have been under far less pressure to take on that task. But circumstances were otherwise. There was a need, and schools were in a position to do something about it. Thus the idea that form follows function offers a way of looking at the world that can be quite thought provoking. The institutional system evolved in order to meet changing needs!

Durkheim did not have much chance to develop his embryonic structural functionalist analysis. Shortly after the publication of *Elementary Forms of Religious Life*, World War I broke out. Almost all of Durkheim's students (including his only child) died in World War I, with significant losses to French sociology starting at the First Battle of the Marne in September 1914. In that battle, pitched French resistance halted the German advance toward Paris and saved France from defeat. But it also plunged Europe into long and bloody trench warfare. The death toll among the small cadre of young and highly nationalistic French sociologists was astronomically high. Durkheim, still a comparatively young man at fifty-nine, died brokenhearted in 1917. Losses during the Great War, the War to End All Wars, were in part a reflection of Durkheim's success. As a professor of sociology and of education, Durkheim had been an early advocate of using flags and other symbols, and pledges and other rituals, as a way of promoting a deeper sense of national identification and commitment among young people.

Durkheim's work was known primarily in France, and it might have been lost to American sociology. But after World War I a number of American sociologists were reading British social anthropology, where they encountered Durkheim's framework and were impressed by its promise. Robert K. Merton was a particularly important conduit, exposing a group of Harvard sociologists who were to become central players in sociology from the mid-1930s through the 1960s (see chapter 11).

Durkheim and the Scientific Method in Sociology

Émile Durkheim was an early and influential advocate of the use of the scientific method in sociology. His study of suicide, first published in France in 1897, is a textbook illustration of the scientific method in action. Reviewing Durkheim's examination of suicide helps clarify how the scientific method came to be employed in sociology.

The first step in the scientific method is to identify some difference among cases (or change over time within a single case) that seems worth trying to understand and explain. Durkheim, along with many other people in his era, identified suicide rate (not suicide as a singular event, but suicide *rate* as an aggregate societal indicator) as a variable worth studying. The focus on rate is critical. Of course, sociologists were interested in what would drive an individual person to commit suicide. But their curiosity was really centered on why rates would be higher in some communities than in others.

The second step is to advance a theoretical principle or set of principles that might explain the kinds of outcomes we are trying to understand. Durkheim began by considering the conventional wisdom of his time. In the late nineteenth century, psychological distress was generally advanced as the explanation for individual suicide, but many people applied this idea to the suicide rate of whole communities. The prevailing view seemed reasonable enough. Suicide rate was probably going to be highest in places and at times of mass distress, such as during an economic depression or after defeat in a war. Part of Durkheim's argument rests on an appreciation for the fact that certain things should be true if psychological distress really does offer a good explanation for variation in suicide rates. This brings us to some research hypotheses.

The third step in the scientific method is to move beyond general discussion of what different people theorize to be true, by identifying (either quantitative or qualitative) empirically testable hypotheses that should be true if the theoretical analysis is accurate. Durkheim chose to look at quantitative statistical data for his analysis. One of the themes in Durkheim's book is that all nations go through periods of greater or lesser distress, and that suicide rates should therefore vary considerably over time within each country, assuming psychological distress is, more than anything else, responsible for variation in suicide rates. Of course, the times of greatest stress would occur in different years in different countries. The defeat of France in the Franco-Prussian War, for example, marked a much lower point for people in France than in the newly united Germany, which coalesced into one victorious nation-state after that war. Nevertheless, all countries and all regions within countries might be expected to have a similar range of high to low suicide rates across time, corresponding with good and bad times enjoyed by those countries. Hence, Durkheim had a set of easily testable hypotheses based on psychological disruption as an explanation of suicide rate. If distress offered a good explanation, the yearly suicide rate in any one country should go up and down rather dramatically over a period of years: down with good times and up with bad times. Reasoning this way, one might also expect that high and low suicide rates for different countries and regions would be roughly comparable in magnitude (at least for countries at somewhat similar levels of economic development), even though highs and lows would probably occur in different years for different countries.

The fourth step of the scientific method is to test empirical hypotheses thought to be consistent with the explanatory framework being tested. Durkheim tested his hypotheses in order to evaluate the utility of an explanatory framework based on psychological distress. The hypotheses were *not* confirmed, however. Most countries have suicide rates that are remarkably stable over time. Good times? Bad times? It doesn't seem to matter much as far as aggregate suicide rates are concerned. Rates in most countries do not fluctuate much from year to year, or even from decade to decade. Moreover, some countries (e.g., Denmark) consistently have high suicide rates, while others (e.g., Ireland) consistently have low suicide rates.

The fifth and final step in the scientific method is to use the results of hypothesis testing in order to fuel theoretical reformulation. Durkheim did exactly that. After looking at patterns in his data, including higher suicide rates in cities than in the countryside and higher suicide rates in Protestant areas than in Catholic ones, Durkheim concluded that well-integrated communities tend to have lower suicide rates, as well as lower rates of other forms of aberrant social behavior. But places where webs of social interconnections are less dense or where collective understandings are weaker tend to have higher suicide rates. Integration matters. Durkheim formulated his insights about integration, summarized earlier in this chapter as what we are calling Durkheim's Principle of Social Control. This is a principle well worth learning. The power of Durkheim's analysis was instantly recognized by his readers at the time.

As a caveat, it is important to remember that what we are referring to as Durkheim's Principle of Social Control was not written out in this specific form by Durkheim himself. Few sociologists have written their predictive insights in such a compact way, and Durkheim was no exception. Most of the axioms and principles found in *Making Senses of Social Theory* offer a more succinct expression of key ideas than can be found elsewhere. The twelve axioms and twenty-one principles in this book necessarily involve interpretation, always keeping in mind the goals of (1) clarity and (2) codifying robust and powerful insight.

Keeping All Our Axioms and Principles in Mind

A concluding remark on the cumulative nature of science is in order. Keeping all our theoretical axioms and principles in mind can help us arrive at deeper levels of understanding. Consider the fact that some teenagers get in serious trouble and others manage to avoid serious trouble. But all teens have to contend with roughly the same hormones, so why does the risk of delinquency differ from person to person? An explanation of differences in risk for delinquency must consider the realities of group membership or exclusion, peer pressure, and involvement in structured activities. Teens in different groups feel pressured to do different things. Teens whose peers get into trouble are themselves more likely to get into trouble. This is especially true if the teen has few countervailing influences because, as Durkheim's Principle of Social Control alerts us, the sway of a group will be greatest when the individual's countervailing ties to other groups are most tenuous.

Our understanding often improves if we look beyond a single axiom or principle. If we add to Durkheim's Principle of Social Control ideas presented in earlier chapters of *Making Sense of Social Theory*, our awareness broadens. Thomas's axiom about Definition of Situation and Homans's Benefit Maximization Axiom and the Principle of Rational Choice can, for example, help us appreciate why the Principle of Social Control is so powerful where "delinquent" teenagers are concerned. If a person's definition of situation is that he has been stigmatized, then the individual will feel very little *stake in conformity*; in other words, there is little reason for following mainstream rules once it is presumed that acceptance into the mainstream is never going to happen. Under those conditions, conformity is viewed by many people in the youth culture, especially those with low socioeconomic status, as a goal only for chumps. This example demonstrates that keeping in mind all our axioms and principles and applying them thoughtfully yields real explanatory power. Of course, perceptions that one has little stake in conformity are frequently wrong. It is common for people to have more to lose than they think. But if one's definition of situation is that she has nothing to lose (by ditching school, for example), then that person's cost-benefit calculations will certainly be affected. The crisp insight we get by applying sociology's theoretical axioms and principles can be used to make sense of much of what happens in this world.

Recap

Durkheim was a monumental figure who left a lasting legacy. That legacy stresses several points. First, sociology should be a science, using data to test and improve on our understanding of the social universe. Second, groups, organizations, communities, and societies are more than collections of individuals. Groups, organizations, communities, and societies have characteristics that are not reducible to an aggregation of traits of individuals. Third, if we want to describe social structure, we have to do so in terms of both attachments (direct interpersonal attachments and systemic connections linking people together) and in terms of shared beliefs. Fourth, in groups, organizations, communities, and societies, form follows function. There is a connection between the systemic needs of the wider community and the social-structure form that subsequently develops. And fifth, social control increases with degree of social integration. To understand Durkheim's legacy is to really begin to understand sociology.

Some Terms to Know

Social Fact: An attribute or pattern of belief and behavior that is true of a group or collective social unit.

Stigma: A belief about an individual that harms that person's reputation in a way that is hard to overcome and tends to limit the scope of interaction others are willing to have with the stigmatized individual.

Collective Conscience: A strong sense of membership and uniformity of deeply held agreement about what is considered good and bad and right and wrong.

Enfeeblement of Collective Conscience: A weakening in the sense of a common belonging that group members have, and an evaporation of any deeply held agreement about what is considered good and bad and right and wrong.

Stake in Conformity: The presumption that a person has a lot to lose by getting in trouble by deviating from social rules or group norms.

Review of Principle

Principle of Social Control: Other things being equal, the degree of social control a group or community exerts over its members (1) increases as a positive function of group/community integration (how interconnected members' activities are and how tightly bound members are by a common set of beliefs), and (2) diminishes to the degree that members have offsetting ties to other groups or communities.

Quiz

Check your answers in the back of the book. If you get any wrong, consider reviewing chapter 7 before continuing.

1. Who is credited with conceiving the possibility of a science of society and terming it *sociology*?
2. Who is credited with pioneering our study of suicide rates and treating them as social facts and as key indicators of the condition of a society?
3. What societal changes did Durkheim say provide new sources of societal integration at the very time that collective conscience is enfeebled by industrialization and urbanization?

Application Exercise

Think of Durkheim's Principle of Social Control with reference to groups pressuring people to conform. Consider an example you are familiar with. What does your own example suggest about the power social groups exert over their members? Under what conditions is group pressure strongest or weakest?

8

Karl Marx on Resistance from Below

PEOPLE IN THE MID-NINETEENTH CENTURY were well aware that the world was being transformed by the juggernaut of European industrial capitalism. At that time, the heart of this industrial juggernaut stretched along the Rhine River from Germany into Holland, down the coast and slightly inland to Paris, across the English Channel to London, and finally up to the mill towns of northern England. That was the industrial center of the world. It is actually a small geographic area with a history of trade and contact among the lowland Germans, Dutch, English, and people of northeastern France. Technological innovation and new commercial ideas always diffused quickly among localities in this region, a fact that turns out to have been an important element in European commercial history.

The Labor Theory of Value

Karl Marx (1818–1883) was a part of this scene, born and raised in Tier in the western part of Germany. Marx went to Berlin during his university years and was influenced by ideas of the recently deceased philosopher Georg Friedrich Hegel (Germany, 1770–1831). Hegel was a leading philosopher in Germany when Marx was young. Hegel advanced the thought-provoking notion that ideas progress through the dialectical clash of opposites. In Hegel's terms, thesis meets antithesis and gives rise to a new synthesis.

Marx always considered himself an economist, but he was not like the utilitarian economists who came to dominate thinking in that discipline. Marx was what is sometimes referred to as a *radical economist* who employed a *labor theory of value.* For Marx, and indeed for anyone believing in a labor theory of value, the worth of something depends on how much effort goes into producing and delivering it. From this point of view, it might be argued that a handmade piece of furniture that was laboriously but awkwardly crafted (like some of the furniture made for home use by the author of *Making Sense of Social Theory*) should be worth more than a piece of well-milled but mass-produced furniture that is churned out quickly by a machine. Another way of looking at the labor theory of value is that all value added during manufacturing (the value of a finished piece of furniture beyond the value of the material the piece of furniture was made from) should be assigned to those actually producing and delivering the product rather than to those making design decisions and managing the process.

The labor theory of value has some problems. Although some handcrafted furniture is both functional and exquisite, some is neither. And although some machine-made pieces of furniture are ugly, flimsy, and impractical, other pieces are functional, sturdy, and quite attractive. For most people, value is a function of more than the amount of time and effort that goes into making something available. There are issues of quality and functional design, of aesthetics, and of simply having goods ready when they are needed. The labor theory of value tends to miss all this. But the labor theory of value does help us to see things we might otherwise overlook. Who actually performs the work that makes industrial wealth possible? Do those people get what they deserve? If not, how does the distribution of rewards really work? Marx looked at the value that corporations produce and decided that capitalists, who were in control of the distribution of rewards, took more of the value being produced than their efforts really warranted, and left workers with less of the value being produced than they really deserved. The difference between the value produced by workers and the wages returned to those workers is a "surplus" in value that those workers create but never see. The extraction of that *surplus value* from businesses and into the pockets of owners is at the heart of what Marx described as the system of capitalist exploitation.

This view led Marx to conceive of *class* in a way that is qualitatively distinct from the understanding most people have of the term. For most people, *class* has come to mean economic well-being. A person with more money is higher class than a person with less money. But Marx's concept of class was different. His concept of class was defined in terms of *social relationship to means of production,* which in a capitalist society means one's *role in the wage-labor system.* Is the person in the role of a wage earner, or is the person in the role of an employer? Marx believed that all people who live by selling their labor for wages have interests in common and should feel solidarity with one another. Wage earners may not know they have interests in common, and may not feel solidarity, but Marx believed that they should because, he argued, all wage earners are exploited, in the sense that they are only employed so long as they produce more value than they create. And most workers are actually wage slaves because of their need to keep working in order to pay bills.

Correspondingly, all those people who are employers and live by purchasing and directing the labor of others share a common set of class interests with all other employers. Thus, Marx's conception of class differs significantly from the most common contemporary use of the term, which is defined strictly by income. According to Marx, someone who owns a small janitorial service with two employees and makes a meager living is a capitalist. As an employer, she or he has interests in common with all other employers, rich and poor. Their interests, as Marx would see it, include protecting private property, minimizing wages and benefits in order to maximize the extraction of surplus value, and having the state create an environment in which it is easy for businesses to operate and difficult for labor unions to organize.

Although Marx believed that class interests are objectively real things, he felt that the ability of people to recognize their objective class interests is imperfect. As long as owners of the means of production also tend to control governments and news media, many wage earners are likely to be misled into supporting policies and programs that benefit owners rather than workers. In fact, Marx argued that people have a tendency to speak and work against their own interests when they fail to accurately understand what their own interests really are. He called this *false consciousness*. True class consciousness is the state of accurately understanding what your genuine class interests are and acting accordingly, in conjunction with others who share the same class interests.

The labor theory of value does not assign much credit to entrepreneurial initiative or marketing genius in the wealth creation process. Many people reject the Marxian approach to economics at its intellectual core because Marx's analysis of capitalism is built on a labor theory of value. But even if we disagree with the labor theory of value, it is important to understand it in order to appreciate how Marx arrived at the revealing insights about conflict for which sociologists remember him. Yet, before leaping to Marx's sociology of conflict, it is important to set the stage by reviewing more of his economics.

Dialectical Theory

While a young adult in Berlin, Marx was a rabble-rouser who caught the attention of the Prussian secret police for his radical, pro-worker, anti-imperialist views. That meant he had to leave. Although Germany was not yet unified into a single country (unification occurred in 1871, after the Franco-Prussian War) Prussia was the strongest of the German states and the Prussian secret police operated throughout the entirety of what would become Germany. This made staying anywhere in the future Germany unsafe for Marx, so he went to Paris, where he was a vocal advocate of radical political change. When Marx overstayed his welcome in France by engaging in political activity, he traveled to England, which had a somewhat more tolerant intellectual climate.

England was a good place for Marx to continue to study and write. Not only was England the seedbed of industrial capitalism, but Marx's close friend and collaborator, Friedrich Engels (1820–1895), was a member of a wealthy family that owned textile factories there. Living in England put Marx in a position where Engels could open doors for him. Marx and Engels even distributed one of the first mass surveys in history: a questionnaire to thousands of British factory workers (they got a low response rate, though).

The ties Engels had to community-minded young factory workers were invaluable. Accounts state that Mary Burns and others acquainted with Engels first showed Engels, and then later Marx, what was happening to wage earners as the Industrial Revolution took hold. Engels and Marx thus acquired insight informed by the daily experiences of some members of England's industrial working class. Engels's own writing about the English factory system, especially his 1844 book, *The Origin of the Family, Private Property, and the State*, was seminal.[1] Although Engels is best remembered as the longtime friend and coauthor of Karl Marx, it is likely that some of the ideas people associate with Marx were actually brought to the collaboration by Engels, who was a formidable intellect in his own right.

Despite the importance of Engels and others, Karl Marx was recognized as the most towering intellect among the radicals attacking the system of power and privilege of nineteenth-century capitalism. As an economist of the mid-nineteenth century, Marx understood economics in substantial measure based on his reading of Adam Smith and David Ricardo, but his understanding also incorporated the labor theory of value. To his study of the economic situation of his times, Marx also imported a Hegelian view that processes of change revolve around a thesis, confronted by some antithesis, leading to a new synthesis. Instead of viewing economic change in cyclical terms involving a business cycle that may be momentarily up or down but goes on forever, Marx came to view economic history in *dialectical* terms. This means he focused on the way an economic epoch, such as feudalism, can give rise to an entirely new economic system. Marx predicted that capitalism would undo itself by sowing the seeds of its own destruction.

The Meaning of Class

Marx, ever the economist, maintained strict adherence to economic determinism. He was firmly convinced that systems of ideas (e.g., religion) and everything else of seeming importance about society (e.g., form of government and nature

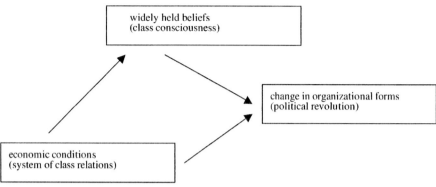

FIGURE 8.1
Marx's Economic Determinism

of legal institutions) are really shaped by the social relations of production in a particular economic system.

By "economic conditions," Marx actually meant, above all else, the class system. He noted that the wage-labor production system is the lifeblood and essence of a capitalist society. In keeping with this approach, Marx defined economic classes in terms of position within the wage-labor system. In capitalism, the social relations of production revolve around who is hiring whom. In capitalism, therefore, Marx would have said the main classes are wage earners (proletarians) and those who purchase and direct the labor of others (capitalists). Marx was convinced that one's class, defined in terms of an individual's role in the wage-labor system rather than his or her level of success, is the single most important factor influencing everything else about a person's experience, quality of life, and beliefs. In capitalism, the wage-labor system unites people who survive by selling their labor (that is, a proletariat class made up of workers who are wage slaves) and people who live by purchasing and directing the labor of others (a capitalist class). Marx described capitalists as despicable parasites who pay laborers less than the value they actually produce through their labor and who enjoy the surplus value workers create but never see.

Marx saw no prospect of real relief for working people except through revolutionary class conflict, because he sensed an unalterable tie between power in the economic sphere and power in political and social domains of society. Marx's understanding of societal dynamics thus rested firmly on an axiomatic assumption that the people in economic power also hold political and social power, and use that power to advance and protect the economic interests of their class.

Structured Inequality Axiom: **The social structural arrangements that survive tend to be those that protect the interests of more-powerful people at the expense of less-powerful people.**

To this must be added a companion axiom, for Marx assumed not only that the fabric of society revolves around ways that the rich and powerful exploit the poor and powerless, but that the rich and powerful will never do anything to change the societal arrangements that benefit them. While the first axiom (Structured Inequality Axiom) captures Marx's reason for feeling that change is necessary, it is the second axiom (Intransigence Axiom) that seems to justify Marx's presupposition that meaningful necessary change can come about only through revolution.

Intransigence Axiom: The powerful do not loosen the grip of exploitation without being pressed to do so.

Taken together, these two axioms make it clear how important the distinction between metatheory and theory actually is. If the Structured Inequality Axiom and the Intransigence Axiom were actually held with deep conviction, one would have little reason to hope that relief from inequality could ever come about as a result of some form of normal evolution from inside the governing apparatus of society itself. The only hope for relief from inequality would have to come from an assault on the governing apparatus from outside the apparatus. This is exactly where Marx found himself intellectually, and we can see this clearly when we formalize the axioms at the root of his theoretical framework. Marx did not think it was within a society's power to fix itself in the interest of the downtrodden, or even in the interest of the rank-and-file citizenry. Hope for progressive improvement developing from within the apparatus of the society, from within *the system* itself, therefore seemed to be a foolish and futile hope.

Lacking hope for progressive improvement, Marx's attention naturally fixed on trying to understand the conditions that might create and mobilize a revolutionary cadre able to take control of the social system by force. He needed to do this because his metatheory (defined by his axiomatic assumptions) excluded the concept of evolution from within the instruments of the society itself as entirely unrealistic.

With Marx fixed on the idea that meaningful change can come about only through a forcible assault on the instruments of society, his intellectual challenge was clear. He needed to understand how the evolution of capitalism transforms the terrain of class relations in a way that produces a revolutionary cadre that is capable of and committed to sweeping change in all aspects of society. This is where Marx's economic analysis, though flawed, allowed him to arrive at certain sociological and political insights that are fundamentally sound. (These are captured in the Principle of Intergroup Conflict, presented later in this chapter.) But to arrive at an understanding of Marx's lasting contribution to political sociology, we must understand the *laws of capitalism*, which he (incorrectly) anticipated would be his lasting contribution to the social sciences.

The Laws of Capitalism

As an economist, Marx is remembered primarily for his analysis of laws or-
daining capitalism's growth and eventual collapse. Marx developed his laws of
capitalism in *Capital*,[2] the first volume of which was released in 1867. The laws
of capitalism as Marx understood them are neatly summarized in a 1978 paper
by Richard Appelbaum.[3] Marx's law of accumulation of capital ordained the
growth of capitalist market economies. Based on his readings of Smith, Marx was
convinced that the market freedoms and productive capacity of industrial capitalism marked a qualitative advance beyond the socially restrictive nature and
lack of material productivity of feudal societies. That is why Marx believed that
capitalism presented the possibility of a more socialistic order: he predicted that
the productive capacity unleashed by capitalism would be able to produce such
great material abundance that the needs of everyone could be easily met. There
would be no reason to fight over possessions because there would be plenty for
everyone, and no reason to fight over control if the employer-employee relations
disappeared. By freeing people to follow the profit incentive, capitalism directs
innovative talent toward the satisfaction of needs and wants. The natural result
is capital accumulation.

In a capitalist society people strive to copy and improve on the success of
others. Profits are reinvested in more machines in order to further expand productive capacity. Still following Smith, Marx believed that competition among
producers would encourage cost-saving innovation and price restraint. In general, this would make life better for people, at least over the short term during the
early stages of capitalism. The amount of physical capital (machines) and social
capital (wage-labor employment arrangements) would grow over time; hence,
capital accumulation.

But Marx predicted that competing capitalists would eventually experience
long periods of falling rate of profit in the battle for market share, especially
during bouts of technology-driven overproduction. Less-profitable companies
would then be absorbed by more-profitable competitors. As a result, ownership
of productive capacity would become increasingly concentrated, ending with
harsher exploitation of workers through the wage mechanism, and greater abuse
of consumers through monopolistic practices. This was the operation of Marx's
law of centralization of capital.

Centralization of capital, Marx predicted, would fuel a trend toward more
extreme class division. That is, the rich would grow even richer, the poor would
grow even poorer, and importantly, the middle class would shrink rather than
grow, as middle-class people (that is, the self-employed) either would become
successful capitalists (by hiring employees) or would join the ranks of wage labor
(by accepting jobs). From this point of view, doctors who give up private practice and go to work for a health maintenance organization (HMO) are joining

the working class. They may not think of themselves as proletarians (because in Marx's view false consciousness can blind people to their true class interests), but Marx would have argued that those doctors are progressively being transformed from small-scale capitalists (if they used to have employees) into wage-earning working people.

With the progression of time, Marx predicted that workers would lose decision-making authority over the work process as a result of the *deskilling* of their jobs. Deskilling occurs as machines are introduced and expensive skilled workers are replaced with less-expensive unskilled workers. Furthermore, workers would become alienated from their work, alienated from other people, and in a sense even alienated from themselves. This comes from loss of a sense of control over one's own time and activity, in combination with a loss of a sense that one is engaged in activity that makes a difference and has any significance.

Marx felt that this combination of factors would necessarily produce economic desperation and extreme class antagonisms leading to some kind of revolution. Capitalism would, in effect, sow the seeds of its own destruction. Thus, in *Capital*, Marx puts a lot of additional analytical detail into the basic model of change outlined some twenty years earlier by Marx and Engels when they wrote *The Communist Manifesto*.[4]

Marx's Contribution to Sociology

Although Marx's economics was based on a labor theory of value that most people reject, the analysis of societal change that he predicated on the labor theory of value led to the development of a principle of social conflict that is insightful and has withstood the test of time. The bigger and more persistent the gap between the privileged and the marginalized, the harder it is to ignore that gap or explain it away. Marx's insights can be communicated in what might reasonably be called sociology's Principle of Intergroup Conflict.

Principle of Intergroup Conflict: **Other things being equal, the degree to which intergroup antagonism is likely to manifest itself in organized conflict is a function of (a) how much homogeneity there is within groups and how much inequality there is separating groups, (b) how much historical or symbolic unity there is within each group and how little historical or symbolic unity there is between groups, (c) how much mobility and communication there is within groups and how little there is between groups, and (d) how often resource competition coincides with differences in group membership.**

Marx was particularly interested in the divide between wage earners and employers. It is through wage relations (which Marx described as the social relations of production in industrial society) that wealth transfers are constantly occurring through the extraction of surplus value. It is therefore this divide between wage earners and the people who hire wage earners that has the potential to really polarize society into warring camps and foment revolution.

Marx anticipated that in any capitalistic society, the middle class would shrink and the gap between wage earners and employers would grow over time. Other important changes would also occur. Opportunities for mobility between classes would dwindle as the gap between the classes increased. And the forces causing a growth in the gap between classes would at the same time result in increased homogeneity within each class. This combination of growing heterogeneity and inequality between the classes and growing homogeneity and equality within each class would, in Marx's view, fuel class awareness and class solidarity. In other words, there would be greater affinity among people who are similar and greater antipathy toward people who are different; hence, intergroup antagonism and conflict.

This Principle of Intergroup Conflict exemplifies good theory in a number of respects. First, it allows for different outcomes in different cases. When there is a lot of movement between heterogeneous groups that are not very different from one another, a person informed by this principle should expect intergroup antagonism and rates of conflict to be low. Revolution is predicted only when there are large and persistent gaps, low rates of mobility, symbolic divisions, and a rise of consciousness about polarizing divisions in society. Second, although Marx was focused on wage earners and employees (specifically because of his interest in sources of conflict that might fundamentally transform capitalism), the principle, at least when stated in generic terms, can be generalized to a number of contexts. For example, we could use the principle to understand why ethnic conflict is more pronounced in some countries and at some time periods than others. Finally, the principle has clear enough operational meaning that it can be used to generate testable hypotheses. It offers significant insight about the way the world operates. And it does so in sufficiently clear yet generic terms that the implications the principle has for a wide range of situations is evident. Like the Principle of Social Control we can derive from Durkheim's work, the Principle of Intergroup Conflict derivable from Marx's analysis provides one of sociology's most clear, robust, and powerful explanatory insights.

Recap

Marx, a self-identified economist, was actually not a world-class economist because his analysis is predicated on a labor theory of value, which has many problems. But Marx, who never saw himself as a sociologist, can be considered a world-class sociologist for developing a predictive principle informing our understanding of something truly significant: intergroup conflict. Importantly, the cumulative body of sociological evidence suggests that the Principle of Intergroup Conflict we can infer from Marx's work is in fact correct, at least in its broad contours. What failed was Marx's economics, which led him to incorrectly predict the demise of the middle class. But the more generic version of Marx's analysis of conflict, captured in the Principle of Intergroup Conflict, adds significantly to our foundation of social scientific understanding of society. He gave us a window for beginning to understand organized resistance of oppressed groups against the rule of those who dominate. And this principle also helps us to better understand certain other types of group division, such as racial and ethnic conflict.

Some Terms to Know

Labor Theory of Value: Calculation of the worth of something is based on how much effort goes into producing and delivering it.

Surplus Value: Wealth initially created through the effort of wage earners but diverted into the pockets of business owners.

Class: Position (selling one's labor or buying the labor of others) within the wage labor system that structures social relationships of production in capitalistic industrial societies.

False Consciousness: Failure to recognize one's own true class interests, to the point of supporting policies and programs that actually work to the detriment of one's own interests.

Review of Axioms and Principle

Structured Inequality Axiom: The social structural arrangements that survive tend to be those that protect the interests of more-powerful people at the expense of less-powerful people.

Intransigence Axiom: The powerful do not loosen the grip of exploitation without being pressed to do so.

Principle of Intergroup Conflict: Other things being equal, the degree to which intergroup antagonism is likely to manifest itself in organized conflict is a function of (a) how much homogeneity there is within groups and how much inequality there is separating groups, (b) how much historical or symbolic unity there is within each group and how little historical or symbolic unity there is between groups, (c) how much mobility and communication there is within groups and how little there is between groups, and (d) how often resource competition coincides with differences in group membership.

Quiz

Check your answers in the back of the book. If you get any wrong, consider reviewing chapter 8 before continuing.

1. What is Marx's Principle of Intergroup Conflict?
2. How did Marx's axiomatic assumptions restrict his theoretical horizons?
3. How did Marx define class?

Application Exercise

Consider race relations and racial conflict in the United States at different points in time. Barack Obama's election as the forty-fourth president of the United States would be understood by almost everyone as an indicator that antagonism and conflict based on race are much less intense than they were one hundred years ago or even fifty years ago. This is a significant change. This is not to say that racism has evaporated—it has not. But it had certainly declined between 1908 or even 1958 and 2008. How would you try to explain this change using the Principle of Intergroup Conflict as a guide?

9

Max Weber on Primacy of Values

M AX WEBER (GERMANY, 1864–1920) IS ONE of the four theorists most sociologists regard as having provided the intellectual cornerstones of the discipline. In comparison with the legacies of Durkheim, Marx, and Mead, Weber's
legacy is somewhat harder to summarize. Nevertheless, he is a particularly important figure in the history of sociology.

Historical Economics in the Background

Weber began his working life as an economics professor. At that time, he was a
young but respected member of Germany's *historical school* of economics. The
historical school dominated economics departments in German universities during the late nineteenth and early twentieth centuries, and differed significantly
from the brand of utilitarian economics dominating in Britain and the United
States. The story of competing schools of economics is worth a little attention
because it helps us better understand Max Weber and equips us to help recognize
some important *founder effects* that continue to have (sometimes underappreciated) impact on contemporary sociology.

What distinguished German historical economics from British utilitarian economics was a conviction among historical economists that (a) each
economy is unique in some way, (b) economists should look to the particulars
of religious and cultural history to discover values that drive those differences
between economies, and (c) economists should look to the particulars of legal
codes, banking systems, and other organizational forms to identify national
differences in the institutional mechanisms that keep economies distinct. Fi-

nally, appreciation for the importance of religion and other aspects of culture, and also sensitivity to the institutional distinctiveness of each society, differentiated German historical economics from mainstream British utilitarian economics.

In this respect, Weber was much like Thorstein Veblen, who himself was influenced by the German historical economists, and Vilfredo Pareto, who shared historical economic interest in belief systems, even though he was exasperated with the historical economists because they were so infatuated with the idea of historical uniqueness. This infatuation with the necessity of taking account of the unique aspects of each system's historical development inhibited the German historical economists from arriving at useful theoretical generalizations; it was also an important factor in the eventual demise of the German school of historical economics because German economists were utterly unprepared to help the German government deal with the hyperinflation of the 1920s. Like Pareto and Veblen, Weber was acutely interested in values. And like Pareto and Veblen, Weber understood that an economy does not function in a sociological vacuum.

Historical economics also differs from the radical economics of Karl Marx. Radical economists tended to see the world as divided between exploiters and the exploited, with each group having diametrically opposed interests. This led radical economists to see the world as neatly divided between saints (the poor) and scoundrels (the rich). Historical economists, by contrast, viewed each national economy as separate from other national economies and presumed that each economic class within a particular country had its fate tied to every other class in that same country. The historical economists believed that the common interests of all classes in one country formed a natural basis of solidarity linking the different classes of that country together. So their use of the terms *solidarity* and *solidarism* closely parallels use of those terms in the contemporary parlance of European Christians, and even that of the Solidarity Movement in Poland, which helped bring an end to Soviet control over Eastern Europe. This is quite different, of course, from *solidarity* as the term is employed by Marxists. Weber's concept of solidarity encompassed workers and capitalists working together on the national scene, while Marx's concept of solidarity pitted international labor against international capital.

It is an interesting historical fact that self-consciously Catholic and Christian approaches to the study of economics, a *social economics* perspective, emerged out of the German school of historical economics. Social economists have spent the last century calling on privileged people to support a living wage and other provisions for the benefit of working people. And why? Not out of pity. Their support comes from a kind of solidarity based on awareness that the fate of capitalists in a country is interconnected with the fate of the workers in that country.[1] Marxist scholars would think of this kind of solidarism, predicated on the idea that a rising tide lifts all boats, as wishful thinking reflecting a kind of false consciousness.

False or not, it is certainly a different consciousness than that which the Marxists possess. Solidarism is based on recognition of the ways in which the interests of different economic classes are intertwined rather than in total conflict. Supporting a living wage and other policies are, from the point of view of solidarism, ways of strengthening the whole society by supporting labor. Pro-labor policies are from this vantage point seen as being in everyone's interest. Likewise, expecting everyone to come to work on time, work hard, work carefully, and work conscientiously is viewed as a way of strengthening the whole society by supporting capital.

Historical economics was in a state of intellectual crisis in Weber's time. German historical economists were aware of the complexity of the social world, and consequently hesitant to arrive at the kind of analytical generalizations necessary in science. Because of their reluctance to embrace the kind of simplification that analytical generalization necessarily involves, German historical economics floundered in its competition with Anglo-American utilitarian economics. This had a heavy impact on Weber, who was strained quite literally to a breaking point by the challenge of trying to develop a science of society informed by both his historical economic training and his rising sociological sensibilities.

Frustrated with the slow pace of theoretical progress being made by historical economists and troubled by his own personal and family problems, including unresolved conflicts with his father, Weber had a breakdown. As he began recovery, he also began writing, first with an attack on the unduly detailed and consequently ultimately confused and uninformative state of theory in the German historical economic tradition, and then with a trailblazing set of books setting out methods, conceptual tools, and a cogent analytical framework for historical comparative analysis of major patterns of change in society at large.[2] By doing so, he contributed greatly to the new and promising science of sociology, and in ways sociologists have yet to fully appreciate.

Analytical Abstraction Following the Ideal Type Method

Max Weber's intellectual interests were broad. Even eighty years after his death, Weber remains among the most widely read sociologists because he touched on so many issues with such penetrating insight. But for that very same reason, Weber's ideas defy easy summary. His strength was his sharp insight about many different topics. And as a workaholic without children, he was prolific and left an immense body of writing that sociologists continue to mine for bits of revelation. An excellent collection of excerpts, drawn from various publications between 1906 and 1924, is available in *From Max Weber*, edited by Hans Gerth and C. Wright Mills.[3]

Weber's impact can be best appreciated if we remember that his way of pursuing scientific advances was to create systems of analytical categories that would simplify the challenge of performing social science investigation. His approach was to highlight categorically important ways in which different social settings can be compared to one another despite obvious differences in particularities of detail. In doing so, Weber often sought to use what he called *ideal type* method. That is, he tried to categorize the major forms that particular kinds of phenomena can assume. An example is *authority.* Sociologists define authority as the legitimate right to make certain kinds of decisions and expect those decisions to be carried out without having to resort to coercion. In contrast, gaining compliance through the use of or through the threat of coercive force is an exercise in raw power, putting it outside the scope of Weber's definition of authority. Weber looked around at all the different systems of authority he was familiar with, through reading as well as through experience, and realized that they clump together into three different categorical types. Weber thought of these major categories as constituting an array capturing empirical variability in its essence.

Authority is an important sociological concept and deserves an illustration. At most colleges, professors have the authority (the legitimate right to make decisions of a particular kind) to decide (within broad limits constrained only a tad by community standards) what students should read in conjunction with a class. But college professors do not have the authority to order students to wash the professor's car or mow the professor's lawn as a condition of succeeding in a class. Stop to think about this. Assigning students to read class-relevant material is legitimate for a professor, and assigning students to wash cars or mow lawns is not. Some professor somewhere may try to somehow compel a student to wash the professor's car, and may even succeed in gaining compliance. But such an order would not be legitimate, so compliance would be in response to something other than rightful professional authority in the pure sense of the term. The student could be an employee at a local car wash and acting in her role as car wash employee (not her role as student). Or the faculty member could be ill and the student could be performing an act of compassion (in a role as a community volunteer or good neighbor). Perhaps the student could be a daughter of the professor (responding in her role as daughter rather than in the student role). Or perhaps the student could simply be responding to coercive force, which would make this an instance of raw exercise of power rather than legitimate authority as Weber defined it. Instances such as these tended to reinforce Weber's conviction that typologies, accompanied by clear categorical definitions, can serve as useful tools to help us notice what is real and pertinent when we study sociological subject matter.

In looking at concepts such as authority, Weber believed that construction of ideal types would assist sociologists in arriving at a better conceptual understanding of societal phenomena. An ideal type is just a listing of common forms (different types of something), or of distinguishing characteristics (features common to a type of phenomenon). Political authority, for example, is present in some form in all societies, but just because all societies can be said to have a system of political authority does not mean that the system of authority is the same in every society. Constructing an ideal type forces us to think clearly about salient distinctions that might be worth focusing on.

Importantly, Weber recognized that identifying common forms was not the same as identifying perfect forms, best forms, or most desirable forms. Ideal types are ideal in Weber's sense of the term when they capture the meaningful essence of a phenomenon in its most characteristic forms. Weber did not mean they are ideal in the sense of being best forms or perfect forms or ultimate forms. But he did feel that by revealing the true character and essential form of things, ideal types can help observers arrive at an epiphany of deep and meaningful understanding. This is to really get it, to really understand, to deeply comprehend. This search for essence is such an important part of what Weber left the discipline that sociologists sometimes use a German word to convey deep comprehension: *verstehen.*

When Weber asked himself about salient distinctions between different systems of authority, he focused on what led people to ascribe authority to a given person. In some societies, the authority of rulers stems from the commitment of ordinary people to a regular, established, procedural system for selecting rulers and making collective decisions. In effect, the system of rules matters, and the authority of the person is grounded in our commitment to procedures. This is what Weber called *rational-legal authority.* For example, rational-legal authority in a democratic society enjoys whatever legitimacy it has to the degree that there is widespread belief that the system of procedures for voting is more or less fair and votes will be counted. (Without that belief, legitimacy grows unstable and weak.)

For a typology (meaning, a list of different types of something) to exist, there must be more than one common form. In addition to *rational-legal authority,* Weber identified two other common types of authority. One is *traditional authority,* in which the authority of rulers stems from a widespread commitment of ordinary people to the right of rule based on historical precedent. When someone says yells out, "God save the Queen!" he is, in essence, saying that the standing authority is legitimate because it is entrenched; it enjoys widespread support because it has a history. Where traditional authority is strong, anyone who challenges entrenched authority risks being treated as a subversive—mistrusted, shunned, or worse.

Weber also noted a third type of authority, based on personal charisma. *Charismatic authority* rests on a cult of personality. This kind of legitimacy is grounded in personal magnetism. Weber called attention to the fact that the type of authority prevailing at any given point in time has a big impact on what happens in society. And Weber correctly noted that the cult of personality, such as that of Juan Perón in Argentina or Fidel Castro in Cuba, with the legitimacy of rule grounded in the magnetic appeal a leader has to some substantial number of citizens, can never be maintained for more than a few years or perhaps a few decades (only rarely, in fact, for more than a few years). Charismatic authority must eventually give way to some other basis of authority.

Weber noted that a common trend in the twentieth century was for charismatic authority to temporarily replace traditional authority and to be replaced in turn by rational-legal authority. One might also argue that countries relying on rational-legal authority may be in need of charismatic leaders at those times when confidence in rule of law and integrity of political process has been deeply shaken.

Weber on Rank Stratification

Another example of Weber's ability to come up with analytical categories can be found in his work on *social rank*. Weber challenged the prevailing view among radicals of his time that economic position determines everything about a person's social station and political opportunities. Weber pointed out that social rank can be based on political position and social honor, as well as on economic resources. And he argued that these three bases of social ranking are largely independent of one another.

Speaking of Germany at the time, Weber noted that a person's rank along one axis may be quite different from ranking along another axis. This was Weber's famous distinction between *class, status,* and *power.* For example, he wrote convincingly that a poor person can be held in high esteem by virtue of having upstanding personal character, while a rich person can be despised for being dishonest or uncaring.

Of course, not all societies are the same, and in some places one's material well-being really does seem to dictate what judgments others will make of a person's worth. That is, after all, why conspicuous consumption can work as a status-seeking strategy in some societies, as Thorstein Veblen aptly noted about the United States. It fact, it is reasonable to think of Veblen as having been driven to study conspicuous consumption because it suggests an obvious way in which countries differ. Weber's analysis of Germany at the beginning of the twentieth century is far removed from the social reality in the United States at the beginning of the twentieth century. The United States was still early in the era of big business and the time of the robber barons. Geographic expanses were so great, economic change so dynamic, and geographic mobility so rampant that it is easy to understand how conspicuous consumption could impart an aura of high social standing and worth, particularly if little else is concretely known about highly mobile people.

Traditional, charismatic, and rational-legal authority, and class, status, and power as bases of social rank, are illustrations of Weber's use of the ideal type method to categorize the different forms of phenomena such as status or authority. But Weber also used the method in another way. Ideal types can be used to identify the most common characteristics of a particular organizational form. An example is *bureaucracy*.

Weber on Bureaucracy

The most widely used of Weber's analytical distinctions is a somewhat different form of ideal type. It was Weber's conclusion that what he called *modern bureaucracy* is the defining organizational form of industrial society. When we use the method of ideal typing to explore a single form characteristic to a particular kind of society or social setting, the goal shifts from describing a variety of different forms to delineating the distinguishing features of one form. Using this modified ideal type strategy, Weber looked at bureaucracy as the form of organization most characteristic of industrial society, and he then identified the most common features of an industrial bureaucracy. Approaching the topic in this way, Weber noticed that bureaucracies in industrial societies tend to be characterized by a constellation of features, including (a) hierarchical chain of command, (b) functional division of labor, (c) hiring based on training rather than nepotism, (d) decisions made according to a system of codified rules that are uniformly applied, and (e) records, as the property of offices rather than of officeholders, being used to monitor performance and guide the development of new rules to further rationalize and improve operations.

Bureaucracy was particularly important, from Weber's point of view, because it became the embodiment of rational action as a value of modern (twentieth century) industrial society. The bureaucracies Weber admired most tended to have a lot of clear rules to promote good performance and avoid repeating mistakes. Rules are made to avoid repeating mistakes of the past; this is a *rational* practice. People of Weber's day were familiar with bureaucracies of antiquity, which were often described as patrimonial or byzantine. Patrimonial bureaucracies were anything but rational. They had rules that were confusing and hard to follow, and they were deliberately so composed in order to forestall improvement-oriented changes that might disestablish sinecure arrangements and upset the balance of vested interests. Positions in these bureaucracies were typically allocated as rewards for past loyal service and as payment for future loyal service in the interest not of the society as a whole but in the interest of those in power.

What seemed to Weber to be rational about modern industrial bureaucracies was what he viewed as an ability to monitor performance and make rules designed to increase efficiency, maximize benefits, and most especially, minimize the repetition of costly errors. Of course, this assumes that feedback mechanisms are functioning properly, and that the organization has not been hijacked by or subverted to the service of special interests.[4]

Variation in the effectiveness of feedback mechanisms is an important sociological matter Weber never really addressed. He did, however, recognize that bureaucracies can become iron cages that trap people into sterile, inflexible responses that deaden individual creativity and undermine individual involvement and personal responsibility.

Bureaucracies can also discourage innovation, especially if people at the higher levels of the organization feel that subordinates may be launching activities that will fall outside the control of superiors. These are all topics that continue to excite sociological discussion. The challenge theorists face is to understand the forces that push organizations in the direction of one set of outcomes (effective use of resources to maximize achievement of organizational goals) rather than another (organizational lethargy, inefficient use of resources, and replacement of commitment to mission with protection of special interests). Fortunately, Weber left us many insights on the question, and these can be given a somewhat more contemporary wording that makes his ideas highly applicable to the realities we confront.

Principle of Organizational Efficiency/Effectiveness: **Long-term organizational efficiency/effectiveness is a positive function of (a) success in maintaining uniform mission awareness and accurate institutional history, (b) depth of commitment to minimizing repetition of past mistakes and taking other steps to improve performance, (c) organizational capacity for assessing challenges and instituting change without interrupting normal operations, and (d) adequacy of alignment of training, information, resources, and operational authority with the tasks people are called on to perform in their roles.**

This principle successfully captures the laudatory qualities Weber attributed to industrial bureaucracy, such as hiring based on training rather than nepotism, and record keeping that would make it possible to have decisions based on real information. But having a generic wording of the Principle of Organizational Efficiency/Effectiveness has additional advantages. Importantly, it makes it easier to distinguish between functional and dysfunctional bureaucracies. Second, this generic wording redirects focus from specific structural features (such as task specialization) to function outcomes. This is important to the degree that the structural features that facilitate success in today's environment may be different from those that seem to have facilitated success in Weber's time (see chapter 6).

Values

Weber is most widely remembered for his analysis of the rise of capitalism in the West. He tried to explain why industrial capitalism took hold in northwestern Europe rather than in China, which in several ways was a more likely place for capitalism to have developed. After all, for centuries literacy was more wide-spread in China than in Europe, science was more advanced, commerce took place in what more closely approximated a single market with commercial traffic along long, navigable rivers, and political and administrative control were more centralized and more effective. But these advantages may have had a downside as well. Good communication and effective administration made it possible for the Chinese government to heavily tax profitable new businesses. Imperial tax policies seem to have sometimes stunted promising new enterprise rather than encouraging its development, especially when new enterprise was viewed with suspicion as a potential power base outside the immediate control of the po-litical establishment. An important part of this analysis is that, in Weber's view, cultural values influence what governments are able and inclined to do, and this ultimately has a big effect on the economy.

The most important difference between China and the West, in Weber's view, involved developments in Christianity fostering rational decision making and what he called a *nondualistic economic ethic.* It was Weber's view that Christianity miti-gates toward insisting that (a) people should weigh available facts and make good choices among such alternatives as may be practically available, and (b) strangers (including traveling traders) should be treated in basically the same way as neigh-bors, rather than being victimized because of their vulnerability. Weber believed that these fundamental belief orientations helped facilitate the steady growth of long-distance trade that became the incubator of Western capitalism. Weber also believed that developments in Christianity fostered an asceticism encouraging frugality, which in turn encouraged saving, capital formation, and investment. Fundamental belief orientations also influence the character of government bu-reaucracy in ways that have deep influence on both taxation and regulation.

In the European context, Weber was originally convinced that Calvinism was responsible for this shift. He forcefully expressed this view in *The Protestant Ethic and the Spirit of Capitalism,* which was originally published as two separate works in 1904 and 1905.[5] Over the course of the next two decades, ending with *General Economic History,* published in 1923, Weber tempered his analysis a bit and came to believe that all of Christianity and in a way the whole of Judeo-Christian tradi-tion and arguably the Islamic tradition (not just Calvinism in any exclusive sense) was responsible for creating the preconditions for capitalism. Randall Collins explains this aptly in a 1980 paper in the *American Sociological Review.*[6]

Whether in historical examination of the European experience or in his study of China and other Asian societies, Weber was inclined toward culturally deter-ministic explanations that put commonly shared values on center stage. This attitude stands in marked contrast with Marx, who explicitly favored economic determinism as a framework for understanding societal change; his economic determinism characterizes prevailing belief systems as reflections of the eco-nomic order and as instruments of ruling-class domination. In Weber's analysis,

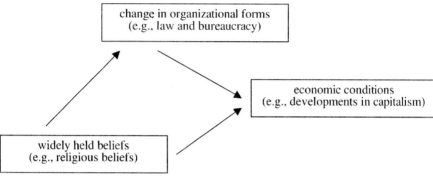

FIGURE 9.1
Weber's Cultural Determinism

the values prevailing in a community are thought to exert a powerful and compelling force on people, shaping organizational forms and economic developments. This definitely differs from Marx, whose distinctive focus was economic power's making it possible for rich people to manipulate public sentiment by hijacking government, mass media, ecclesiastic hierarchy, and other social institutions. Weber's insights on these matters can be expressed in the form of an axiom conveying his view that social structural arrangements embody, reflect, and reaffirm social values.

Values Axiom: **As a set of values becomes more deeply embedded and more uniformly held by people in a society, common social roles and widely institutionalized systems of rules are progressively modified in ways that manifest and maximize adherence to core values.**

This axiom, which was integrated into later sociological analyses by Talcott Parsons (see chapter 11), is accepted by some sociologists and contested by others. This is a good time to reiterate the fact that differences in metatheoretical perspectives are primarily defined by differences in the axiomatic assumptions different groups of theorists make. Developing a better theoretical understanding of the relationship between behavior and beliefs is one of the biggest challenges sociologists now face. And the Values Axiom, along with Weber's strategy of constructing ideal types and recognizing the importance of historically unique particulars, left a lasting impact on subsequent generations of sociologists.

Recap

There is general agreement that Max Weber is one of the most important sociologists ever to have lived. Weber successfully counteracted the Marxian premise that values are mere reflections of ruling-class strategy for controlling the masses. He catapulted values onto center stage as independent variables or intervening variables rather than as dependent variables in sociological models. Weber also influenced subsequent generations of sociologists by using the construction of ideal types as a method for arriving at conceptual clarity that could lead to better understanding of sociological phenomena.

One of the beauties of these chapters is that, when understood together, they help us realize just how differently Durkheim, Marx, and Weber understood the same fundamental phenomena. When trying to understand the forms of social organization that evolved, Weber always looked first to cultural values emerging over the course of history. Thus, he saw contemporary organizational forms of the West becoming increasingly rational as an embodiment of values sparked by religious developments which over the course of time influenced the civil arena. This view is quite different from that of Marx, who would view the organizational forms evolving in any society as an embodiment for the strategies of the powerful to control and exploit everyone else. Both differ from Durkheim, who understood change as something emerging from within social structural arrangements themselves, compelled in the direction of advancing the common good, more than as the consequence of cultural forces or vested interests at work, pushing the evolution of society's organizational and institutional apparatus in a particular direction.

Some Terms to Know

Ideal Type: A typological scheme used either (a) to categorize the major forms a certain kind of phenomenon can assume, or (b) to identify the distinguishing characteristics of something.

Authority: The *legitimate* right to make certain kinds of decisions and expect those decisions to be carried out without resorting to threat of force.

Power: Ability to gain compliance through the threat or use of coercive force.

Rationality: Characterized by forethought and calculated planning intended to minimize costs and negative side effects while maximizing benefits.

Review of Axiom and Principle

Values Axiom: As a set of values becomes more deeply embedded and more uniformly held by people in a society, common social roles and widely institutionalized systems of rules are progressively modified in ways that manifest and maximize adherence to core values.

Principle of Organizational Efficiency/Effectiveness: Long-term organizational efficiency/effectiveness is a positive function of (a) success in maintaining uniform mission awareness and accurate institutional history, (b) depth of commitment to minimizing repetition of past mistakes and taking other steps to improve performance, (c) organizational capacity for assessing challenges and instituting change without interrupting normal operations, and (d) adequacy of alignment of training, information, resources, and operational authority with the tasks people are called on to perform in their roles.

Quiz

Check your answers in the back of the book. If you get any wrong, consider reviewing chapter 9 before continuing.

1. An ideal type
   a. identifies what the best and practically achievable forms are.
   b. identifies what the archetypical forms are and captures the essence of those forms.
   c. identifies what the impossible utopian forms are.
2. Weber's ideal type of authority has three forms. What are they?
3. What are the characteristics of a bureaucratic organization as identified in Weber's ideal type?
4. What is Weber's Values Axiom?

Application Exercise

Try developing an ideal type by listing some common forms of household units that are prevalent in the United States. Recognize that in order to do this, *you must first narrow your conceptual ground*. Are you, for example, more interested in defining who the members are (e.g., single parent, cohabiting natural parent, blended) or in defining the nature of role definitions (e.g., traditional, egalitarian), or in something else?

Assess whether you have used the ideal type method in a way that would help someone else think specifically and clearly about the narrow conceptual ground you have chosen to look at. (To the degree that you have done this, the method has achieved its purpose.)

10

George Herbert Mead
on Individual Agency

FAR FROM THE INTELLECTUAL FERMENT OF WESTERN EUROPE, where lively discussion about macroeconomic change dominated the attention of pioneering sociologists, most of the first American sociologists were influenced by philosophy and psychology, and they were preoccupied with trying to understand how people adjust to one another in face-to-face human interaction. In the world's first sociology department, at the University of Chicago, a distinctly American approach to sociology coalesced in the viewpoints of George Herbert Mead. Mead's insights formed the bulwark of what would later come to be known as the *symbolic interactionist* perspective (see chapter 13).

Pragmatism

The University of Chicago was founded with Rockefeller money at the end of the nineteenth century. Chicago, the rail hub of the nation, viewed itself as a kind of spiritual as well as industrial heart of the United States during the era of industrialization. The Chicago World's Fair (the "World's Columbian Exposition") of 1892 and 1893 (precisely when the University of Chicago was forming its sociology department) marked a great celebration of optimism about things to come, symbolized by a huge dynamo, a generator for producing electrical current to make things happen.

The first administrators of the University of Chicago intentionally sought to hire faculty who would be intellectually bold and creative, and when it came to this sociology department they certainly succeeded. A small group of sociologists at this university produced theoretical breakthroughs of major importance in sociology:

(a) formation of the symbolic interactionist perspective, treated in this chapter as well as in chapter 13, and (b) the development of urban ethnography (chapter 4) as a methodological approach leading to significant theoretical developments.

George Herbert Mead focused on a single, pivotal question: how do people manage to adjust to one another? This was a question of interest to psychologists and philosophers at the time, and Mead found himself in a circle of colleagues who were among the top minds of their era. One of those people was John Dewey, the person most often credited with America's most notable contribution to philosophy, *pragmatism.* Pragmatism stresses doing what works rather than sticking to failed models of the past. To illustrate in a way that has universal resonance, we can point out that Dewey was responsible for weakening the hold of the lecture style of teaching in schools by introducing field trips and emphasizing the importance of hands-on experience in K–12 education. Hands-on approaches work, Dewey argued, so we should use them. Do what works. That is pragmatism.

A pragmatic focus on what works was well suited to Chicago's dynamic character in the midst of America's industrialization. While New York may have been the nation's financial capital and Washington, D.C., its political center, Chicago was its rail hub and arguably its most diverse and robust manufacturing center. Pragmatism seemed to fit the city of Chicago's character at the time, but it also melded nicely with the ideas that were percolating in Mead's sociology at the University of Chicago.

The Self as a Part of Social Situation

To the pragmatist orientation borrowed from philosophy, the Chicago sociologists added a concern with self-concept drawn from the work of the most influential social psychologist of the era, William James. But the concept of *self* was given a less introspective psychological meaning and a decidedly more social flavor when employed by early sociologists such as Charles Horton Cooley at the University of Michigan. Remember that a symbolic interactionist question is, how do people manage to adjust to one another? And recall the partial answer Mead drew from pragmatist philosophy. Consider the situation, weigh the alternatives, select a path that may get you what you want, and get on that path. But what is the situation? And what does one really want? The psychologist William James recognized that the *self* each of us brings to a setting, with all our personal drive and our baggage of personality, actually becomes a part of the setting.

Sociologist Charles Horton Cooley, in his 1902 book *Human Nature and the Social Order*, provided what is for sociology an absolutely pivotal insight by recognizing the social origins, in other words, the group origins, of self. Cooley's insight came when he realized that people think of themselves in ways that mirror how they believe themselves to be seen by others.[1] This was Cooley's famous concept of *looking-glass* (or mirror) *self.* Cooley recognized, for example, that children who daydream a lot and are then called dumb or slow or retarded by family members, teachers, schoolmates, or neighbors are at risk of growing up questioning their own abilities. Once that happens, those children may have difficulty ever gaining confidence in their own intellectual ability. Self-concept can be heavy baggage. *Self-concept,* then, deals with seeing oneself as an object. It is an individual's perception of her own fairly enduring qualities (such as degree of physical attractiveness, strength, speed, endurance, coordination, cleverness, memory, intellectual sharpness), in combination with the individual's assessment of her own immediate performance in the situation.

We are sometimes consciously aware of how we see ourselves as objects. At other times, however, how we really see ourselves is partially buried in the recesses of the subconscious. In either case, we all have some degree of awareness of ourselves. And yet, our sense of self may not be entirely accurate, because awareness of ourselves flows, in some manner, out of the way in which others have responded to us in the past. And it then influences our process of adjustment in our current day-to-day interactions with other people. The beautiful young woman who grew up feeling awkward because she looked unlike others in the community she grew up in is likely to still view herself in a way that is influenced by the reactions of others to her long ago. Deep memories can recede somewhat, but they often hide just beneath the surface. Sometimes we even try to hide them from others, by overcompensating in some fashion, yet those feelings often express themselves in our reactions to unexpected or uncomfortable situations.

Each of us (1) literally carries deep-seated self-conceptions with us as we move from one situation to another. But (2) we also continually update a portrait of our situational self, reflecting how we feel we are doing in the eyes of others right now, in the present where we are. This means that how we respond to situations is, to some extent, a function of what kinds of people we believe ourselves to be in general, and is also a function of how we feel we are performing in the immediate setting. For example, people who feel themselves to be clumsy are less likely to try new things when the opportunity unexpectedly arises. And people who crave more respect yet really doubt their own abilities tend to react according to these feelings of doubt. They may, for example, be particularly sensitive to anything that could be interpreted as a sign of being slighted. In workplaces, for example, insecure managers who feel their own performance may be in question often tend to quickly retreat to the rules to justify actions and deflect scrutiny, while managers with more secure senses of self tend to quickly invite greater scrutiny, in the form of outcomes assessment. This sociological concept thus illustrates why different people react in different yet predicable ways to what appear from the outside to be similar situations.

Contemporary sociologists also focus on *identity,* which is a sense of having a highly meaningful membership in a group, or a highly salient sense of belonging to a certain category of people.[2] The distinction between self and identity is an important one for sociologists. *Identity* does not have exactly the same meaning as *self-concept*. Self-concept denotes qualities we feel we have that are essential to our own character as individuals or reflective of our own current performance potential as individuals. Thus, *self* has to do with what makes us unique in comparison with people who are otherwise similar (other young African American men or other college-educated women). *Identity* refers to a group or categorical membership (e.g., gender) that is highly salient and inescapably important, usually because others react to us in terms of that group membership rather than in terms of our truly individual qualities and character traits. Identity becomes salient to the degree that the groups that we are a part of seem to matter, and matter a great deal, to others. It is usually defined by what others seem to notice and respond to. Identity captures how we have come to expect to be treated because of our appearance or our memberships without regard to the true nature of our individual beliefs, actions, or performance. Most sociologists take it as axiomatic that self and identity mirror the treatment we have received from others in the past.

Self/Identity Axiom: **The individual qualities we feel we have (self) and memberships we regard as salient (identity) reflect how other people have responded to us in the past and seem to respond to us in the present.**

This axiom relates well to Veblen's vital insight that all people want respect and are deeply conscious of their own social acceptance or lack of it. The hunt for acceptance is at the heart of the human social condition and human social experience.

Being part of a particular group or social category (e.g., gender, age, race, ethnicity, religion, gang membership, or profession) can be tremendously important in how others treat us and in how we come to believe we will be treated. But understanding identity is complicated by our difficulty in disentangling identity from self. It is also complicated by the fact that people will frequently magnify an identity out of self-defense, after being stigmatized or excluded by others.

It is important to recognize that, on some level, sense of both identity and self are kinds of baggage we carry with us from place to place. If two people have trouble reaching for something and a person who happens to be watching begins to laugh, possible reactions vary, depending on the self-concept held by those persons who are unsuccessful with their reach in this situation. The laughter may be entirely unrelated to these two people straining to reach for something, but tell that to someone who is sensitive about matters of height. We all carry baggage, but we seldom stop to calculate how that baggage may influence our perceptions and alter our behavior. When a person is accused of being too sensitive about something, it often means the accuser is getting close to an important part of that person's self-concept or identity. People who are particularly sensitive about height are usually those who have been made, by others, to be acutely aware of their height. How we have come to view ourselves as objects does influence how we interpret and respond to situations. And those who are particularly sensitive about race are usually those who have been made aware, by others, that much of the world still reacts to what is on the outside (race or gender or age) instead of what is on the inside (character—honesty, empathy, responsibility, altruism, sincerity).

George Herbert Mead's Theoretical Synthesis

A handful of very bright people with a handful of very good ideas all came together at the same time and in the same intellectual community at the University of Chicago; intellectual ferment was bubbling over in sociology at Chicago in the years around 1920. A synthesis was about to emerge, and George Herbert Mead was the person who would put this revealing new synthesis together. Mead synthesized a number of different ideas to describe the process that goes on as people adjust to one another during interpersonal communication.[3] He came to realize that people adapt cooperatively to the social world, and also actively remake their social worlds, by engaging in an ongoing five-step process during interaction:

1. People observe the gestures of others, taking note of verbal and nonverbal cues.
2. While observing some gestures, people decipher those gestures. This includes a process of orienting to the role of the other person to better understand what the other person actually wants and intends. Sociologists call this *role taking*.
3. Role taking simultaneously invokes some degree of self-reflection. We each have some sense of *core self* that we carry from situation to situation, and by triangulating on the reactions of other people toward us, we gain some degree of fluid situational self-concept about how our performance in the immediate situation can be viewed.
4. After *taking the role of the other* and gaining some sense of the way we appear to others in the immediate situation, each of us is able to engage in *imaginative rehearsal* of different lines of potential conduct and select a path that we judge has the best chance of producing the results we want, or at least ending in an outcome we find acceptable. This would include the face-saving work of departing a situation after presenting a sense of self that we feel is accurate and/or resembles the way we would like to be seen.
5. Having gone through these various mental exercises based on interpretation of the actions of others, we must then take the step of modifying our own contact as we continue the interaction.

Most sociologists accept the accuracy of this five-step description of the recurring process we go through as we adjust to others in daily life. It was as an unprecedented tribute to the power of Mead's ideas that his most important books, including *Mind, Self, and Society* (1934), were not actually *written* by Mead. Rather, they are collections of class notes that his students compiled and published under his name after his death. Mead's students did this because they recognized both the originality and the enormous importance of his contribution to sociology and to sociological theory.

Mead believed that one's ability to engage in symbolic interaction requires a set of social skills that must be learned. Human beings are not born knowing how to understand language or interpret most gestures. They are not born understanding how to identify roles or interpret what role another person is assuming. People must learn how to read gestures and to role take, and they typically learn these crucial social skills during childhood play.

For infants, interaction with caregivers is particularly important for learning the meaning of words and gestures. As children grow, interaction with peers becomes more important, especially when playing games (such as baseball) in which each person occupies a different role and must be aware of the roles other participants are simultaneously playing. Acquiring the social skills necessary to play these games empowers individuals with what Mead described as the capacity of *mind*, which is the ability to adjust one's actions in light of the responses of others. Ipso facto, people become true *social* beings capable of the constant adjustments social life requires.

A clear presumption built into Mead's analysis is that individuals have what sociologists sometimes term *agency*, or free will, with the power to alter the flow of events. People make decisions about how to react to situations. Each individual has the power to alter relationships and change social meaning. Mead concentrated on the way people respond to immediate situations and how these responses subsequently change the flow of events and transform the understandings people have about events.

Role Redefinition

The daily relevance of Mead's ideas is immediately apparent when we try to customize the way in which our role relationships with other people are defined. Right now, my own role as husband includes about 10 percent of the cooking and 65 percent of the kitchen cleaning. There have been times when I was expected to do more and times when I was not expected to do as much. Each long-term shift in role responsibilities involves a period of complex negotiated adjustment tied to other things, including child supervision, pet care, yard work, income-generating activity, elder care, community commitments, and even personal maintenance, such as exercise. How does a particular definition of responsibility emerge? And when will people have the most or the least latitude in customizing their role obligations? Once a role definition does take hold within a relationship, how is it sustained? Questions like these continue to be of fundamental interest to sociology,[4] and Mead gives us some answers that can be stated in the form of a principle.

Principle of Role Redefinition: **Other things being equal, the latitude people have to redefine a role relationship is (1) a positive function of the degree to which (a) role occupants listen to and understand one anothers' points of view, (b) role occupants agree about the kind of change they would like to see, (c) the role relationship is shielded from direct observation by others, and (d) there is peer support for change, and (2) is an inverse function of the levels of (e) anticipatory socialization for current definitions and (f) validation for adhering to current definitions.**

This principle gives us a way of understanding how much customization of roles will take place, although the Principle of Role Redefinition does not tell us what the outcomes of role redefinition will be. We will revisit this question in chapter 13. But for now, we can appreciate the great insight Mead and his colleagues had about roles. Strong normative expectations, reinforced by anticipatory socialization and peer pressure for conformity, discourage people from creatively redefining the expectations associated with their roles. This is especially true if role-related behavior is readily observable by a wide range of people outside the relationship. But in relationships enjoying a great deal of symbolic interaction between role occupants, especially when people in the relationship want a change and desire change in the same direction, change is likely and the likelihood of role redefinition goes up to the degree that role-related behavior is largely shielded form observations by others and when there is peer support and encouragement for change. When applied to spousal relations, Mead's ideas ushered in a strikingly modern view at a time when many people felt that traditional husband-wife rights, responsibilities, and division of labor were part of God's divine plan, and to be followed without question rather than to be modified.

Appreciating Mead's Genius

How do people manage to adjust to one another? Mead's answer is that people use their social skills to consider their situations, recognize their own roles in those situations, weigh the alternatives, select different paths, and try to negotiate with others to redefine commitments and expectations. If this idea seems rather ordinary and pedestrian, one has only to remember the ideas that had previously prevailed in order to appreciate the genius of Mead and his colleagues.

Social science before Mead was typified by the work of Italian criminologist Cesare Lombroso. Lombroso was a humanitarian who believed society should treat criminals with care and compassion because many criminals, he argued, were actually protohuman rather than fully human. He thought many people were in jail because they were not far evolved beyond the apes and, as a result, were impulsive and lacked control over their basic animal instincts. In these cases, Lombroso did not see criminal behavior as a matter of free will exercised by callous people. His view was that the poor creatures just couldn't help themselves. The poor beasts should be isolated from society—for society's protection—but treated with genuine compassion.

To put it politely, Lombroso's views sound extreme to a modern ear. But his ideas were consistent with the conventional wisdom of his time. In fact, he was viewed as being rather progressive. And remember that Lombroso (1836–1909) lived during the same period as Mead (1863–1931). Mead's ideas and those of his contemporaries marked a dramatic change in the accepted way of making sense of human behavior. If Lombroso's ideas seem silly and the ideas of Dewey and Mead and Cooley seem commonplace, it is because the insights of Mead and his colleagues were such an obvious improvement that they were fully absorbed by society. Their uncommonly perceptive insights have become our common sense. But today's common sense was actually a striking departure from the world as most people understood it one hundred years ago. At that time, the prevailing view was that behavior was for the most part dictated by genetic tendencies. Bad boys were thought to be bad because their badness was *in the blood*.

Recap

Early European sociology focused on what was outside the individual and in some sense predetermined by social forces beyond a person's control. Of course, European sociologists understood that Americans were right when they said people have agency. Likewise, American sociologists understood that Europeans were right when they said many of the features of social reality we have to deal with were created without any help from us as specific individuals and would still be a part of the social landscape even if a completely different set of people were there to contend with them. Micro-, meso-, and macrodynamics are all important.

Mead's work dramatically advanced sociology by formulating an understanding of individual agency. He brought an understanding that people really do have agency, and he brought acute recognition of the ways in which agency plays itself out in our daily interactions. An important element in this picture is how we see ourselves as a reflection of the way others have responded to us in the past. Once formed, self-concept and sense of identity are kinds of baggage we carry with us from situation to situation. They influence our interpretation of, and our reaction to, each new situation. In the mix of interpersonal communication that takes place, people are able to use their interaction skills to collect information about, reflect on, negotiate in regard to, and adjust their conduct with others. In fact, we are constantly doing these things; this is why many sociologists are convinced that George Herbert Mead's work tells us about the very heart of what it means to be a social being engaged in social life.

Some Terms to Know

Self-Concept: A sense of one's own being as a distinctly separate person having particular internal qualities and tending to perform in certain ways.

Identity: A sense of having a highly meaningful membership in a group or highly salient association with a category of people.

Role Taking, or *Taking the Role of the Other:* Recognizing what role another person is in, what objectives he has, and what constraints he faces.

Agency: Free will, with the power to alter the flow of events.

Review of Axiom and Principle

Self/Identity Axiom: The individual qualities we feel we have (self) and memberships we regard as salient (identity) reflect how other people have responded to us in the past and seem to respond to us in the present.

Principle of Role Redefinition: Other things being equal, the latitude people have to redefine a role relationship is (1) a positive function of the degree to which (a) role occupants listen to and understand one anothers' points of view, (b) role occupants agree about the kind of change they would like to see, (c) the role relationship is shielded from direct observation by others, and (d) there is peer support for change, and (2) is an inverse function of the levels of (e) anticipatory socialization for current definitions and (f) validation for adhering to current definitions.

Quiz

Check your answers in the back of the book. If you get any wrong, consider reviewing chapter 10 before continuing.

1. What was Mead's central question?
2. Match the theorists with the concepts they have come to be identified with.
   a. Charles Horton Cooley   i. pragmatism
   b. John Dewey   ii. looking-glass self
3. Explain the difference between *self-concept* and *identity*.
4. Describe the process of symbolic interaction people work through as they adjust to others.

Application Exercise

Describe a role relationship you are familiar with that has been redefined over time.

What can you say about the process of role redefinition as it unfolded in that particular relationship? Based on what you have observed, can you suggest any improvements in the Principle of Role Redefinition?

Did the events you observed suggest that self-concept or identity were involved in an important way?

PART IV

MAKING SENSE OF SOCIOLOGY'S THEORETICAL PARADIGMS: GRASPING THE BASICS

I N PART I OF THIS BOOK, we explored the meaning of theory in a science. Theory is activity aimed at clearly expressing how we think differences are produced. The differences sociologists are interested in are differences in the nature of (a) interpersonal attachments, (b) shared beliefs, and (c) systemic interconnections, including regulatory constraints, for example. When we practice sociology *as a science*, we try to describe these three things; to understand the dynamic processes that give rise to differences within or between settings over time; to understand how and why consequences result from having particular kinds of interpersonal attachments, shared beliefs, or systemic linkages; and finally, to utilize our growing body of knowledge for helping groups and organizations operate more effectively and for the purpose of promoting community-level institution building for the common good.

We know we are making progress in identifying theory when we can express axioms and principles in a form that can be uniformly understood by careful readers, and that, after research and refinement, enhance our ability to explain social reality. Research is activity designed to test axioms and principles using real-world data, with the conviction that testing our ideas will allow us to refine and improve our understanding. That is the scientific process.

In part II we considered the way sociologists, including students of sociology, can use theory in an active way in their own research. This includes trying to better understand the world we are confronted with, developing testable hypotheses to use in research, and engaging in our own efforts at theory construction in an attempt to advance sociological understanding.

In part III of *Making Sense of Social Theory* we discussed seminal works of the key intellectual pioneers who launched sociology as a discipline. With historical hindsight, we can see that the most important of these figures were Émile Durkheim, Karl Marx, Max Weber, and George Herbert Mead. Durkheim, Mead, and Weber all self-consciously identified themselves as sociologists, although Weber began his academic career as an economist, Mead was heavily influenced by philosophy and psychology, and Durkheim held a joint appointment in education. Marx always thought of himself as an economist or political economist, but he nevertheless contributed in important ways to the base of theoretical insights that have motivated subsequent sociological investigation. The interdisciplinary roots of sociology are important to consider. The early figures came to sociology with a practical interest in the world and tried to develop theoretical insights that explain meaningful kinds of variation and change. From the start, sociology has been a discipline with relevance.

Durkheim, Marx, Weber, and Mead were most important as first founders because they asked the big questions that have continued to capture sociologists' attention over the years: (a) In what ways does society impose itself on the individual, and how do we understand that process (Durkheim and Mead)? (b) How is it that segments of the society become polarized against one another, and what long-term consequences does polarization have (Marx)? (c) To what extent do values dictate how people will go about constructing their social worlds (Weber)? (d) How do individual people adjust to others and exert agency over the course of events (Mead)?

People thinking about sociology's big questions have taken the work of the first founders in a variety of directions, coalescing into four distinct and recognizable perspectives. The first of these developed around the time of World War II, when the insights of European sociologists and economists were being synthesized by Talcott Parsons and others into a structural functional framework influenced by Durkheim and Weber, as well as Vilfredo Pareto and the British utilitarian economists. By the late 1950s, partly in response to what were seen as the blind spots of American structural functionalism, conflict theory and symbolic interactionism coalesced out of work being done to extend the basic insights of Marx (conflict theory) and Mead (symbolic interactionism). Somewhat later, exchange theory emerged out of an amalgamation of concerns raised by the people working in each of the other emerging traditions.

Part IV attempts to offer manageable introductions to these four perspectives. Our goal is to provide a useful framework for firmly grasping the basics. Part IV is intentionally brief. It is skeletal by design, in order to retain clear and explicit focus on the most fundamental points. We promote conceptual clarity by staying away from the sort of all-encompassing detail that can make it hard for people to arrive at a holistic understanding.

11

Structural Functionalism on Systemic Efforts to Adapt

EACH OF THE FOUR THEORETICAL PERSPECTIVES covered in part IV was formed as a creative synthesis of the ideas of several different theorists. Each is useful and illuminating once its central premises are properly understood. The chapters that follow convey main points in a clear way and do not attempt to cover much detail.

The first of sociology's paradigms to take definitive shape was structural functionalism. By about 1955, the structural functionalist perspective had assumed its basic form, but the inspiration for contemporary structural functionalism can be traced to Harvard University in the 1930s, where it evolved out of intellectual activity swirling around Talcott Parsons. Parsons creatively integrated ideas he drew from Vilfredo Pareto, Émile Durkheim, Max Weber, and British utilitarian economists. This synthesis was one of the most intellectually ambitious efforts ever undertaken by a sociological theorist. Although Parsons's effort was not a total success, this work is intriguing and marks an important point in sociology's disciplinary history.

Each of sociology's established theoretical paradigms offers revealing explanations of important sources of variation in the real world. Each of these paradigms has a metatheoretical core that consists of a set of orienting questions, sensitizing concepts, and axiomatic assumptions that provide some direction for us whenever we employ any of the frameworks.

Structural Functionalism's Basic Metatheory

Structural functionalists treat societies as social systems. They recognize that systems change in significant ways over time. The structural functionalists assume that societal change tends to be driven by a search for better ways of organizing activity to provide for the well-being of the social system and the people in it. Applying structural functional metatheory consequently emphasizes a particular set of orienting questions. There are purely descriptive questions: What do we mean by a social system? What needs can social systems be said to have? What are the observable properties of a social system? Then, there are orienting questions that more directly anticipate the scientific ambitions of structural functionalists to explain differences between social systems and change within social systems. How does a social system recognize that it has unmet needs? What is the process through which change then develops?

These are not simple questions to which there are incontrovertibly correct answers. Instead, they are questions that invite us to experiment with different definitions and different ways of conceptualizing what we are looking at. Importantly, metatheoretical orienting questions only direct our inquiry to certain topics. The questions do not dictate what we will conclude about these topics over the course of our inquiry.

In the past, the sociologists who have applied a structural functional perspective in their work have found it useful to look to a particular set of sensitizing concepts. Sensitizing concepts identify features of the work that seem to us to be real and important, given the kinds of orienting questions we are interested in. Some of the sensitizing concepts used by sociologists applying a structural functional framework have been: social system, functional need, dysfunction, feedback, institutionalization, social structure, culture, roles, values, and authority.

Sensitizing concepts have practical importance because they encourage us to approach our orienting questions in a particular way. The analytical baseline for structural functionalism always involves a focus on at least one social system. This can be a society, or an analytically distinct sector of a society such as the military or the educational system, or perhaps a single organization or a community. With a social system focus rather than a focus on individual people, structural functionalists always wonder about the functional needs the social system has and may be meeting to some degree, and about *dysfunction*, which is persistent failure to adequately meet needs. *Feedback mechanisms*, the arrangements that alert a social entity to functional success or failure, are an indispensable part of a structural functional framework. The changes structural functionalists are most interested in explaining are changes that become *institutionalized* as enduring rather than fleeting aspects of social structure (most often detectable in the kinds of roles one finds in a social system) and culture (largely defined by the values that gain currency among people who are a part of that social system). Finally, authority is a key concept in most structural functional analyses because it is useful in identifying the kinds of decisions made within the system, in locating where and describing how those decisions are made, and in determining how those decisions are enforced; all these ideas turn out to be key to understanding the systemic character of any social entity we study.

The sensitizing concepts are important aspects of any metatheoretical perspective, and are important tools for analysis. But to complete a metatheoretical perspective it is also important to explicate central axioms. The pivotal structural functional axiom will be discussed later in this chapter, but is simple enough that we can introduce it in a preliminary way right now. This is the Form Follows Function Axiom, asserting that social systems tend to develop features that are useful in meeting the needs those social systems confront.

Form Follows Function Axiom: **Form follows function in the sense that widespread patterns of structural change emerge as systemic responses to meet new needs or correct for poor performance in the face of old needs.**

At the heart of structural functionalist metatheory is the simple assumption that social units do change over time and tend to change in a way that results in improvement for the system and the people in it. It is also worth remembering two other axioms, introduced earlier in this book. The Founder Effects Axiom has special relevance because it calls attention to the important premise that social systems are more than the sum of the individual people in those systems. Social systems often acquire characteristics that outlive people. This helps account for the distinctiveness of one social system (organization, community, society) when compared to another system of like kind (another organization or community or society).

Founder Effects Axiom: **Those interests and concerns of earlier figures that became active parts of institutional memory or are deeply embedded in institutionalized practice shape the activities of others for a long time to come.**

The Values Axiom is also well worth remembering because it calls attention to the important structural functional premise that shared beliefs are important in shaping what a system is like. Values are (for structural functionalists) not merely reflections of what a system is like: deeply held values help shape social systems. Shared beliefs matter.

Values Axiom: **As a set of values becomes more deeply embedded and more uniformly held by people in a society, common social roles and widely institutionalized systems of rules are progressively modified in ways that manifest and maximize adherence to core values.**

Add these axiomatic assumptions to the orienting questions and sensitizing concepts already introduced in this chapter, and we have a distinctive metatheoretical framework. This framework grew out of the hallmark of structural functional analysis, *efforts to recognize and understand systemic tendencies for progressive change.*

But without principles, a metatheoretical framework cannot be thought of as mature theory or good science. It is true that metatheory is essential to science. It is also true that metatheory is always present in scientific work (though sometimes in an unstated and implicit way). But a metatheoretical understanding, though necessary, is never sufficient to constitute good scientific work. Without principles, all the structural functionalists really have is blind faith that tendencies for progressive change always win out, which is simply not true.

The Boundary between Structural Functional Metatheory and Theory

Even when our first instinct is to employ a structural functional perspective, we have to be clear about the fact that a system has to work well in order to have good outcomes. That is, the social system (e.g., organization, society) must be structured in a way that makes sense (in terms of the constraints the system faces and resources that are at the disposal of people to use) in order for the system to be functional (i.e., the system does a satisfactory job of meeting the demands placed on it). If the system is not structured in a way that makes sense in terms of constraints and resources, it is not likely to do a good job of meeting needs. Consider health care in two developing countries with high rates of infant mortality related to sickness and dehydration. In one country the health-care system spends scarce resources to provide some additional information about infant dehydration to a great many poorly educated rural people, and to provide those people with distilled water to be mixed with sugar and a small amount of salt when their children are having trouble keeping fluid in their bodies. This is an inexpensive (cost effective) system that can work under challenging conditions. It suggests a health-care system that matches available resources to the types of needs that are most widespread and significant. This would perhaps be more functional for a country than a health-care system spending all its money on expensive high-tech equipment for the one best hospital in the capital city.

It is important to understand that to employ a structural functional perspective (or any other theoretical perspective) well, in a scientific way, a person needs to be a realist. Even if one way of structuring health-care delivery would be most functional for a particular society, this does not mean that the society will automatically gravitate to that solution. In poor countries, there are a lot of pressures in favor of spending scarce health-care dollars on a world-class hospital in the capital city. Structural functional *metatheory* would lead us to assume that a social system will make the best decision, in this example, spend money in the ways and places it has the most positive impact. But to be scientifically oriented, structural functional *theory* must move beyond metatheory in ways that predict when functional outcomes are most likely and explain how they are likely to develop if in fact functional outcomes do occur. The same set of theoretical principles should, at the same time, identify conditions under which dysfunctional outcomes are most likely and explain how dysfunctional results come about. People interested in developing structural functionalism as a scientific theory ask: What mechanisms function to move a social system toward optimal solutions, and how do those mechanisms malfunction in moving a social system in the direction of suboptimal solutions? When and how are those tendencies activated? When and how are they stopped?

If we accept Comte's vision for the goal of sociology, which is acquisition of knowledge we can use to make society better, then it is critical to understand functional systemic tendencies supporting progressive improvement and dysfunctional tendencies subverting progressive improvement. One cannot be adequately understood without the other. Deep understanding of one is tantamount to understanding both.

Structural functionalists do not believe the answers to their questions are to be found in personality. The fact is that you will have a hard time finding many structural functionalists who think things get better over time because the world is made up entirely of warmhearted humanists who want to do good things for their less-fortunate neighbors. Nor will it be easy to find structural functionalists who automatically assume people in power are benevolent, truth-seeking civil servants. For a structural functionalist the key is to be found in understanding systemic mechanisms that can function in spite of the fact that there are some bad people in the system. What kinds of mechanisms, if operating properly, can contribute to keeping any social system (society, organization, etc.) functioning well despite the less-than-worthy leaders social systems sometimes find themselves with? The Principle of Organizational Efficiency/Effectiveness (chapter 9) offers a good theoretical understanding of the structural sources of function and dysfunction in complex organizations.

Principle of Organizational Efficiency/Effectiveness: **Long-term organizational efficiency/effectiveness is a positive function of (a) success in maintaining uniform mission awareness and accurate institutional history, (b) depth of commitment to minimizing repetition of past mistakes and taking other steps to improve performance, (c) organizational capacity for assessing challenges and instituting change without interrupting normal operations, and (d) adequacy of alignment of training, information, resources, and operational authority with the tasks people are called on to perform in their roles.**

The insights captured by this principle have been more broadly extrapolated to society at large by Talcott Parsons and others. Structural functionalists maintain that there are four types of dynamics that can work in favor of preserving system integrity even when special interests lobby for outcomes that, from a system point of view, would be suboptimal. (1) To the degree (but only to the degree) that feedback mechanisms work properly, early detection of shortfalls in meeting important goals and realizing core values can stimulate some corrective response before overshoot is too noticeable. (2) When there is enough structural resilience to allow some experimentation, creative response to evolving challenges is possible (but only when there is sufficient structural resilience to allow some experimentation). (3) To the degree (but only to the degree) that shared values are clear and receive validation, they can help people distributed throughout the system to remember key priorities and evaluative standards. Motivated by a common set of commitments, operatives in various parts of the system are more likely to push in a consistent direction, manifested in a constellation of goals and practices that give the system its distinguishing character. (4) When there is enough awareness of institutional history (but only to the degree that there is awareness of institutional history), stability in adherence to ways of the past retards change in some measure. Ideally, this resistance is sufficient to discourage change without reflection, but not all change.

Using a long time horizon, structural functionalists find it easy to maintain a positive outlook. Feedback mechanisms push for change and resilience in the system facilitates experimentation. At the same time, the presence of shared values and a well-understood institutional history provide some basis for stabilizing the change process, keeping it on as straight a line as possible with as steady and stable a trajectory as possible. Feedback is especially important in this respect. Among other things, problematic decisions will have mounting consequences that will eventually be absorbed as costs for someone. That produces sources of "push back" that, in theory, make societies self-correcting systems.

But as scientists, structural functionalists have to be realists. They fully understand that good outcomes are always contingent on things working right, but that things do not always work right. That is why the goal of structural functionalism must ultimately be to discover how feedback and equilibrium processes operate in social systems, where communication among subunits can be sporadic and connections can be subtle. Some of the things that can malfunction from the standpoint of a social system's being successful are (1) absence of regularly functioning feedback mechanisms or misdirection away from assessment of things that should really be the key priorities, (2) inadequate structural resilience to allow experimentation, (3) fundamental conflict or ambiguity over central priorities and core values, and (4) insufficient sense of institutional history to appreciate potential downsides of change.

Distinguishing between Functional and Dysfunctional Social Entities

Functional systems

1. Well-functioning social entities have feedback mechanisms that generally provide accurate and early warning of impending problems;
2. Well-functioning social entities tend to invest significant resources in the search for better solutions to emerging challenges;
3. Well-functioning social entities are usually characterized by a widespread sense of agreement about key values and central priorities;
4. Well-functioning social entities maintain sufficient knowledge of institutional history to avoid repeating mistakes and avoid implementing changes undermining important organizational competencies.

Dysfunctional systems

1. Dysfunctional social entities have feedback mechanisms that often misidentify problems early on and provide late warning once challenges are accurately identified;
2. Dysfunctional social entities generally to fail to significantly invest resources in the search for better solutions to emerging challenges;
3. Dysfunctional social entities are usually characterized by either lack of clarity in or fundamental conflict over key values and central priorities;
4. Dysfunctional social entities fail to maintain sufficient sense of institutional history to avoid repeating mistakes and avoid implementing changes undermining important organizational competencies.

The pivotal point of this discussion, and the central theme of *Making Sense of Social Theory*, is that metatheory is only a starting point. The Form Follows Function Axiom is indispensable, to be sure. But real scientific progress—theory and not just metatheory—comes in the degree to which we understand why and how change occurs in some places and not others. The Principle of Organizational Efficiency/Effectiveness gives us a good start toward understanding why some social entities at certain points in time seem to function rather well, while others do not.

Systemic Origins of Change

It is important to recognize that structural functionalists appreciate two broadly conceived and analytically different sources of change. First, the obvious one is a need to change in response to new, growing, or evolving challenges in the environment where a social system operates. To the degree that climate change results in lower crop yield, will that pose a new or evolving problem facing society (in contrast with a problem merely facing the individuals in the society)? Structural functionalists try to understand the ways societies and other organizational forms become aware of problems and change themselves in response to evolving problems. Second, social systems confront problems of strain that result when different parts of a social system are not coherently organized and coordinated with other parts of the same social system. If a society is organized on the basis of 8 a.m. to 5 p.m. employment for parents and 9 a.m. to 2 p.m. schooling for children, there are some obvious scheduling gaps in child-care coverage. One way the institutions in American society changed in the 1980s in order to cover these gaps was to offer on-site child care at many schools, both before and after normal school hours. The idea that different parts of a system can and will change to accommodate other parts of the social system is an important aspect of structural functional theorizing.

Structural functionalists have made some significant progress in developing explanatory principles. The main purpose of this chapter is to reveal how structural functionalists have come to view the world, and to gain an understanding about how their framework has evolved over time. In the process, we will also gain a clearer understanding of the work that remains to be done by all sociologists in the future if we are to develop a more mature theoretical framework following a structural functional perspective. We next turn to key moments in the development of structural functional thinking, beginning with the work of Vilfredo Pareto.

Interest in Vilfredo Pareto and the Concept of Equilibrium

To understand the development of structural functionalism in the United States after 1930 requires that we remember the earlier theoretical contributions of Vilfredo Pareto, Max Weber, and Émile Durkheim. Vilfredo Pareto (France/ Italy/Switzerland, 1848–1923) was a famous economist known for his use of equilibrium modeling to understand changes in price and long-term trends in supply and demand. Between about 1887 and 1897, Pareto was consumed by the task of building mathematical models for economics. But with each passing year after 1897, he devoted more time to the study of sociological factors influencing the economy. He spent the last twenty years of his life trying to develop a sociological theory that lived up to Comte's vision of sociology by producing an overarching sociological theory that could subsume the study of economics and political science, more or less as subdisciplines within a grander and more encompassing sociological framework.

Pareto did this by applying equilibrium analysis to the study of society as a holistic system composed of interdependent spheres of social, economic, and political activity, where each sphere is understood to have specific kinds of impacts on every other sphere. For example, Pareto thought economic prosperity changed social values so that people became more hedonistic and interested in short-term gratification. But when consumer debt builds to the point that a tipping point is reached, the economy contracts and people in general became more cautious (a dynamic introduced in chapter 6). Then they begin to save again. Notice a stable *equilibrium* process, with change in one direction stimulating a series of reactions that eventually return the society to something approximating its prior state.

For Pareto, this was a tremendously exciting intellectual endeavor. He viewed society as a social system with interdependent social, economic, and political domains. And he understood that by identifying ways in which social, economic, and political phenomena influenced one another, he could model societal change.

Pareto's concept of equilibrium involves the property of *elasticity,* or an ability to increase or decrease quickly and easily in response to changing conditions. Sometimes there is only a little elasticity in a system and sometimes there is a great deal. For example, the United States has a large army, so the military enjoys a lot of flexibility in how it will deploy troops during relatively tranquil periods. But when hostilities cause large numbers of troops to be committed to battle or occupation, the military has less flexibility. Elasticity varies over time. When changing conditions require adjustment, some adjustment can be made with relative ease. But when changing conditions continue to require more supplemental effort, elasticity can disappear and more dramatic steps are forced.

Pareto's switch from economics to sociology came about because he wanted to include relevant sociological factors in his models. He was a real social scientist. Pareto's genius lay in adopting equilibrium models for the study of the whole social system and not just the economy. He did this by examining the ways in which cyclical shifts between periods of regulation and deregulation in government, and cyclical shifts between periods of liberalism and conservatism in popular mood, both influenced and were influenced by shifts in the business cycle.[1]

Pareto's equilibrium analysis of society as a system intrigued Joseph Henderson, who early in the twentieth century was an influential senior professor of physiology at Harvard University. In the early 1930s, Henderson gathered a circle of bright young social scientists around him. Among them were George Homans, who would later become a major advocate of exchange theory in American sociology; Robert K. Merton, who arrived at Harvard familiar with the works of Durkheim before Durkheim's books had been translated from French into English; and Talcott Parsons, who arrived at Harvard familiar with the works of Max Weber before Weber's books had been translated from German into English. All three of these discussion group members would later become presidents of the American Sociological Association, as would some of their students. There were several other young social scientists in this circle. This discussion group, described in a 1968 paper by Barbara Heyl, was the seedbed that produced structural-functional thinking in American sociology.[2]

Talcott Parsons Brings Weberian Content to the Harvard Pareto Circle

Talcott Parsons (United States, 1902–1979; PhD, University of Heidelberg, 1929) was studying in Germany shortly after the death of Max Weber and while Max Weber's brother, Alfred, was still teaching sociology at a German university. Parsons became Weber's first major conduit into American sociology. Importantly, Parsons completely absorbed Weber's notion that the value system of a society has immense impact on events; this is captured in our Values Axiom (see chapter 9). In addition, Parsons fully adopted Weber's method of constructing ideal types as a strategy for trying to better define analytical distinctions, Weber's recognition that whether social systems function well is problematic (sometimes they do and sometimes they do not), and Weber's appreciation of the importance of feedback systems in understanding performance differences between systems (also described in chapter 9).

Although a great synthesizer, Parsons was first and foremost a Weberian. Parsons assimilated Weber's analytical approach while studying in Germany. By the time he was recruited into the Harvard Pareto circle, Parsons was already a convincing advocate for Weber's position that societal values are among the most important things sociologists should be looking at.

Weber's work was the intellectual starting point and foundation for Parsons. You might say that Parsons added Durkheim's and Pareto's insights to that Weberian foundation. But there is another way to look at what was going on at the time. Having the ideas of Durkheim and Pareto swirling within the Harvard Pareto circle helped Parsons see how to bring more intellectual order to Weber's approach.

Weber's work is so sweeping in scope that it can seem haphazard and in need of analytical focus and direction. Parsons found focus and direction in the main points Pareto and Durkheim emphasized. Society can be viewed as a social system (Pareto) in which needs have to be met (Durkheim). Structural forms evolve over time to meet those needs (Durkheim), and the nature of society as a system of interrelated domains means that the repercussions of any change can be tracked in order to better understand how the society operates as a system (Pareto). These were all convictions Weber shared, but they remained rather implicit in Weber's work, and Weber never worked out their theoretical implications. Parsons saw working out these implications as his special task.

Weber's concern with social values is at the heart of Parsons's scheme, but Parsons infuses his Weberian analysis with the awareness of society as a system composed of interconnected domains influencing one another (Pareto), having needs and responding to those needs with the adjustments in structure and culture that allow the social unit to better meet the challenges it confronts (Durkheim).

Pattern Variables as Social Values Embodied in
the Expectations that Come to Define Social Roles

Parsons, like Weber, wanted to treat values as variables. Doing so required that he find a way of gauging qualitative differences between the systems of values prevailing in different places, or between the systems of values prevailing in one place at different points in time. Parsons was enough of a scientist to know that variables imply measurement, and that the act of measurement is a step on the road to conceptual clarity.

Parsons looked to Weber's work for guidance about measurement and found clues in Weber's discussion of qualitative differences in role expectations. Weber recognized that values have impact on what roles come to mean in different societies, and influence how people live out their commitments in everyday life. So Parsons quite naturally looked to differences in roles as a source of information about qualitative differences in societal value systems. Since Parsons was trained in Weberian method, the next logical step he needed to take was to develop a categorical system he could use in his effort to identify qualitative differences in roles that might reflect deep cultural differences at work.

Parsons did this comparatively early in his career. The task occupies an important part of his 1951 book, *The Social System* (a title drawn from Pareto). In *The Social System*, Parsons offers what he calls a *pattern variables* scheme for contrasting the value systems of different societies.[3] Parsons observes that the value system of every society can be placed on a series of continua. Following Weber, he observes that the way in which roles take shape in any one society are in part a reflection of the core values of that society.

Parsons speaks of four different sets of pattern variables (initially five, but one was dropped later, as his theory matured). For purposes of illustration, one is the continuum running between (a) *affectivity*, or the degree to which people think it is good if role relations are characterized by a lot of strong emotional feeling and expression, and (b) *affective neutrality*, or the degree to which people think it is good if role relations are characterized by some emotional distance and high levels of both social control and emotional self-control. Germany and Italy do not fall at exactly the same point on this continuum, and we can see this by contrasting the same role title in the two societies. What it means to be a teacher in Germany is slightly different from what it means in Italy, and this difference is, at least in Parsons's view, a reflection of underlying cultural standards about what is or is not appropriate.

Approached in this way, comparing roles can allow sociologists to identify qualitative differences in value systems separating different societies. Just how much emotional involvement are teachers supposed to have with their students in Germany? Is it the same in Italy? The degree of emotional attachment or emotional distance deemed most appropriate differs according to the prevailing values of the social system (again, so says Parsons). Can we see this in other roles as well? Parsons thought so. Should this enable us to describe deep-seated differences between societies or other social units? Parsons thought so. (The Principle of Evolution would lead us to anticipate that the differences between Germany and Italy may have narrowed since Parsons's time, because isolation has been reduced by improvements in communication, expansion of trade, and establishment of the European Union.) But the central point holds. What it means to be a father in one society is not exactly what it means in another society. Parsons thus posits that societal value differences manifest themselves in the character of broadly institutionalized roles (roles found widely throughout the society).

Parsons settled on four sets of pattern variables that he felt capture key societal differences. These are (1) affectivity, or preference for feeling and expressing emotional bond in role encounters, versus affective neutrality, or preference for minimizing the expression and even the experience of emotional bond in role encounters; (2) universalism, or preference for uniform standards applied to everyone in the same way, versus particularism, or preference for having differences in standards as appropriate for different groups; (3) specificity, or preference for imposing limited and well-defined obligations on a role, versus diffuseness, or preference for expecting role occupants to respond to a wide array of demands that are not always clearly defined in advance; and (4) ascription, or preference for allocating opportunities and assignments on the basis of demographic memberships (e.g., gender, ethnicity) and origin (e.g., neighborhood roots, family background, socioeconomic class), versus achievement, or preference for allocating opportunities and assignments on the basis of individual performance.

Following Weber, Parsons believed that values are particularly important drivers of history and determinants of social structure development. Parsons was convinced that every society could be located with some degree of accuracy on each of these continua at a given point in time, and that doing so would tell us something valuable about the prevailing social values of that society. The approach is an interesting one, though a new generation of theorists may decide some other set of value standards would offer a more useful contrast between belief systems prevailing in different places.

A Structural Functional Framework from Durkheim

Parsons thought of values and roles as major components of *structure* we organize our lives around. Parsons then added Durkheim's concept of *function*, or requirements for the continuation and success of social entities. He then asked what consequences each element of structure has for the ability of a social entity to have its needs met. What consequences for system function or dysfunction does a particular configuration of values have? This approach reveals the most basic axiomatic assumptions underlying the structural functional perspective (the Form Follows Function Axiom already introduced in this chapter).

Remember that axioms are analytical devices that help us look for things that may be important. They are not taken to be *absolute* truths, even by the theorists who use them most often. When applying a structural functional framework, sociologists know that not everything is functional. But thinking about what would happen if the natural flow of events were toward functionality should help us to identify both convergent and divergent cases. Then we can study these cases for important clues about the way social entities actually operate in reality. This is the scientific way of proceeding. We try to describe how things work in theory. Then we collect the data about convergent and divergent cases, knowing that by working with data from divergent as well as convergent cases, we will have our best chance of revising our theories to arrive at more penetrating, more revealing explanations of why things work as they do.

This means that when we use a structural functional perspective, it makes sense to look for dysfunctions. Robert K. Merton was particularly skilled at looking for negative side effects. He offered a scheme for conducting structural functional analysis that was more open than the one Parsons developed. Merton advocated that sociologists should examine every aspect of structure and ask two useful questions: (1) What are the negative as well as the positive consequences? (2) To what degree are consequences planned and intended to help meet systemic problems or help satisfy collective needs? Conversely, to what degree are they unplanned from the standpoint of the system, either accidental or perhaps designed to satisfy special interests without regard for the integrity of the social system or the common good of the people in it?[4]

Asking these questions, Merton discovered that there are a lot of unintended consequences to organizational and systemic activity. These unintended consequences are of real interest to sociologists—they are data to help us better understand how the world works. Sometimes these unintended consequences are negative and sometimes they are positive, but they are always revealing.

While Parsons focused on societies as his units of analysis, Merton's attention was usually riveted on smaller social units, including organizations and communities. In other words, Merton believed that every social entity has functional needs of its own, and might therefore evolve in ways to better meet its own needs. Thinking the way Merton did requires us to view the weave of society as somewhat loose—sometimes loose enough to allow autonomous, independent action on the part of different organizational units and subunits.

While Parsons certainly understood that Merton's belief is often true in practice, his own interest was in understanding how a society as a whole could acquire such a powerfully systemic character that its seemingly autonomous organizational components would assume goals and develop structural qualities such that they contribute more effectively to the satisfaction of societal needs, even when that is to the apparent disadvantage of the subunit. In this respect, Parsons and Merton approach structural functional analysis in starkly different ways. In Merton's view, a single organizational unit or subcomponent might be expected to hinder the wider social whole by pursuing its own agenda. For this pattern to be generally true, systemic feedback mechanisms need to be understood as primarily local and internal. In Parsons's view, for the whole society as a powerful system nudging component units to do what is in the best interest of the society at large, feedback mechanisms need to be understood as much more expansive and encompassing. In either case, careful empirical study of and theorizing about feedback processes will be required for scientific advance of the structural functional framework.

The Merton–Parsons debate hinges on the important social science concept of *coupling*. We know from organizational research that tight coupling most commonly involves ties based on (a) hierarchical relationship in the same chain of command; (b) a system for administrative constraint, review, and possible reversal of actions taken in subordinate units, including placement of people in roles and retention of people in roles; (c) high levels of accurate communication between subordinate and superordinate units; (d) high levels of resource dependence of subordinate units on superordinate units; (e) a strong sense of common fate; and (f) a commitment to a common set of uplifting values and objectives, presuming the set of objectives is understood by people as coherently integrated rather than mutually competing. Weak coupling is common when these conditions are reversed.

Although not very explicit about this, Merton tended to write about society as a weakly coupled system. It is important to recognize that in developing his approach to structural functionalism, Merton stressed weak coupling. As a consequence of weak coupling, relatively isolated or autonomous units can focus on provincial goals and pursue their own (provincial) goal-related activity with comparatively little concern for either what they contribute to the broader system or how their actions might inadvertently generate costs for other units (i.e., little concern for what economists call *externalized costs*).

Parsons thought about society differently, as a tightly coupled system. For theorists who are heavily involved in discussion of structural functionalism, this is an important point. Parsons implicitly viewed society as a tightly coupled system. When coupling is tight, subunits are not organizationally isolated or autonomous. There are few truly provincial goals because local units define their particular goals in concert with goals of the wider whole. Accountability is in terms of what the local unit contributes to the wider whole rather than what the local unit does or gets or keeps for itself. Part of the calculus of contribution must be the drag one unit places on other units. Consciousness of externalized costs is consequently high, and local units are prevented from adopting practices that generate high levels of externalized costs.

Stated as a general principle, Merton's and Parsons's ideas can be applied either to organizations or to societies, and can be used to explain either the relative proliferation or the relative absence of provincial objectives that distract attention from broader objectives.

Principle of Systemic Coupling: **Other things being equal, the ability of a system of organization to maintain mission focus (and avoid mission creep) is a positive function of the extent to which (a) a stable and shared awareness of common ends can be maintained, (b) lines of communication remain open and honest, (c) subordinate units remain resource dependent on higher-level units, (d) resource allocation is aligned well with mission involvement, and (e) people at different locations within the system of organization have a sense of common fate.**

This takes the fundamental disagreements between Merton and Parsons and puts them in their proper place within a science framework. Instead of assuming the outcomes one or the other has in mind (the loosely coupled world Merton envisioned or the tightly coupled world Parsons was thinking about), both outcomes should be recognized as quite possible and indeed common. If both are possible, they are for that same reason both problematic. This returns us to science. Our scientific goal in this case is to understand how and why some organizational subcomponents of a social system largely subordinate their own provincial interests to the interests of the more encompassing social whole, while other organization subcomponents pursue what are primarily local agendas to the apparent disregard and possible detriment of the wider system.

Merton looked at cases that made him aware of how often provincial interests could sideline societal concerns. Local political corruption was one of his more vivid illustrations. Parsons, by contrast, looked at instances that made him appreciate how much societal needs, commonly shared values, and government authority could override provincial concerns. The spread of universal compulsory education was an important example in Parsons's view. Once we introduce the concept of coupling, however, our level of predictive insight increases substantially. For treating the strength and intensity of coupling as an independent variable enables us to explain (1) why some centers of power are more effective than others in exerting control over subordinate units, and (2) why some—but only some—subordinate units pursue autonomous agendas that may even conflict with the goals of wider social system. This brings us one step closer to Comte's vision of a body of social science principles we can use.

Parsons, for his part, never denied that the current structure of the social world has negative consequences. Nor was he blind to the fact that social entities such as government units can be hijacked to serve special interests. He knew such things happened and thought of outcomes as problematic rather than certain, which requires asking a particular set of questions. Why don't those with power always succeed in hijacking private organizations or government agencies to serve their own special interests? How is it that there are times when change does seem to work to the general benefit of a society and its members? Parsons believed that answering these questions would lead to discoveries that could be used constructively to shape a better world. The Achilles heel of structural functionalism has been an unscientific tendency to blindly assume that feedback processes will work well to promote system improvement; instead, what is necessary is a scientific effort to more adequately understand how feedback mechanisms work in some social units and malfunction in others. Fortunately, this is a flaw that can be rectified through intensified research effort.

The Four Function Scheme

Parsons is best understood as a great synthesizer. He began his career by working for a decade on a book integrating Durkheim, Weber, Pareto, and the British economist Marshall. It was this book, *The Structure of Social Action* (1937), that inaugurated Parsons's career effort to build a comprehensive structural functional synthesis out of earlier social science theories.[5] For the next forty years, Parsons labored to develop a structural functional framework for describing how societies work.

Parsons's structural functional framework really took shape after publication of *The Social System*. His starting point for analysis of structure was to use Weberian ideal typing as an analytical technique, guided by Weber's preoccupation with the importance of societal value differences and the way those value differences express themselves in social roles. So by *structure*, Parsons meant regularized role relationships, the wider organizational units in which those role relationships are embedded, and the values and norms that encourage role occupants to act in particular ways.

The other key for Parsons is *function*, or key needs faced by a social system. Parsons accepted Durkheim's focus on the need social entities have to be integrated, and accepted another piece of social science wisdom of his time, that social entities need to adapt to their environments, to be able to set and pursue goals, and to be able to maintain some semblance of agreement about fundamental matters of right and wrong.

Putting the ideas of structure and function together yielded the structural functional framework. A society thrives only by evolving structural solutions to the functional problems it faces as a social system. Thus, Parsons applied the ideas he acquired from Weber about social structure, and added to these Durkheim's preoccupation with integration as one of the functional needs of social systems. He drew from Pareto to conceive of structural solutions (à la Weber) to functional problems (à la Durkheim) as being fine-tuned through equilibrium feedback mechanisms (à la Pareto).

Parsons's explanatory approach took on more clarity over time, as he came to believe that most human activity is directed by one of four component elements of social structure, which he termed *values, norms, collectivities,* and *roles.* Parsons maintained that these four elements of social structure change over time to better meet one of four social system needs, which he termed *latent pattern maintenance* (basic value agreement), *integration* (the development of a stable and coherent

Adaptation	Goal Attainment
Latent Pattern Maintenance	Integration

FIGURE 11.1
Parsons's Four Function Scheme

pattern of unifying relations tethering people together), *goal attainment* (setting collective priorities and deciding how to meet those priorities), and *adaptation* (mobilizing resources for pursuit of collective priorities). Parsons was somewhat arbitrary in designating what he thought of as *the* set of problems common to all social systems and *the* analytically distinct forms of structure common to all social systems. But in this respect he did what good scientists do, which is to take a stand, exposing ideas for critical examination and testing by others.

Parsons and his followers often used the term *AGIL* as shorthand for *adaptation, goal attainment, integration,* and *latent pattern maintenance* (seen by starting in the upper left-hand corner of figure 11.1 and moving clockwise). Consistent with his use of the Form Follows Function Axiom as a theoretical footing for structural functional analysis, Parsons posited that structural variation and change result from the attempts of different social entities to better meet the challenges they confront.

Because Parsons thought of structural change as something that results in response to changing needs, he organized his ideal type of elements of social structure to overlap with his ideal type four function scheme (figure 11.2). Roles

roles	collectivities (organizations, etc.)
values	norms

FIGURE 11.2
Parsons's Four Elements of Social Structure

are in the upper left-hand corner because they are more explicitly related (in Parsons's view) to changes for purposes of adaptation and so forth.

Parsons believed that if faced with the same four basic social system challenges, every society would blunder along in more or less the same direction when seeking solutions to problems common to all social systems. In other words, whether through independent invention or copying successful innovations developed elsewhere, societies would typically follow the same general evolutionary path.

The four types of evolutionary change Parsons predicted corresponded with changes in his four elements of social structure. Thus, he suggested that inasmuch as form follows function, we should anticipate that structure will change as problems change form. These changes are role upgrading (better training for everyone), structural differentiation (functional separation and operational semiautonomy for organizational subunits), inclusion (moving toward norms that apply to people more uniformly—more nearly one set of rules for men and women, for example), and value generalization (achieving unifying agreement about commitment to a few overarching values, such as freedom in the United States). This evolutionary scheme is outlined in one of his more accessible books, *Societies, Evolutionary and Comparative Perspectives* (1966),[6] and it is developed in more detail in Parsons and Platt's *The American University* (1973).[7]

This is how Parsons integrated key ideas from Weber (especially the primacy of values, exemplified by the shift toward a more rational society in which professionals tend to be governed by a sense of responsibility to clients, to their professions, and to the society at large), with key ideas from Durkheim (especially the idea of social structure, in the form of attachments and beliefs, evolving to better meet system needs under changing circumstances), and with ideas from Pareto (especially Pareto's analysis of societies as systems in which feedback mechanisms are at work and equilibrating processes can be observed). Parsons was always interested in *big* patterns of change, such as the Industrial Revolution, the democratic revolution, and the educational revolution. He wondered why these big patterns of change occurred when, where, and how they did. He tried to be aware of vested interests, but he assumed the hold of special interests could be broken by constant pressure of the compelling needs of society at large.

Getting Practical about Functional Outcomes

The optimism captured in the Form Follows Function Axiom is rejected by many, especially those informed by Marx, because they are justifiably suspicious of power.

This disagreement between those applying the metatheoretical perspectives of conflict theory and structural functionalism allows us to identify some central questions that will have to be addressed before sociology can successfully integrate structural functionalism with conflict theory. Under what conditions should we expect feedback mechanisms to work, resulting in problem-solving structural change?

Conversely, under what conditions should we expect to see feedback systems malfunction? Under what conditions should we expect well-positioned special interests to hijack public organizations and use them for private ends? And conversely, how can commitment to general betterment be maintained in public and private organizations? When social scientists have better answers to these questions, we may see an integration of the different theoretical perspectives into a single framework that offers coherent explanations for different outcomes under different circumstances.

Structural Strain

Parsons was clearly more influenced by Weber's intellectual style than by that of Durkheim, or for that matter Pareto, Mead, or Marx. What we see in Parsons, as a result, is a career-long exuberance for generating typologies rather than for developing explanatory principles. But there are explanatory insights to be found in Parsons's writings.

Parsons calls attention to what he terms *structural strain*, or inconsistency among the various elements of social structure. This inconsistency can take the form of poor coordination between different organizational units. An example would be the widespread pattern of 8 a.m.–5 p.m. parental work schedules simultaneous with 9 a.m.–2 p.m. school schedules without any organized before- or after-school care. If work schedules and school schedules fail to align well, Parsons would say there is structural strain constituting a need for change. A second type of structural strain is found in the inconsistency between values and widespread practices. If the country's values are centered on equality of opportunity and blind justice, but the only work opportunities women have are to make coffee for men in the office, there is a flagrant inconsistency, or a strain, in structure. Here too, Parsons would say persistent structural strain needs to be relieved through structural change.

At the time when Parsons was beginning his work in the 1930s, the civil rights movement was not visible enough to have much public recognition in the mainstream press. Most Americans, whatever their race, did not expect much change. But Parsons did. His theory brought him to expect change and to welcome it as both inevitable and desirable.

Parsons and the other structural functionalists were adamant in pointing to the fact that American values stressing equality of opportunity did not square well with the common pattern of exclusion from opportunity on the basis of race. The sociologists were painfully aware of the contradiction between American values of equality of opportunity and the reality of discriminatory practices in American society at the time. Structural functionalists reasoned that serious structural strain, that is, dramatic inconsistency between societal values and widespread social practice, had to be relieved through structural change. Either the values had to change or practices had to be modified. Moreover, Parsons was convinced that when change comes about as a result of structural strain, values normally win. This means that practices generally change to conform to values rather than the other way around. For this reason, the long-run outcome of the civil rights movement was never in doubt for structural functionalists. This was the interpretation in Gunnar Myrdal's 1944 book *An American Dilemma*.[8] Although there is not yet a Nobel Prize in sociology, Myrdal, the second sociologist to win a Nobel Prize, shared the award for economics in 1974. (Jane Addams had won a Nobel Peace Prize in 1931.)

This important structural-functional idea about values and reality can be captured as the Principle of Structural Strain, but the principle needs to be written somewhat more generally in order to account for structural strain resulting from other kinds of misalignment, such as the necessity to develop new organizational arrangements for child care that results from the fact that school days are shorter than parents' workdays.

Principle of Structural Strain: **Other things being equal, the pressure for change grows internal to systems of organization as a function of degree of (a) incompatibility among the various demands people face as role occupants and (b) inconsistency between expressed values and common patterns of behavior, with change of behavior in the direction of greater consistency with core social values when there is general agreement about the value that seems most relevant, and with values changing in the direction of greater alignment with behavior when there is disagreement about which values apply.**

The centrality of this principle is attested to by the fact that in all the writing Parsons left about institutions (education, family, religion, law), there is an emphasis on the role institutions play in inculcating and defending core values.

Contrasting Structural Functional and Conflict Perspectives at a Metatheoretical Level

A brief analysis of the Enron debacle of 2001 or the home mortgage crisis beginning in 2007 can illustrate the basic metatheoretical differences between structural functional and conflict perspectives. Conducting this analysis is useful because it highlights some of the questions sociologists need to address in order to make more theoretical progress.

The Enron scandal had to do with bookkeeping and reporting practices that were used to make Enron stock look like a much more profitable and secure investment than it really was. Individual investors, mutual funds, and pension plans paid a premium price to buy Enron stock because they were misled into thinking it was a low-risk, high-return asset. Executives were rewarded for their creative accounting because it made the company look good. But when the truth came out, the corporation collapsed and government regulators were criticized for not having uncovered the problem earlier.

The home mortgage crisis of 2007 occurred in much the same way. A large number of mortgages were issued to people who would have trouble paying them back if the economy experienced a downturn. This happened for three reasons. First, financial institutions were making a lot of money issuing new mortgages. Second, the companies issuing the mortgages were not risking much because they quickly bundled the mortgages together into large packages and then sold them to investors. That is, the companies got paid for creating toxic assets, and then quickly turned around and sold those toxic assets so that the toxic assets would be someone else's problem. Third, investors tended not to have much fear because real estate kept appreciating in value. As long as real estate prices were continuously rising, a person having difficulty paying off a mortgage could sell at a profit and repay the loan. This does not work in a time of declining real estate prices, however, and what goes up must eventually come down (at least if Pareto was correct about the world).

There were already regulations in place when these crises occurred. Some of these regulations were passed in the aftermath of the 1929 stock market crash and the Great Depression of the 1930s. Even tighter regulation followed followed both the Enron scandal and the home mortgage crisis. This all leads to a nice test question. Does increased regulation mean the society is really evolving, becoming stronger and better able to meet challenges?

There is a case to be made for, and also a case to be made against, a structural functionalist interpretation that increased regulation is a sign that society has changed in ways that represent a positive response to crises. To make the case for this interpretation: The stock market crash of 1929 and the Great Depression of the 1930s made it clear that excesses had to be controlled. The Securities and Exchange Commission and other regulatory agencies evolved to offer some oversight and constrain excesses. These developments meant that the crises after the year 2000 were less serious than they would otherwise have been because some regulations were in place. The U.S. government is developing even better regulatory capacity now. The system works in the sense that evolution improves the ability of society to deal with future challenges.

A compelling case can also be made for the conflicting interpretation that the system remains exploitive and changes only in ways that are designed to hide the exploitation. That interpretation is this: The few times people are caught, the penalty is insignificant in relation to the damage done. Tightened enforcement is just for show, and lasts only as long as public attention is focused on the issue. Even those organizations (in this case auditing firms and regulatory agencies) that are ostensibly devoted to the defense of the public interest against special interests seem to be co-opted over time. Once auditors and/or regulators are co-opted, the situation may be worse than ever because the existence of auditors and regulators creates an aura of legitimacy around whatever is happening and the general interest of the public is lost in the process.[9] Finally, even if we are fixing problems a little bit, we may not be fixing them fast enough to do any good.

There can be legitimate disagreement over interpretations of events. The proper social science response is not to deny the other position or demonize people holding the other position, but to search for the kinds of evidence which one could use to resolve the question.

The challenge sociologists face is to move beyond axiomatic statements and make more efforts to articulate predictive principles. The implicit promise of science is that we can make progress by advancing principles that explain and predict variation.

Recap

Structural functionalism is often mischaracterized as opposing change. Quite the opposite is true. Structural functionalism is based on the premise that change is necessary (and desirable) to adapt to shifting circumstances. So structural functionalism as a theoretical framework is definitely not antichange.

Structural functionalists emphasize the importance of things being done in ways that are consistent with core values. This often means changing the way the society operates, so structural functionalism cannot be understood as inherently supporting every instance of status quo. But structural functionalists do tend to assume that change works toward rather than away from the greater collective good. Of course, in certain instances this seems to be the case, and in other instances it seems not to be the case. Consequently, structural functionalists need to do more to understand how feedback and other processes work, in order to explain why real-world outcomes sometimes seem more detrimental than beneficial.

Robert Merton's more open treatment of functions (positive and negative, intended and unintended), and consideration of all kinds of social units (organizations and organizational subunits as well as communities and societies) can provide us with useful conceptual tools as we try to better understand how countervailing pressures and tendencies come to be resolved in a complex world.

Some Terms to Know

Stable Equilibrium: The tendency of a system to return to its original state, as when increasing demand generates higher prices and demand then softens (returning to its original point) in response to higher prices.

Elasticity: Having resources and discretionary authority in place to try some changes without the requirement of major alterations elsewhere in preparation for the change.

Structural Strain: Inconsistency among the various elements of social structure.

Review of Axiom and Principles

Form Follows Function Axiom: Form follows function in the sense that widespread patterns of structural change emerge as systemic responses to meet new needs or correct for poor performance in the face of old needs.

Founder Effects Axiom: Those interests and concerns of earlier figures that became active parts of institutional memory or are deeply embedded in institutionalized practice shape the activities of others for a long time to come.

Values Axiom: As a set of values becomes more deeply embedded and more uniformly held by people in a society, common social roles and widely institutionalized systems of rules are progressively modified in ways that manifest and maximize adherence to core values.

Principle of Organizational Efficiency/Effectiveness: Long-term organizational efficiency/effectiveness is a positive function of (a) success in maintaining uniform mission awareness and accurate institutional history, (b) depth of commitment to minimizing repetition of past mistakes and taking other steps to improve performance, (c) organizational capacity for assessing challenges and instituting change without interrupting normal operations, and (d) adequacy of alignment of training, information, resources, and operational authority with the tasks people are called on to perform in their roles.

Principle of Systemic Coupling: Other things being equal, the ability of a system of organization to maintain mission focus (and avoid mission creep) is a positive function of the extent to which (a) a stable and shared awareness of common ends can be maintained, (b) lines of communication remain open and honest, (c) subordinate units remain resource dependent on higher level units, (d) resource allocation is aligned well with mission involvement, and (e) people at different locations within the system of organization have a sense of common fate.

Principle of Structural Strain: Other things being equal, the pressure for change grows internal to systems of organization as a function of degree of (a) incompatibility among the various demands people face as role occupants and (b) inconsistency between expressed values and common patterns of behavior, with change of behavior in the direction of greater consistency with core social values when there is general agreement about the value that seems most relevant, and with values changing in the direction of greater alignment with behavior when there is disagreement about which values apply.

Quiz

Check your answers in the back of the book. If you get any wrong, consider reviewing chapter 11 before continuing.

1. It is often said that form follows function. What does this mean?
2. Parsons believed that social change follows an evolutionary progression. That is, over the long course of time, structural change tends to move in predictable directions. What is one of the directions he thought change tends to move in, over the long course of time? Generally speaking, does this seem accurate to you?
3. What are the two analytically distinct sources of structural change, according to structural functionalists?

Application Exercise

In the United States during the first decade of the twenty-first century, there was sharply divided opinion regarding freedom of choice relating to abortion. When strongly divided public opinions about matters of deeply held values persistently dominate public attention, the social system has what Parsons would have called a *latent pattern maintenance problem*.

Shortly after being inaugurated as the forty-fourth president of the United States, Barack Obama tried to encourage both sides of the abortion debate to unite in the common cause of reducing the number of abortions being performed, but by reducing demand rather than by restricting access to the procedure. Obama offered a threefold strategy for reducing demand: (a) taking educational and family-planning steps in an attempt to reduce the number of unwanted pregnancies; (b) taking steps to make life in the United States more friendly toward and more supportive of people with young children, in the interest of making it more workable for people to bring a pregnancy to term and keep their child; and (c) easing the path to adoption for people who do bring a pregnancy to term, but for whatever reason feel unable to raise the child.

Decide whether or not you are inclined to view Obama's effort as an attempt to bring about what Parsons meant by "value generalization." Briefly explain your assessment.

12

Conflict Theory on Battles over Benefits

S TRUCTURAL FUNCTIONALIST IDEAS WERE BEING DISCUSSED at Harvard University and elsewhere throughout the 1930s and 1940s, but they did not emerge as a clearly articulated theoretical paradigm until the early 1950s. As that was happening, many people rejected the metatheoretical assumptions that structural functionalists tended to make about a society being a system organized to progressively redesign itself for the common good. Their views eventually coalesced into conflict theory as an alternative intellectual framework. As an alternative to structural functionalism, the conflict perspective suggests different orienting questions, a different set of sensitizing concepts, and a distinctive set of axiomatic assumptions about exploitation, conflict, and system change.

Conflict's Rejection of Structural Functional Metatheory

To understand the conflict perspective, one has to appreciate its basic metatheoretical rejection of the structural functionalist position that seemed predominant in American sociology by 1955. From outside the discipline in 1955, sociological theory could easily have appeared to be structural functionalism. But strong axiomatic objections were stirring in reaction to the intellectual hegemony of the structural functionalists. This intellectual reaction gave rise to two alternative metatheoretical perspectives: symbolic interactionism and conflict theory. Symbolic interactionism, to be discussed in chapter 13, was a reaction to the structural functionalist preoccupation with societies as units of analysis. Many people felt that structural functionalism paid too little attention to individual people and undervalued the role of human agency in shaping social events. The conflict theorists were generally comfortable with the macrolevel focus of most structural functionalists but had serious misgivings about assuming that change tends to move in the direction of maximizing the common good. Conflict theorists rightly pointed out that structural functional metatheory, if used without effort to add explanatory principles, encourages *teleological* reasoning implying that if a social structural arrangement exists, it must have evolved for a reason and must be good. Conflict theorists correctly argued that reasoning of this kind is patently unsound and indefensible. Structural functional axioms used in the absence of explanatory principles seem particularly prone to the problem of teleological reasoning.

The teleological character of structural functional metatheory was particularly worrisome to conflict theorists because they felt that the automatic concern for the health and integration of society leads to an implicit desire to support the status quo against destabilization. This can, for example, amount to uncritical support for repressive regimes. Some sociologists oriented toward conflict theory consequently suspected that a structural functional approach must be inherently antipopulist and in favor of political reactionaries. This was an unfortunate mischaracterization because it slowed theory discourse within sociology for a long time.

Conflict Metatheory: Exploitation of the Powerless by the Powerful

Conflict theorists tended to assume that power corrupts, and that the institutions of society develop in ways that are intended to keep the rich and the poor in their respective places. This makes for an interesting comparison between structural functionalism and conflict theory precisely because the perspectives share so much. People applying both perspectives tend to have a macro focus, often using societies (or sometimes communities or organizations) as their units of analysis. People using both frameworks also tend to be alert to social structural arrangements, how they work, and what consequences they generate (including consequences that are difficult to recognize). And sociologists using both perspectives tend ultimately to be interested in predicting when societies or other social systems will change and how they will change. It is at this point that the perspectives diverge, however: they offer distinctive metatheoretical frameworks for looking at change.

The difference starts with the orienting questions asked by people employing a conflict perspective: Who benefits from the way the social system operates? How does the social system work to benefit those groups of people? How do people in social systems understand and interpret the distribution of benefits in that system? When and how does resistance develop against the system of benefit distribution? How is resistance forestalled by those in power? What ultimately happens when conflict occurs, and why? Because of the orienting questions they employ, the key sensitizing concepts most conflict theorists focus on are class, vested interests, stratification, power, and oppression. By the late 1950s, a conflict paradigm was successfully challenging the intellectual hegemony of structural functionalism in sociology, and social science research was focusing more attention on these variables.

Conflict Theory's Main Metatheoretical Axioms

In addition to orienting questions and sensitizing concepts like the ones listed here, conflict metatheory is based on two fundamental axiomatic assumptions, each of which was introduced in chapter 8.

Structured Inequality Axiom: **The social structural arrangements that survive tend to be those that protect the interests of more-powerful people at the expense of less-powerful people.**

A companion suggests that people in power must be forced to give up their grip on power if inequality is to be relieved.

Intransigence Axiom: **The powerful do not loosen the grip of exploitation without being pressed to do so.**

The conflict perspective thus emphasizes the self-serving nature of powerful people, and calls into question whether any reform-oriented structural change brokered by people in positions of power will be genuine or meaningful. Conflict theorists tend to suspect that change brokered by people in power will always be designed to protect and extend the interests of those who are already advantaged. While structural functionalists are convinced that greed can and should be curbed when doing so is for the good of society as a whole, conflict theorists do not see that happening. They tend to think that any apparent altruism on the part of the powerful is merely for superficial appearance.

The disagreement between conflict theorists and structural functionalists will be resolved only when we have principles stipulating the conditions under which and processes through which altruistic values will subordinate the power of special interest groups, or vice versa. Conflict theorists have already made some significant progress in developing explanatory principles that help us understand how conflict actually unfolds in the real world. In this chapter, we will review how the conflict framework assumed some of its current form.

Unmasking the Power Elite by Rediscovering Marx

American sociology's rediscovery of Marx began with the urban ethnography of Robert Lynd and Helen Merrell Lynd, who spent several years studying Muncie, Indiana. In the 1920s, America was rapidly urbanizing, and church leaders in

Muncie were concerned about the decline in church attendance and the spread of urban-style social problems. In order to gauge the problem and suggest ways of getting people back to church, a consortium of churches hired the Lynds, a husband-and-wife team of sociologists, to conduct a study.

The Lynds spent several years interviewing people and conducting surveys in and around Muncie. One of their principal discoveries was exactly what readers of Marx had anticipated: class matters. The businesspeople of Muncie made most of the important decisions in government and in civic circles, as well as in the economy. Although the Lynds did provide Muncie's religious leaders with useful information about declining church attendance, their lasting sociological contribution was to improve our understanding of class in the United States.[1]

A revealing set of community studies followed in the tradition of the Lynds' *Middletown* and showed that businesspeople have enormous political and civic as well as economic clout. Studies of movers and shakers have confirmed this, discovering what C. Wright Mills aptly describes as *the power elite* in his 1956 book by that title.[2] In addition, William Domhoff is one of many people to try to discover how the power elite exerts control over local, state, and national government, and over organizations of every kind, from behind the scenes. In his 1974 book, *The Bohemian Grove and Other Retreats*, Domhoff describes how private social clubs can serve as meeting grounds for the rich, enabling them to develop a sense of group feeling and to chart strategies for promoting shared interests.[3]

One of the interesting offshoots of the power elite literature charts interlocking directorates. The boards of directors of power-wielding organizations such as banks, big corporations, and high-profile civic groups often have overlapping membership. Working together on boards of directors of corporations and nonprofit organizations, and sitting on advisory panels for a variety of government agencies, a few individuals can communicate with one another and have profound influence. Needless to say, those well-connected individuals come from the top of the society and not the bottom, and their positions give them real voice. They are not a silent majority; nor are they a voiceless underclass.

Of course, there is significant variation from place to place. A power elite seems to hold almost monolithic power in some times and places, such as in cities with only a few industries that are tightly controlled by a small number of people from a few interrelated families. Where education and human capital are scarce, as in Atlanta during the 1940s and early 1950s, when Floyd Hunter wrote *Community Power Structure* (1953), it is hard for voices of dissent to be heard.[4] Political power and civic influence seem to be more pluralistic in cities where there are many industries, where a diverse array of people are less thoroughly interconnected, and where education and human capital are relatively abundant and widely dispersed, as Robert Dahl found in New Haven when he wrote *Who Governs?* in 1961.[5] The studies by Hunter and Dahl, with their varied findings, suggest an explanatory principle.

Pluralist versus Power Elite Perspectives as a Way to Mark the Boundary between Conflict Metatheory and Conflict Theory

Within the social sciences, there has been an engaging and long-running debate between *pluralists* and *power elite* theorists. Pluralists have described communities in which many people have voice in determining what will be on the public agenda. Often the outcomes of the political process, at least in these communities, seem to benefit the community broadly. But other social scientists have described communities in which the rich and powerful seem to exert more or less monolithic control over government, and the government agenda and outcomes of governmental process seem, at least from some points of view, to benefit only the rich.

This mix of research results presents us with an important question: Does the power elite always rule, and rule in its own interests? Or does it never do so? A scientific way of approaching the question would be to treat the outcome as a dependent variable to be explained. Enough has been learned from prior research that it is possible for us to offer a principle informed by research findings.

Diversity of Voice in Governance Principle: **Other things being equal, the diversity of voices heard in the public arena is a function of (a) the breadth of distribution of control over economic activity, (b) the organizational density of social life, (c) the level and breadth of distribution of human capital, and (d) the number and openness of channels of public communication.**

Some structural functionalists might blindly assume that the normal operation of power yields changes that serve the collective good. And some conflict theorists might blindly assume that the normal operation of the system really benefits only those in power. The truth seems to be that both descriptions are more or less accurate, but for different times and places. The social science challenge is to understand how special interests make themselves felt in corridors of power. This is the kind of question the conflict framework is well positioned to help us answer. Conversely, we also want to better understand how the grip those in power have over the public arena can be broken. In addressing this question, both the structural functionalist metatheoretical framework and the conflict metatheoretical framework will be exceedingly useful, though their value will appear in different ways. Conflict metatheory helps keep us alert to the interest of individual actors and the groups they form, as well as to the ways the interests of powerful people come to be reflected in institutional arrangements protecting those in power and influencing the flow of resources. Structural functional metatheory does little to sensitize us to the vested interests of different players, but it does alert us to systemic processes that might counterbalance those vested interests.

Moving forward in this respect has meant moving beyond Marx. When Marx laid out the basic theoretical premises of conflict theory in the mid-nineteenth century, the *era of big business* was only beginning. That was before anything that we would recognize as a modern industrial economy had developed anywhere. It was before cars, before department stores, before any antitrust legislation, and before the establishment of the Federal Reserve Board. It was nearly a century before the establishment of the World Bank and the International Monetary Fund. Aware of all the historical developments postdating Marx's description of early industrial capitalism, Marxian writers have (beginning with the Lynds) tried to analyze current conditions from the vantage point of Marx's theoretical framework, but as they think Marx would apply the framework if he were alive today and aware of contemporary events. Making Marx's ideas more contemporary has, in fact, been the single biggest preoccupation of people who identify themselves as working within the conflict tradition.

Appreciating the Scientist in Marx: Neo-Marxian Analysis of Class

For conflict theorists informed by a Marxian conceptual framework, all questions ultimately return to descriptions of the class structure. But modern class structure is not as simple as Marx imagined it would be when he and Engels wrote *The Communist Manifesto* in 1848.[6] Marx observed that owners and workers were fundamentally different from one another in almost every respect in early capitalist society. And he was convinced that these differences would grow more pronounced as capitalism matured. He predicted that owners would have total workplace authority and wage earners would have no voice at all in making workplace decisions. In an age of automation, Marx thought that the jobs of most wage earners would be deskilled over time, and that the wages of employees would then be driven down to a starvation level.

But contemporary reality is somewhat different. For one thing, many wage earners actually have a great deal of job authority and autonomy. If we look at the economy as a whole, we see that some of the largest occupational categories (e.g., manager and foreman) fall into the *ambiguous class position* of being employees themselves, yet having supervisory authority. Managers and foremen are typically accorded more respect, higher wages, and better benefits than other workers. Nevertheless, they are still wage earners who must continue selling their labor in order to survive.

Another important dimension of contemporary class relations concerns the skill level of the average worker. While *deskilling* has proceeded quite far in some occupations, many new occupations (e.g., computer design, computer repair) require a great deal of training. Moreover, occupations requiring great skill are not as easy to supervise as semiskilled jobs on an assembly line. A worker who has trouble keeping up with an assembly line is easily (if perhaps incorrectly) judged to be "slow" but it is much harder to arrive at a judgment about whether someone in the field of computer repair or even air-conditioning repair is fast or slow. In aggregate, the human capital of working people has grown rather than shriveled as a consequence of technological change. At the same time, conditions for tight workplace supervision and control have diminished. While it is true that some old crafts have largely disappeared, a technology-based economy requires people with more skill rather than less. Certainly in comparison with the world Marx envisioned, many more employers need to offer higher wages and better working conditions in order to attract and keep the kinds of employees needed to remain competitive. This is particularly clear in those sectors of the economy where success is predicated on a firm's ability to produce a steady stream of useful innovations. In sum, even during economic downturns, today's typical worker is simply not in the dire position in which Marx anticipated capitalism would deposit all workers with the passage of time.

All these factors combine to create a contemporary class structure in which many people, perhaps the majority of workers in the United States, are in fact wage earners who share some of the characteristics Marx associated with being a member of the capitalist class. As Erik Wright points out in his 1978 book, *Class, Crisis, and the State*, this puts people in ambiguous class positions where their class interests can seem somewhat murky and conflicted.[7] Wright and other neo-Marxian conflict theorists wonder what it will mean if most people come to have, or at least feel that they have, one foot in each of the main classes Marx described. The answer seems pretty obvious to most sociologists: class ambiguity discourages class conflict by mitigating against polarizing class consciousness.

In this respect it is easy to appreciate the scientist in Marx; his Principle of Intergroup Conflict (see chapter 8) allows us to understand why class conflict has been muted in modern society. Informed by Marx's analysis, we should only expect class conflict to intensify at such times as the gaps between different groups grow, opportunities for mobility diminish, and the sense of solidarity of interests within divided groups becomes stronger.

Pressed to better understand the operation of contemporary class dynamics, conflict theorists have also developed deep appreciation for the important and pervasive ways in which class manifests itself through control of knowledge and manners, apart from control of financial resources and means of production. Bourdieu and Passeron write about *culture capital*, or manners and knowledge that signal one's right to be treated as a person of special worth.[8] Having culture capital in the form of impressive knowledge and preferred manners also helps people build *social capital*, or useful contacts and network connections expanding one's scope of opportunity.

One especially interesting aspect of this work is the concept of *symbolic violence*. Just as the people with culture capital tend to feel entitled to the good things in life, those people who lack much of what is approved as standard culture capital tend to feel that they are undeserving. Getting poor people to blame themselves for the fact that they have few advantages in life constitutes symbolic violence to the degree that it directs the substantial psychological costs of poverty inward in the form of self-loathing. It also increases the likelihood of continued failure.

Neo-Marxian Efforts to Move beyond Marx: Conflict Theories of the State

Among the conflict theorists interested in seats of political power, some of the most interesting discussions have swirled around attempts to understand the role of the modern state. Nicos Poulantzas is one of many people to ask what Marx might have said about the role of the state if Marx were alive today. Poulantzas, in his 1978 book, *State, Power, and Socialism*, argues that Marx would reject simpleminded notions that the state is controlled by individual capitalists. Instead, Poulantzas's Marxian view is that the state functions as a sort of capitalist clearinghouse, promoting the general interests of business without necessarily supporting every vested interest of every business owner.[9] What happens, for example, when oil companies want high gas prices that increase their profits, but at the same time, auto manufacturers prefer low gas prices so they can sell larger cars that are typically sold on a higher profit margin? This also begs the question, are the interests of Toyota the same as the interests of Ford? Conflict theorists struggle with such questions.

How can we make sense of the interests of all those who are economically powerful? This is highly relevant if we think of a power elite's hijacking control of the government for its own interests. Which interests are we talking about? Are we talking about the interests of only those few who happen to be in momentary control? Or are we talking about the interests of some broader class or grouping? What can we say about the processing through which special interests and common public interests gain definition and vie for influence? Poulantzas and most other conflict theorists believe that the ruling class as a whole, as distinguished from individual people with wealth or power, has some collective interests.

The flip side of this equation, explored by general conflict theorists, concerns the efforts of government to maintain its legitimacy in the eyes of common people. To maintain legitimacy, governments can be expected to utilize propaganda tactics to deflect blame for any problems away from themselves and toward internal opposition or external enemies. Government might also be called on to provide safety-net protections and maintain official mechanisms for the adjudication of grievances. Gurtov and Maghroori capture these insights in their 1984 book, *The Roots of Failure: United States Foreign Policy in the Third World*, in which they attribute the fall of governments to the loss of legitimacy that comes from a widespread perception that the interests of average people are ill served by those in power.[10]

Principle of Legitimate Authority: **Other things being equal, the degree of legitimacy enjoyed by a government is a positive function of (a) the reliability with** which the rights or ordinary citizens are protected and services are provided, (b) enforcement of laws is viewed as fair, and (c) ideology and information are skillfully used to deflect blame in the direction of internal opposition or external enemies.

Correlated with this idea, it is important to recognize that domestic crises often come to a head after long periods of fiscal overextension (deficit spending) and/or projection of military power.[11]

General Conflict Theory

Most conflict theorists focus on traditional Marxian concerns. These include (a) inequality between business owners and wage earners, (b) control of government and manipulation of media and ideology to protect the interests of business owners, and (c) class conflict. There are, however, conflict theorists who have tried to develop more general frameworks for studying conflict of all kinds. This general conflict tradition started in Germany with Georg Simmel, who was a friend of Max Weber's and one of the original founders of the German Sociological Society. As we noted earlier, Simmel was fascinated by conflict as a category of phenomena that is pervasive in everyday life. One of his great insights is that conflict between groups tends to lead to increased cohesion within groups (Conflict/Cohesion Principle).

Simmel, like his friend Max Weber, was ever alert to the ubiquitous nature of conflict, and he was convinced that sociology needed to broaden its focus beyond Marx's preoccupation with societal change stemming from the revolutionary clash of business owners and wage earners. Weber's analytical separation of (economic) *class* from (social) *status* and (political) *power* is evidence of an approach to conflict that is much broader than that of Marx. And Simmel's concern for conflict in ordinary, day-to-day human interaction is broader still. Among other things, the positive consequences of conflict need to be appreciated; this is a point developed in Lewis Coser's *The Functions of Social Conflict* (1956).[12] Conflict, Simmel recognized, has all sorts of positive consequences, not the least of which is alerting people when something is not working well and needs to be addressed.

The German intellectual interest in conflict in all its many forms crystallized in Ralf Dahrendorf's *Class and Class Conflict in Industrial Society* (1959).[13] Dahrendorf focuses on the fact that relationships between people with different levels of organizational authority are inherently conflict ridden. His theory of conflict is as revealing as it is elegant in its simplicity. Dahrendorf said the following:

1. Conflict tends to occur between those who have organizational authority and those who do not.

2. Conflict is orchestrated into group action more rapidly (a) if grievance procedures exist and there is a history of using them, (b) if people at the same authority level are able to communicate with one another, (c) if a leadership cadre exists among those at subordinate levels of authority, (d) if ideologies pinpoint rather than obscure lines of division between those with and without authority, (e) when the range of similarities within authority levels and differences between authority levels are greatest, and (f) where ties across authority levels are limited in number. (Note the incorporation of Marx's fundamental insight about intergroup conflict, reviewed in chapter 8.)

3. The more often conflict is played out, the less likely it is to turn violent and the more likely it is to lead to modest, steady, progressive change (of the kind structural functionalists often think about) than to dramatic, punctuated, deeply fundamental change (of the kind Marxists often think about).

4. When conflict is played out, it eventually leads to structural change relieving old pressures, though it often creates the conditions under which new ones will develop.

Dahrendorf's scheme has the beauty of being applicable to any situation where there are authority differences built into organizational roles. The pattern Dahrendorf noted and assumed to be characteristic of organizations in general is amply covered the Intransigence Axiom.

There is intuitive logic to this axiom. The existence of authority differences gives rise to the possibility of abuse or perceived abuse of power. When conflict arises in response to abuse, structural change aimed at reducing friction becomes more likely. But Dahrendorf treats this scenario as an inevitability to be assumed rather than a possibility to be explained. He would say that in every organization there are ways for people in authority to get special benefits (which is obviously true) and furthermore, that people in authority are compelled by inner drives to pursue those benefits (which is not necessarily true) and unchecked in their efforts to do so by a lack of organizational controls (which is also not necessarily true). Over time, the unchecked use of authority for self-serving purposes generates resentment and conflict. The more resentment that is generated, the more conflict erupts. And the more conflict erupts, the more likely structural change becomes. Dahrendorf presumes that change brought about in this way will correct some problems. But he also presumes that those newly elevated to positions of authority will find their own path through which to benefit, and that resentment and conflict will consequently follow.

Level of violence is one subject that Dahrendorf does treat as a variable to be explained. Some conflicts turn violent, but not all conflicts do. Which conflicts are most likely to turn violent? Which are least likely to do so? Dahrendorf notes that conflict is more likely to turn violent if it is episodic rather than chronic, and when it occurs outside of an arena with rules and procedures.

Principle of Violent Conflict: **Other things being equal, the likelihood of a conflict's turning violent is inversely related to (a) how frequent conflict is and (b) how thoroughly regulated conflict is.**

One of the restrictions of Dahrendorf's approach and the approach of many other conflict theorists is that these approaches explicitly focus on situations in which conflict occurs along a fault line defined by differences in wealth or power. However, if we use experience as a guide, we know that conflict also occurs among peers or between groups that are at the same level of organizational power or economic wealth. Theodore Caplow, in his 1968 book, *Two Against One: Coalitions in Triads*, builds on Simmel's basic insights to explore how conflict dynamics change as soon as an association of people, such as a family or a collection of friends, grows from two individuals (a dyad) to three individuals (a triad).[14] The possibilities for coalition formation instantly make themselves apparent. And coalitions that pit one set of actors against another can shift over time. The fundamentally important observation is that conflict can be found in any setting and while lines of conflict can be relatively stable for long periods, there are also times when lines of conflict can shift like sand. Broadly conceived, conflict is such a ubiquitous feature of the social world that its treatment needs to be a central part of any effort to build a comprehensive sociological theory.

Dependency and World System Theory

One feature of conflict theory that has special appeal is its applicability to different units of analysis. At one extreme, Caplow examines coalition formation within triads, for example, a parent and two children. At the other extreme, Andre Gunder Frank, in his 1967 work *Capitalism and Underdevelopment in Latin America*, considers the dependence that he says elites in poor nations develop on rich nations,[15] and Immanuel Wallerstein, in his *The Modern World System*, examines the flow of events that tie the fate of nations producing resources (lumber, sugar, cotton, minerals, and fuel) to manufacturing countries in a *world system*.[16] Both dependency theorists and world system theorists try to explain why some countries are relatively rich and others are relatively poor. They generally perceive that relationships of dependence ensure that the wealth of the developing world will slowly gravitate into the banks of the industrial West, where those profits will be used to bolster the continued development of the most powerful countries rather than the relatively impoverished lands from which profits were generated. Similar ideas have been used to point toward a kind of internal colonialism in which the financial resources of poor rural or poor urban areas end up being siphoned out of those communities rather than invested locally. This situation has broached questions being explored by sociologists in Latin America, including ex–sociology professor Fernando Cardoso, the inflation-fighting president of Brazil (1994–2002), in his 2001 book, *Charting a New Course: The Politics of Globalization and Social Transformation.*[17] But the conclusions these theorists reach are still controversial and contested among academics. Theorists are busy grappling with these questions, as the current debate over neoliberalism and globalization attests.

A Concrete Point of Departure between Paradigms

Having a coherent sense of sociology as a discipline requires being able to make sense of the ways different paradigms inform our understanding of the world. Education provides a concrete point of departure for understanding what conflict theory and structural functionalism have in common and how they differ. Both paradigms assume the existence of institutionalized features of society that are bigger than any individual and have enormous consequences. For example, people working in both paradigms assume that industrial societies mobilize collective resources (e.g., taxes) and commit those resources to schools that are monitored and controlled to some degree by government. People employing both paradigms work with the common presumption that school curricula are designed to achieve some planned purpose extending beyond the wishes of a particular group of students and their parents. The curriculum is more or less imposed on students by school systems. It is widely understood that most students have little recourse but to go along with what they are instructed to do, and that each student's future opportunities as well as present experience are shaped by the nature of educational institutions and the curricular and delivery decisions those institutions make.

At this point, the similarity between conflict theory and structural functionalism ends. Structural functionalists regard educational institutions as having emerged and undergone steady change oriented to promote the common good. Schools are seen by structural functionalists as imparting technical knowledge, cultural graces, and democratic civility. They are viewed as promoting altruism as a social value, so that well-educated students will mature into adults working in the common interest. And they are appreciated as the training grounds where most people learn necessary occupational and citizenship skills. But from a conflict perspective, schools are viewed as instruments for solidifying the class structure, ensuring that the children of rich and powerful people will themselves be helped along on the road to their own wealth and power, and that the children of lower-income workers are molded into compliant followers who will settle for whatever they are given and be thoroughly unprepared to exercise leadership on any meaningful scale.[18]

Conflict theory and structural functional theory lead us to expect different things. It is good that we be alert to both scenarios because both outcomes are possible. But if our goal in science is to explain variation, our ultimate task as theorists will be to discover principles that allow for the possibility of both outcomes and help us understand why different outcomes come to pass in different cases.

Recap

Conflict theory is not a tightly integrated body of thought. Instead, it consists of a wide-ranging collection of works applying the same set of metatheoretical assumptions in different settings, and then trying to move beyond those axioms to the discovery of principles explaining meaningful kinds of variability in the real world. Most work in the conflict tradition seeks to reveal inequality, to explain how inequality is created and maintained, and to understand its consequences. Research in this tradition has fundamentally transformed our understanding of the social world by revealing just how deeply rooted inequality is and how destructive it can be.

The conflict tradition is informed by Marx's critique of the nineteenth-century class situation. But it is also more. The critique of class and power has been revised in light of developments as they have unfolded with the passage of time. Moreover, conflict in all its forms has been brought under examination, with the result that the perspective has relevance to situations of all kinds.

Some Terms to Know

Culture Capital: Ways in which upper-class status manifests itself through control of knowledge and manners.

Social Capital: Useful contacts and network connections that influence one's access to opportunities.

Symbolic Violence: Self-imposed limitations and distress caused by blaming oneself for problems caused by others.

Review of Axioms and Principles

Structured Inequality Axiom: The social structural arrangements that survive tend to be those that protect the interests of more-powerful people at the expense of less-powerful people.

Intransigence Axiom: The powerful do not loosen the grip of exploitation without being pressed to do so.

Diversity of Voice in Governance Principle: Other things being equal, the diversity of voices heard in the public arena is a function of (a) the breadth of distribution of control over economic activity, (b) the organizational density of social life, (c) the level and breadth of distribution of human capital, and (d) the number and openness of channels of public communication.

Principle of Legitimate Authority: Other things being equal, the degree of legitimacy enjoyed by a government is a positive function of (a) the reliability with which the rights or ordinary citizens are protected and services are provided, (b) enforcement of laws is viewed as fair, and (c) ideology and information are skillfully used to deflect blame in the direction of internal opposition or external enemies.

Principle of Principle of Violent Conflict: Other things being equal, the likelihood of a conflict's turning violent is inversely related to (a) how frequent conflict is and (b) how thoroughly regulated conflict is.

Quiz

Check your answers in the back of the book. If you get any wrong, consider reviewing chapter 12 before continuing.

1. If the axioms in this chapter are correct, how much likelihood is there that established power will voluntarily reform itself in order to relieve inequality?
2. Under what conditions is a local power elite likely to exert the most monolithic control over local government?
3. How many people have to be in a group before we begin to see coalitions form?

Application Exercise

Reasoning from the principles reviewed in this chapter, how do you expect the Internet to shape class conflict in the future, and why?

13

Symbolic Interactionism on Fluid Meaning and Action

TWO ARTICLES OF FAITH IN SCIENCE ARE THAT (1) all understanding is provisional (because we assume all knowledge can ultimately be improved on) and (2) those of us who are engaged in the quest for better understanding must be willing to articulate our provisional (and therefore potentially flawed) understandings as a part of the process of moving toward a somewhat more realistic and more informative body of theory. The rise of theoretical paradigms in sociology aptly illustrates this point. The structural functional paradigm, taken by itself in its 1950s form, was unrealistically optimistic about the benevolence of societal institutions and power brokers. Many sociologists recognized this, and the conflict paradigm emerged as a corrective.

Sometime in the future, we may be able to link and perhaps integrate structural functional theory and conflict theory by identifying when and explaining how special interests are able to hijack government and other social institutions, and by learning how institutions can be better protected from hijacking so that the common good can be served. At that point, we will be able to consolidate the conflict and structural functionalist paradigms into a single and more powerful theoretical framework. A good natural science analogy is the integration of the early twentieth-century theory of electricity and the early twentieth-century theory of magnetism to produce a theory of electromagnetism. This integration took a lot of effort by theorists and it took a lot of years to achieve. But it did eventually happen, and when it did, it marked a major scientific leap forward. Bridging the divide between structural functional and conflict theoretical approaches to understanding social systems will require an equally significant leap forward in understanding, and one that will undoubtedly require us to take into account the role individual people play in influencing social response to the challenges of daily life. This is where symbolic interaction comes into the picture.

The Symbolic Interactionist Critique of
Structural Functional and Conflict Theory

As those contributing to the development of the conflict paradigm were loudly questioning structural functionalist assumptions about the benevolence of social institutions, another set of voices began to be heard in greater number. Those were people who questioned the implicit assumptions shared by structural functionalists and conflict theorists, most notably an implicit assumption of *structural determinism.*

Both the structural functional and the conflict perspectives give primary attention to structural arrangements. For structural functionalists and conflict theorists, the degree of stability in the way things are done year after year, even as the years pass and people change, suggests that those social structural arrangements actually act with compelling force on people. The turnover in the population of students at a college is virtually complete over a ten-year time horizon (even when graduate students are taken into account). Over the same ten-year time horizon there can also be substantial turnover in faculty and staff. The people who do remain are in some respects changed, and sometimes changed significantly, by virtue of being ten years older and finding themselves with more experience and being at a different stage of the life cycle. (Over the course of ten years, staff members who begin as young adults with small children accumulate some gray hair and find that they have teenagers.). Yet, most colleges at time 2 have a great deal in common with what they were at time 1. Organizations, institutions, and societal patterns are, from structural functional and conflict points of view, real social entities. They are more than the sum of the individuals who are members, and people who are members of organizations or have institutional roles do tend to accommodate themselves in significant ways to those roles because organizational structure and organizational culture are real and imposing.

By way of contrast, we can see that sociologists most inspired by George Herbert Mead understand that social structure, while real, is always subject to being reshaped and redefined by the very people who live out their social lives within the context of those structurally patterned relationships. People informed by the work of George Herbert Mead assume that individuals have considerable agency to shape their commitments, to redefine shared meaning, and to remold the organizations and institutional settings they find themselves a part of.

The work of many of those inspired by Mead and interested in agency coalesced into what has come to be known as the *symbolic interactionist* perspective. Symbolic interactionists have always regarded both the conflict theory and the structural functional perspectives as unduly deterministic, paying too little attention to the fact that individuals can reshape their situations, among other things by redefining what is expected in their social commitments. The determinism of structural functional theory and conflict theory implies that the beliefs, behavior, and fate of individuals are all shaped by organizational, institutional, and societal requirements. Characteristics such as institutional arrangements of family and education, the class structure, legal codes, the police enforcement apparatus, and theological teachings of prevalent religions all assuredly influence people. But interactionists tend to believe that individuals have more *agency* than early structural, cultural, and class determinist models would allow.

Symbolic interactionists all recognize that every society has structural features and cultural characteristics, and that the features and characteristics of the society are critical to understand. Each of us is indelibly marked by the kind of society we live in and our location in it. Symbolic interactionists know and appreciate this. Nevertheless, symbolic interactionists stress that cultural and structural determinism is limited in its consequences, and that individual people do exercise agency and are able to significantly reshape the social world, or at least that part of the social world that they personally inhabit.[1] In fairness, it is important to recognize that structural functionalists and conflict theorists also recognize that individuals have agency and can reshape the world in which they live. But symbolic interaction accords much more weight to the capacity of people to free themselves from constraints of the past, and in the process, to transform social structure as much as to conform to it.

Symbolic Interactionist Metatheory: Agency and Adjustment

As sociological theory was maturing in the 1950s, there was a great deal of explicit interest in macrolevel analysis of society as a whole. Structural functionalists and conflict theorists shared an interest in understanding long-term change in the character of society. They tended to think in terms of social structure and culture influencing people, rather than the other way around. People are obviously involved in bringing about change, but both structural functionalists and conflict theorists tend to think in terms of individuals doing things in response to inexorable social forces that can be understood only in terms of broad historical conditions. The main disagreement between structural functionalists and conflict theorists is not over macro- or mesodeterminism (social systems determine individual actions), but merely whether the built-in logic of superorganic entities (societies, communities, organizations) is to evolve structural features and cultural attributes benefiting the whole social entity and the people in it (as structural functionalists tend to believe) or benefiting the privileged groups in control (which is what conflict theorists tend to believe). The structural functional and conflict paradigms really took shape in the mid-twentieth century, as sociologists tried to integrate and/or work out apparent inconsistencies in the analyses of Durkheim, Weber, Marx, Pareto, Veblen, and their contemporaries.

While all this was happening, growing numbers of sociologists came to feel dissatisfied with both the structural functional and conflict approaches because of the macrodeterministic tendencies found in the works most often associated with those perspectives. By the 1960s, people who drew heavily from the work of George Herbert Mead came to identify themselves as sharing a symbolic interactionist perspective that was quite distinct because it emphasized the primacy of individuals. Symbolic interactionists challenged the view of human beings as mere pawns of their surroundings, and focused on the process through which people engaged in direct communication can come to share new understandings and redefine the ways in which they relate to one another.

Focusing, as they do, on symbolic communication in relationships, symbolic interactionists have tended to ask a particular set of orienting questions: What factors have the most impact on the ways in which people interpret daily events? What makes some social interactions more meaningful and salient than others? How can beliefs and role relationships be redefined in social encounters with others? How does interaction, as it unfolds in discrete relationships, have impact on widely shared beliefs and institutionalized roles (for example, influence what people in general come to see as a good mother, teacher, or employee)? When considering these questions, symbolic interactionists have tended to employ a special set of sensitizing concepts that only partially overlaps with those used when the other paradigms are being employed. Symbolic interactionists tend to be acutely aware of definition of situation, self-concept, identity, stigma, emotional arousal, peer groups, reference groups, role, role strain, and role distance. By the early 1960s, symbolic interactionism had coalesced into a paradigm that was broadly recognized by people in the discipline, having its intellectual roots in the work of George Herbert Mead at the University of Chicago.

The Chicago School of Symbolic Interaction

Interactionists trained at the University of Chicago emphasized that events are fluid. How people define their situations can be altered. Roles can change as a result.

Most people need little convincing of this. Marriage illustrates the point quite well. Some marriages are filled with affection, while others are shrouded in hurt and bitterness. Some marriage unions are warm and cuddly, while others are rather distant or even cold in their outer appearance. The point is that marriages vary enormously in character. Very few marriages are cookie-cutter versions of cultural norms or legal institutions, as a simplistic reading of structural functionalism might lead one to anticipate. Nor are many marriages simply mirrors of a society's system of class relations or interest-group divisions, as a simplistic reading of conflict theory might lead one to anticipate. The character of a marriage cannot be prescribed by law or ordained by a fate in a way that leaves role occupants powerless to modify the relationships they find themselves in. If for no other reason than this, sociological theory needs to take adequate account of the microdynamics through which people directly involved in relationships coconstruct new meanings and co-redefine the role relationships that bind them together.

We know that couples actually shape and forge the particular character of their marriages through their actions and reactions over time. Interactionists watch as marriages once fresh and full of affection come to the point where they hit a fork in the road, when the accumulation of things done and said either takes the married couple on a path heading in the direction of deepening respect and mature affection (the well-aged fine wines of marriage) or on a path heading in the direction of mutual emotional abandonment or even contempt (the sour old vinegars of marriage). The fact is that people actually do have agency to act, and their actions and activities do make a difference.

People in a relationship have considerable ability to remold and reshape what exists between them: both the tenor of emotional feelings and the practical division of tasks and activities defining the relationship. But this can happen only on one condition: both people must want to reshape their relationship in more or less the same direction, and they must want this at the same time. It takes two to tango—to build a relationship permeated with more passion and respect takes two people simultaneously trying to kindle more passion and grow a deeper sense of mutual respect. One person acting alone is just spitting into the wind.[2] Symbolic interaction is *inter*action. Individual action is what is left of interaction when the *inter* has been amputated. It is not much fun for anyone at moments when a marriage is in this state. Relationships can fall into a pattern of having one person act unilaterally, forcing the other person to accommodate or leave. But when this happens the range of eventual outcomes, particularly in the tenor of feelings of connection between people, is severely limited. At that point the relationship ceases being a partnership of cocreation. It is natural for people who find themselves in a relationship like this, and who feel this way for a prolonged period, to become alienated not only from the other person but from themselves as well. This is surprisingly comparable to the kind of alienation from one's own self that Marx ascribed to workers in a capitalist society. Your time and effort become enslaved to goals and task assignments over which you have no control. They are imposed on you rather than owned by you, yet you watch your life essence dissipate in furtherance of those things while your own dreams languish without your ever really having an opportunity to try to make them materialize.

This is a pretty sad state of affairs, but a condition in which many people live out long stretches of their lives.

Mead was interested in *inter*action where people each adjust to the other, and in the process of sustained interaction can coconstruct an evolving relationship. He posited that this kind of adjustment takes place through layers and layers of interaction in which people *read gestures* of others, *role take* to imagine what those others are thinking, consciously reflect on their own *selves* both as they are (in any objective sense) and as they may seem to appear to others in this situation, engage in *imaginative rehearsal* about possible alternatives ways of responding, and then give the *adjusted response* they make after deciding what to do next. The work of role taking, reflection, and adjustment to others is part and parcel of what it means to have an interactive relationship in the sense Mead meant, with a great deal of cocreation over time.

The marriage example reveals a fundamental characteristic of the Chicago school of symbolic interaction. Symbolic interactionists of the Chicago school do not focus heavily on *why* things happen. Their concern is with process, with *how* things happen. In examining the unfolding of events, symbolic interactionists working within the Chicago tradition have found that reactions can be just as important as initial actions. What is subtly communicated is just as important as what is explicitly vocalized. What is perceived (definition of situation) is even more important than what is real when trying to understand and predict human behavior.

Consider an argument among college roommates. Depending on the flow of interaction, the argument can lead to big changes—one person moving out, for example. Short of severing a relationship, an argument can also lead to a fundamental redefinition of roles and relationships. This is positive when redefinition takes the form of people finding better ways of respectfully enjoying one another and accommodating to each other. Sometimes forms of redefinition are more negative, regularizing expressions of contempt through which people intentionally offend one another's sensitivities and sensibilities.

The dynamic character of everyday life, and the essential hollowness of deterministic models, was brought to life in Chicago interactionist works such as Tamotsu Shibutani's compelling story of a U.S. Army unit during World War II, *The Derelicts of Company K* (1978).[3] This work merits lengthy discussion because it puts deterministic models to a clear test. The pertinent historical factors are as follows. First, the United States was at war with Japan from 1941 to 1945. Second, at the time the war broke out, there were approximately 130,000 people of Japanese ancestry living in the Hawaiian Islands (then an overseas frontier territory that would not become a state until 1959), while another 130,000 people of Japanese ancestry were living on the mainland, mostly along the West Coast in places such as Seattle, Los Angeles, and California's Central Valley. Of these Japanese Americans, about half were citizens who had been born in the United States.

The remainder were noncitizens—at that time U.S. race-based laws prohibited immigrants from Asia and Africa from becoming naturalized citizens. Third, the U.S. government forced most of the mainland people of Japanese ancestry into what the government usually called *relocation camps*, located in remote areas away from the seacoast. These were in fact concentration camps (although they were nothing like the Nazi death camps people commonly think of when the term *concentration camp* is used). Fourth, a high proportion of young male U.S. citizens of Japanese ancestry volunteered for the army or were conscripted into the army, and most of them were sent off to war having been clearly told by their families that they needed to fight bravely for the United States to earn the trust of other Americans. Fifth, at the time, the U.S. Army was racially segregated, and most Japanese American soldiers were assigned to a single segregated fighting unit. That fighting unit was the 442nd Regimental Combat Team. During World War II, the 442nd became the most highly decorated unit of its size in U.S. military history, with over 9,000 Purple Hearts being awarded to soldiers of the unit during the war. In a single battle lasting five days in 1944, 121 men died and 700 were wounded in pitched fighting that saved 211 Texans from a battalion that had been cut off from the 36th Infantry Division and completely surrounded by enemy forces. Sixth, as young Japanese American men turned eighteen, many were eager to join the army and enter the ranks of what was regarded by them and many others as America's best fighting unit. This sentiment was typically encouraged by their families. These new recruits were prepared to run any risk for their country, the United States. It is with this historical background and this definition of situation that Shibutani's analysis starts.

By mid-1944, people in the United States could see an end to the war in Europe, perhaps in less than a year, but an end to the war in Asia seemed much further off. So by late 1944, the army stopped sending new Japanese American recruits to replenish its units in Europe, where the 442nd had been fighting Italians and Germans. Instead, the U.S. army now began sending new Japanese American recruits to language school at Fort Snelling in Minnesota. The troops being sent to Fort Snelling for language training were supposed to become interpreters for an anticipated invasion force to land in Japan.

The army wanted and expected the kind of eager young spit-and-polish recruits it had come to expect Japanese American soldiers to be, and that was exactly the mind-set of recruits who stepped off the bus at the beginning of training. Then symbolic interaction kicked in. A couple of white officers assigned to this particular Japanese American group were regarded by many of the soldiers as insensitive racists who viewed the recruits as inferior because of their ancestry. Progressively, the recruits' definition of situation changed, as they accumulated face-to-face experiences with those few officers and, importantly, as they talked among themselves about what their experiences with those officers said about the army. Peer groups thus shaped an emerging new collective awareness. As the recruits talked to the point of shaping a collective interpretation of events and therefore reshaping their definition of situation, they decided that the army was "racist" and "chickenshit." They came to feel that the defining quality of army life (as they were coming to view it after discussing and processing their experiences with those particular officers) was occupying the whole day with meaningless things, without effective coordination and often without apparent forethought by people with rank who hold you in contempt.

The views and feelings of this particular group of soldiers were aimed at the whole army even though their experience was localized to a few people and a relatively small number of events and encounters. This suggests a generalizable observation that can be communicated in the form of an axiom.

Social Location Axiom: **People tend to think that what they have personally encountered or heard from the people closest to them is authentic and representative and generally true.**

When definitions of situation changed, role redefinition was quick to follow. Some soldiers assumed roles as ringleaders and actively organized efforts to trivialize training activity. In the Fort Snelling case, the situation deteriorated to the point that several recruits intentionally began trying to be "screwup" soldiers for the express purpose of making their officers look bad. (To the American military's credit, it learned from the Fort Snelling case. It should also be mentioned that the U.S. military was formally integrated in 1948 and played a leading role in desegregating America and in socializing people to judge others on the basis of responsible performance rather than skin color.)

Shibutani was an intellectual grandchild of George Herbert Mead. That is to say, Shibutani's friend and teacher was the young student who took over Mead's role at the University of Chicago. This was one-time Chicago Bears football player Herbert Blumer. As Blumer's own work matured, and with his 1969 book, *Symbolic Interactionism*, he became the most articulate spokesperson for the view that society is defined by the kind of symbolic interaction taking place within it.[4] But while Blumer articulated the intellectual position, it was work such as Shibutani's that proved the point with extraordinarily detailed observation. The group of soldiers Shibutani studied seemed almost predestined to be model recruits instead of mess-ups. The army's structure, plus family needs and anticipatory socialization, almost guaranteed that this group would be made up of exemplary spit-and-polish soldiers. But something happened. This company of recruits took on a life of its own as soon as people began to interact and then process their experiences with peers. Orientation to the wider setting (in this case, the army) was redefined in light of direct experience and the peer discussion and processing of experiences that occurred in emerging social relationships within the unit. The same thing happens in every setting. How people process what is done and said forms meaning and gives rise to patterned response. Blumer said society is social interaction, and Shibutani was one of the symbolic interactionists doing the research to demonstrate that it can be.

Shibutani was particularly struck by the importance of peer groups, or groups of equals we associate with, and reference groups, or the groups we look to as yardsticks for measuring our own performance. A lot of socialization, or learning about behavior and expectations, takes place in these groups, as does anticipatory socialization, or learning about behavioral expectations applying to some role we expect to enter in the future. These are ideas found throughout the symbolic interactionist literature, and they provide us with predictive insight about socialization.

Principle of Socialization: **Other things being equal, socialization will be more effective to the degree that the person being socialized (a) depends on the socializing agent, (b) trusts the socializing agent, and (c) has an opportunity to act out or practice new norms and roles with peers.**

Ultimately, the Chicago school of symbolic interaction emphasizes the fluid nature of shared beliefs and role obligations when people deal with one another in sustained relationships over time. As Shibutani and many others have pointed out, trust is a crucial ingredient in the equation. The role occupants in a relationship tend to rely on one another more when trust builds over time, but they generally seek to limit their interdependence when experiences lead to mistrust. Importantly, trust differs from similarity, liking, or likability. Trust comes from experiences that suggest a person will do what he is counted on to do, rather than what is in his own immediate and personal self-interest (including leaving the work for everyone else to do). People have a built-in tendency to want to be surrounded by others who are reliable and show at least some indication of altruistic tendencies. Where trust is lacking, people tend to seek to limit interaction if possible, or to circumscribe interaction through rule-bound procedures if limiting interaction is not possible.

Trust Principle: **Other things being equal, people withdraw from roles/relationships if practical, and tend to use formal and informal rules to minimize their obligations and reduce room for ambiguity if withdrawal is not practical, (1) as a direct function of perceived vulnerability in the setting and (2) as an inverse function of degree of trust in the people in that setting.**

One more example may serve to further illustrate the extent to which, in Herbert Blumer's terms, society really is symbolic interaction. In a single generation, the United States has gone from a society in which women were relegated to subservient positions in all realms to something closer to parity in many job sectors. A massive social transformation like this requires new laws, changes in school policy, and so forth. But as much anything else, symbolic interactionists feel that it takes one-on-one communication to open minds and change world-views. Symbolic interactionists maintain that expanding horizons is something that sometimes has to be done the hard way, one person at a time, although legal and other institutional changes can certainly create conditions in which this is more likely to happen. Winning people over to a different way of think-ing and acting, one person at a time, often necessitates challenging interpersonal encounters rife with symbolic meaning. Interactionists are inclined to feel that everything starts with discussion and symbolic encounter. They tend to believe that it is only after receptive ground is tediously prepared that laws are passed and changes in occupational structure emerge. Fifty years ago, almost no women were accepted to medical school. In fact, women were thought by many of those who sat on medical school admissions committees to be unsuited for work in the medical professions. Now half of all those who become doctors are women. The change did not come easily. But from the vantage point of someone draw-ing on the symbolic interactionist perspective, the change was more bottom-up than top-down, requiring a great many hearts and minds to be opened through individual one-on-one encounters before success was possible. To the extent that the social interactionists are right, society really is symbolic interaction, and people really do have agency.

The Iowa School of Symbolic Interaction

The first long-running debate among symbolic interactionists concerned the source of fluidity in social encounters. Does interaction among people in a set-ting produce change purely out of happenstance? For example, consider an in-stance in which Aaron turns on the garbage disposal just as Joe is talking, result-ing in Sally's mishearing Joe and inaccurately concluding he is making a snide comment, to which Sally responds with anger and Joe counters in a disrespectful way, which makes Sally reply with disgust. Joe ends the exchange by storming out, leaving Sally feeling contempt and Joe looking for new friends (or a game of pickup basketball). If only Aaron had not turned on the garbage disposal at that particular moment, Sally and Joe might have remained friends. This is one of the kinds of scenarios Chicago school interactionists are alert to. Change is some-times planned out, but at other times it is rooted in unplanned or coincidental events. Chicago interactionists are interested in the fact that people can act and react in unexpected ways, making outcomes highly fluid and role/relationship change often subject to happenstance and seemingly somewhat random.

Symbolic interactionists of the Chicago school expect this kind of unfolding of events to occur in real life, and they consequently look for it. But there is a way to be a symbolic interactionist without giving so much credence to happenstance. That is, it is possible to think that society really is symbolic interaction, with roles and relationships given genuine shape by the people immediately embroiled in the situation, and nevertheless view outcomes as highly predictable because of the personalities involved. This describes the view of symbolic interactionists of the Iowa school and their intellectual descendants. They believe events tend toward predictable outcomes as a result of the convergence of a particular combination of personalities. No relationship is a mirror image of other relationships of the same kind because, even if the roles are the same (boss–employee, police officer–civilian, student–teacher) the personalities are different. Everybody carries their own baggage with them into situations. If one dad feels deep down that he is very smart but not very hip or coordinated, and another feels he is very hip, but not very smart or coordinated, and a third feels he is very coordinated, even if not very smart or hip, these three dads are likely to respond differently, and consistently and predictably so, when confronted with different kinds of situations involving their children and their children's friends. At least, this is what people influenced by the Iowa school of symbolic interactionists tend to think. The core self-concepts of these people will push interaction with their own children, and their children's friends and the parents of those friends, in a consistent direction. This puts a cast on things, and relationships with others evolve distinctively from that point.

Similar dynamics have been observed in organizations. Bosses who have doubts about their own ability commonly react in a predictable way. When confronting unexpected situations, they generally tend to retreat to role scripts. We see a very different pattern of reaction among those who are self-confident. They tend to respond to situations by moving away from routine and showing more tolerance for ambiguity. People in positions of authority with little self-assurance often tend to redefine roles in the direction of more routine, greater ritual in interpersonal relationships, and more power games. In contrast, people with high self-assurance who occupy positions of authority often tend to redefine roles in the direction of less routine, less ritual in interpersonal relationships, and fewer power games.[5]

This issue presents a nice contrast of how different groups of theorists would approach the situation. All interactionists would be interested in distinctions that arise within the particular relationship or setting, and all interactionists would study how these distinctions develop. Symbolic interactionists influenced by the Iowa school tend to emphasize that core self-concepts and most salient identities of the people in a relationship persistently push interaction in a consistent, predictable direction. Long-run outcomes are therefore constrained by a mix of personalities.

Self and *identity* are notions that do travel with people from role to role and from setting to setting. To the extent that self and identity influence the way a person interprets and responds to things, these concepts provide us with a solid framework for predicting outcomes of particular situations and the way in which roles and relationships can be expected to evolve.

Symbolic interactionists of the Chicago school counter that each ongoing relationship can easily become more distinctive and individualized over time as the course of events unfolds. Personality (core self) is thought to exert less influence. Eventual outcomes are thought to be more fluid and less predictable. But symbolic interactionists of all schools credit people with having agency and with being able to reshape the relationships they are engaged in. This is to some degree different from conflict theorists, who focus on the consistent pressures placed on people by their location in the class structure. From the perspective of conflict theory, long-run outcomes receive their basic contour from systems of wealth and privilege. And structural functionalists focus on the consistent pressures placed on people by existing cultural patterns, institutional arrangements, and legal restraints. Structural functionalists believe long-run outcomes are constrained by a variety of pressures originating in all those institutional spheres of activity.

The Chicago versus Iowa debate raises a serious issue. What determines the unique configuration that an ongoing relationship gravitates toward over time? People informed by the Iowa school are inclined to think core self-concept and salient identities are continually injected into interaction, and often in critical ways at turning-point moments. But people informed by the Chicago school are more likely to withhold a prediction about final outcomes because they are conscious that events can take unexpected twists and turns, and they tend to think core self ultimately takes a backseat to the *situational* self. (The situational self is how we think we look to others right now in the immediate situation, given what has just been done and said.)

If the core self is switched off a lot of the time—this is a premise built into Mead's Chicago school description of interaction in *Mind, Self, and Society*—then outcomes of any single interaction will be harder to predict because the baggage of core self will not always be contaminating every encounter and dictating the contour of every outcome.[6] If core self is switched off, or at least turned down most of the time, each single situation presents a new set of possible choices. The range of outcomes increases geometrically with all the permutations and combinations involved in long chains of interaction. But Iowa school interactionists do not believe the core self is switched off or turned down that easily. They think core self actually gets amplified precisely at those emotion-laden moments when a person has to consider an adjustment that could make a difference.

It was Manford Kuhn who led sociologists at the University of Iowa to explore the role of core self-concept in determining people's reactions to situations. Part of the method he and his colleagues pioneered was to ask people to answer the simple question "Who am I?" by writing down words or phrases to describe themselves.[7] It turns out that many people tend to define who they are using nouns to name key roles they occupy, for example, I am mother/father, daughter/son, sister/brother, student/teacher, employee/boss, boyfriend/girlfriend, team member. This suggests relatively strong identification with social structural positions. Other people respond with adjectives that have more to do with style or quality of performance in roles than with precise social structural position, for example, I am smart, hardworking, clever, diligent, and so forth.

It is hard to deny that on some level, sense of core self is a kind of baggage we carry with us from place to place. We all carry baggage but seldom stop to calculate how that baggage may influence our perceptions and alter our subsequent behavior. This is what Kuhn and his colleagues of the Iowa school of interaction call on us to do. The Iowa-Chicago debate will ultimately be resolved when we articulate theoretical principles explaining when, how, and to what degree different aspects of self-concept and different aspects of identity shut on and off or intensify or moderate with respect to how much influence they exert on the way people interpret and react to situations. To summarize, then, the discrepancy between the Iowa and Chicago schools centers on a long-running debate focused on the degree to which change in an interaction setting is (a) fluid and relatively unpredictable, because the activated self-concept tends to be situational and therefore highly variable from moment to moment; or (b) relatively predictable, because the aspects of core self-concept and salient identity are carried by people from situation to situation.

There has been plenty of interesting work done by sociologists attracted to this question.[8] We have found, for example, that people who feel they are being evaluated in unjustifiably positive terms sometimes act in ways that convey the fact that they actually do not deserve such a high rating. In other words, some people subconsciously seem to shape interactions to make the way they look to others correspond with what they believe themselves to be really like. This was a position advanced by David Heise in what he described as *affect control theory* in his 1979 book, *Understanding Events*, which looks deep down inside people where the core self lives.[9]

One of the difficulties in dealing with this subject is conceptual imprecision leading people to use terms in different ways without fully appreciating the differences of meaning that are masked by sloppy use of language. For example, *self* is often confused with *identity*. But how we see ourselves in terms of qualities, which are the real substance of who we are as individuals (i.e., the core self), is not the same as our identity. Having an identity is feeling that our memberships in groups or social categories are vital; in fact, the notion of identity is so salient that it can sometimes shape our perceptions and reactions. This normally happens when we have come to believe that many people relate to us in terms of our group memberships rather than because of the quality of our individual performance or the content of our individual character. For instance, many of the people who have a strong sense of racial or ethnic identity are the people who have learned from experience to expect that they will be treated differently by appreciable numbers of people because of their race or ethnicity rather than in terms of anything for which they are individually responsible. Of course, the line between self and identity is sometimes blurred. With gender, for example, many people feel they both are distinctively "manly" or "feminine" on the inside, in a way that is intrinsic to themselves and more than a label imposed by the world.

Although self and identity are analytically distinct concepts, sociological findings about both self and identity converge in an important respect, suggesting a principle that has broad application.

Commitment Availability Principle: Other things being equal, the intensity of a person's commitment to a social unit, and one's inclination to make sacrifices for collective purposes, (1) increase to the degree that one's sense of self and identity are acknowledged and valued in the setting, and (2) decrease to the extent that one's sense of self and identity are unrecognized, unappreciated, or demeaned in the setting.

The Commitment Availability Principle contains what proves to be a critical recognition about organized social settings. In order for there to be at least moderate levels of efficiency and effectiveness in satisfaction of mission-critical activities in any organized setting, it is important that people in a setting have senses of their own personal attributes and group memberships that are consistent with conscientious role performance in that setting. To the degree that these conditions are compromised, it becomes easier to divert people to alternative agendas. Sometimes those personal agendas merely diverge from the organizational agenda. Sometimes they actually oppose the organizational agenda. In either case, they divert focus and energy.

The concepts of self and identity, so important in symbolic interactionist discussions, illustrate the importance of being careful with our definitions. The terms are often used interchangeably in everyday conversation. Even among sociologists, the definitions used for one term or the other are not always consistent. Indeed, there is a good reason sociological theorists let one another define concepts like self and identity in a variety of ways. Tolerance for individuality of approach allows people to have the intellectual latitude necessary to carry their thinking out to its logical conclusion. But because so much individuality of approaches is fostered, in the interest of communicating accurately with readers it is important for every social scientist to strive as much as possible for definitional precision.

Dramaturgy

Symbolic interactionism of both the Chicago and Iowa varieties explores the work of *coconstruction* as people modify their relationships over time with the natural unfolding of interaction. Nothing stays the same. Not only can new feelings be created, but old feelings atrophy if they are not revitalized. We are all familiar with the example of young married people, very much in love, turning into couch potatoes with seemingly independent relationships with the same living-room television screen. Unless people in love do things to keep the fire alive, love atrophies. Maintaining feelings takes work (the second law of thermodynamics). It takes work on the part of both people who want the same (or something close to the same) thing out of the relationship. Of course, if married people are fortunate enough to keep the fire alive, being passionately and playfully in love at fifty or sixty or seventy means something different from being passionately and playfully in love at twenty or thirty or forty. This does not happen automatically; it needs to be molded and shaped and then periodically shored up and reinforced or it does not happen. When it does happen, it does not stay around unless actively and continually enticed to stay. Note, then, that the defining feature of the symbolic interactionist perspective is concern with people's mutually interacting in ways that shape change in the relationship. For both the Chicago and Iowa interactionists, this is collaborative work. But it must always be remembered that the interactionists focus on agency and adjustment because they find these things to be interesting, important, and desirable. This does not imply that they are always common. Habitual patterns of behavior are often developed to "get the job done" or to "stay together" when there are sharp and potentially irresolvable visions of what the relationship should be.

When Blumer said society is symbolic interaction, he could (as a former football player) have just as correctly said symbolic interaction is a team sport. This is crucial to remember when coming to really understand symbolic interactionism. The shape of change evolves within the give-and-take of *inter*action (involving meaningful role taking, reflection, and effort to adjust) among the people embroiled in relationships where there is a basis of trust that people will act in ways in which you count on them to act and where there are similar ideas about the direction of change that would be desirable.

Even though most people think of it as a variety of symbolic interactionism, dramaturgy is fundamentally different from both the Chicago and Iowa schools. Specifically, dramaturgical analysis focuses on the way people symbolically communicate in order to project views or convey impressions. Dramaturgical analysis, which is nicely summarized in Erving Goffman's 1959 book, *The Presentation of Self in Everyday Life*, specifically deals with impression management. Goffman characterizes all the world as a stage and uses the theatrical concepts of a *front stage* (what the audience sees), a world of controlled and manipulated impressions broadcast outward for the consumption of others; and a *back stage* (what the actors know), a world of more honest and sincere interaction that few people are privy to.[10]

We are all familiar with front-stage efforts at *impression management*. This is what makes itself apparent whenever anyone is straining hard to look impressive. Goffman's focus is on the crafted images, usually positive, that people try to project of themselves.

We can also speak of *alter-casting*, whereby one person tries to portray someone else by projecting crafted, often negative, images of that person.[11] Because it is a major way in which feedback is distorted and conflict plays itself out, alter-casting may prove to be an important concept when symbolic interaction is integrated with structural functionalism and conflict theory.

There are many settings in which some people are in a position to demonize or otherwise alter-cast opponents. Dismissing people or their positions through mockery or straw-man argumentation is a common technique. (Even though bearing false witness is proscribed by the ninth commandment it is commonplace.) To the degree to which impression management and alter-casting become commonplace in a setting, the adjustment processes Mead describes are impaired and a mechanism for functional change is compromised.

The fact everyone understands what "impression management" means is proof enough that Goffman identified something that is very real. But while most symbolic interactionists feel comfortable identifying dramaturgy as an interactionist perspective, there is a fundamental distinction between Chicago and Iowa on one hand and dramaturgy on the other. The Chicago and Iowa frameworks are both explicitly about coconstructed change. Impression management is often about a relatively static and fictional image that is projected from a single source and aimed at a receiver. The focus moves from what is cocrafted by two people who are synergistically changing both sides of their relationship at the same time with ongoing interaction, to one person's projection of an illusion he or she hopes other people will respond to as real. Recognizing this distinction makes it easier to appreciate the real root concerns of the symbolic interactionist traditions. By contrasting Iowa and Chicago with dramaturgy, we can more fully appreciate that symbolic interactionists of the Iowa school and, even more, the Chicago school, are fundamentally interested in creative change as a collective product. They focus on how people can work together to modify what they started with.

Role Theory

From the beginning, some symbolic interactionists were grappling with the challenge of dealing with social structural realities. The fact that there are people in recognizable roles as students all over the world, doing similar things with other people who are in recognizable teacher roles, and often interacting in similar places recognizable as schools, should be enough to establish that we individuals do not simply go out and imaginatively construct unique worlds for ourselves. Instead, we inherit some things by virtue of being born in a particular society.

What we inherit includes a preexisting framework of social institutions (which structural functionalists are especially interested in) and a preexisting framework of class and stratification (which conflict theorists are particularly interested in). We take those preexisting things that we inherit and then shape them somewhat as we take one small corner of the social world and make it our own (which the symbolic interactionists are particularly interested in). And this always involves negotiated exchanges of different kinds (which the exchange theorists are particularly interested in). All this is captured in the Principle of Role Redefinition, developed in chapter 10.

We are not completely free agents when shaping our own little corner of the world, because other people are also in the mix and seeking their own accommodations. We have agency, but other people do as well. It is together with others that we shape and mold the reality we will live with. This idea is nicely conveyed by Peter Berger and Thomas Luchmann in their 1967 book, *The Social Construction of Reality*.[12] We are all social carpenters and psychological plumbers and management electricians engaged in constantly remodeling that portion of the social world we traverse. But the remodeling jobs each of us engages in take place within a preexisting framework defined by the institutions, organizations, and class structure that permeate the society. Our connection with those institutions, organizations, and class structure is based on the roles we occupy.

Role theorists try to deal with structural realities while keeping faith with the most basic tenets of symbolic interactionism. They do so by focusing on roles (rights, responsibilities, and dignities that would be expected of anyone occupying a particular position) and on interpersonal relationships (aspects of role performance that are unique to particular combinations of people and would most likely change in the event that the role occupants were replaced).[13] Of course, all sociologists recognize that roles are among the basic building blocks of social organization. This makes role theory a natural connection point among all the theoretical frameworks.

Role theorists, among them Ralph Turner in his 1990 article on role change,[14] ask fundamental questions about the roles and relationships inside institutions and organizations: How is it that people get assigned the roles they have? Why do those roles have the general form that they do? Once people are in a role relationship, how likely are they to individualize that relationship, and how does that process of improvisational change really occur? How does the wider environment influence the degree of latitude people have in recrafting a role or relationship? Can people make their own deal? How can people be pressured to pull their own weight if they are inclined to leave all the work for others (perhaps often expecting an equal or greater share of credit for themselves and being dismissive of those more deserving of credit)?

William Goode was one of many important developers of role theory. Goode's concept of *role strain*, or the demand overload we experience when we consider all our various role commitments and obligations, is one of the most powerful concepts sociologists have.[15] How do people respond as role strain mounts? Arlie Hochschild explores the challenges posed by role strain in her 1997 study of the difficulty of balancing work and family. She argues that role strain is a pivotal factor driving social change in contemporary America. Hochschild's research demonstrates that as people spend more time at work, family members have less time and emotional energy to give one another. The very texture of our lives is changing as a result. In the past, people tended to be relatively private at work and to look to the family for the bulk of their socioemotional support. But increasingly, large numbers of people find that they are growing more private in the family context while looking to the workplace for the bulk of their socio-emotional support.[16]

Hochschild's work thus convincingly implicates the connection between (a) the symbolic interactionists' primary interest in the unfolding adjustments of ordinary people in roles that are common in a society, and (b) the structural functionalists' primary interest which ways that one institutional sphere of life (say, family) is transformed over time, either (i) in response to changes external to the structural and cultural features of the society itself (as an example, be-cause of evolving technology) or (ii) changes in the society's other institutional spheres (for widely observable alteration on family dynamics in response to pervasive changes in the nature of work large numbers of people in the society are engaged in). All this makes role theory a natural bridge between symbolic interactionism and structural functionalism, as illustrated by Hage and Pow-ers in *Post-Industrial Lives*. Complex organizations, social institutions, and class structure are all real, and they do determine a great deal. But life in them abso-lutely necessitates a degree of adjustment. The types and degree of adjustment required are variable and open to social science explanation. But adjustment is always required to some degree, and that adjustment occurs through a process of symbolic interaction.

While the old-style bureaucratic workplace called for comparatively little adjustment beyond accommodation to rules, the innovation-producing work-place emblematic of a postindustrial economy requires more interactive play and flexibility from workers. Increasingly, the individual who has the best idea at the moment, not the person with the highest job title, is the one people listen to. More people have a career trajectory of being shifted from one project team to another every several months or couple of years, instead of going to work in the same section of the same building with the same people for one, two, three, four, or five decades. To the degree that the teams are engaged in developing or delivering innovative or customized products and services, there needs to be a lot more nuanced communication among team members and clients and outside vendors, in order to find a good solution for the problem at hand. Thus, change in the things organizations need to do in order to remain competitive (a move from overwhelming preoccupation with cost efficiency to the primacy of efficacious problem solving) dictates greater levels of coconstruction and change as functional requirements, and structural change is necessitated in order to encourage and sustain interaction of that kind. It does not happen automatically.

All this implies something about structural functionalist thinking and the relationship between symbolic interactionism and structural functionalism. We should not ask whether early structural functionalists were right or wrong when they seemingly took structural determinacy for granted. A more contemporary structural functionalist view would be that, to be able to function well, all organizations need people to exercise a certain degree of agency. Symbolic interaction, then, is an absolutely necessary process that needs to unfold within organizations in order for those organizations to be able to function. Remember, though, that this is symbolic interaction as Mead defined it, characterized by real listening, reflection, and earnest effort to meaningfully change in order to contribute more to an enterprise shared with other role occupants. In other words, we have to speak sociologese and not fall back into English. If we were using ordinary English meanings, more interaction would simply mean more words exchanged between more people. That is *not* Mead's meaning as applies in this case. Mead's meaning for more "symbolic interaction" is more profound listening; deeper reflection about what there might be in the observations, concerns, and suggestions of others; more openness to experiment with coconstructued solutions; and willingness to adopt and sustain those changes that pragmatically yield good results.

The treatment offered in *Making Sense of Social Theory* suggests a scientific approach to theory construction. We should not bother to ask whether early symbolic interactionists were "always right" or "always wrong" when those interactionists seemingly took human agency for granted. "Always" is a metatheoretical way of looking at the world that can only be quasi-scientific. To be more scientific we need to adopt a "sometimes" way of looking at the world. We need to ask, "when?" "where?" and "how?" And we subsequently need to advance theoretical principles that might help us understand, explain, and predict "when," "where," and "how." Organizations that need to generate a steady stream of innovations have to encourage more agency than organizations doing the same routine work over and over again. Symbolic interactionists have always appreciated that there are practical limits to agency in any environment. A structural functional approach to this subject gives us a way of understanding the variations in those limits, at least in complex organizations, based on the goals of those organizations and their organizational structure. This affirms one of the starting points of this book. The different theoretical perspectives do not invalidate one another. Instead, they work together in an additive way. Each gives us a different piece of a bigger puzzle.

It does not end social science inquiry to say that symbolic interaction is a functional requisite for certain kinds of organizations operating under particular kinds of conditions. From a science point of view, this only gets our inquiry off to a good start by identifying types of variability we need to explain. Organizations are not all the same in terms of the amount of agency they need people to exercise, or the issues over which agency needs to be exercised for the organization to function effectively. These are things we want to understand and explain, although we already have a first approximation answer in the form of the Innovation/Complexity Principle, introduced in chapter 6. The same conditions that privilege certain alliance structures over hierarchy and markets also necessitate the exercise of more agency in order for inter- and intraorganizational activity to be coordinated effectively. Agency is essential for success to the degree that challenges are complex and conditions require innovation.[17]

Recap

Symbolic interaction is distinctive in its focus, not just on individual agency, but on coagency. Symbolic interactionists focus on ways in which meaning is cooperatively constructed. Everyone has some voice, and arrangements that are concluded are a synthesis resulting from give-and-take. The outcomes of that give-and-take are influenced by the self-concepts and identities people bring with them into new situations. But the degree to which self-concepts and identities affect outcomes is still under study. Class structure, institutional arrangements, and location in organizations greatly influence people's lives, but wherever people find themselves, they use their social skills to modify and temper their social surroundings, generally by modifying roles and relationships. Keeping this in mind helps us connect symbolic interaction with the conflict and structural functionalist perspectives.

Some Terms to Know

Peer Group: A group of equals we associate closely with.

Reference Group: A group we look to as a yardstick for measuring our own performances.

Socialization: Learning from others, especially about behavioral expectations.

Anticipatory Socialization: A type of socialization, specifically, learning about behavioral expectations applying to some role we expect to enter in the future.

Core Self-Concept: Traits we see as deeply ingrained in and significantly defining our character.

Situational Self-Concept: A sense a person has of the quality of his or her performance in an immediate situation.

Interpersonal Relationship: Aspects of role performance that are unique to particular combinations of people and are likely to change in the event that the role occupants are replaced.

Role: Rights, obligations, and dignities defining what would be expected of anyone occupying a particular social position.

Role Strain: The cumulative weight of all the demands a person confronts in his or her various roles.

Review of Axiom and Principles

Social Location Axiom: People tend to think that what they have personally encountered or heard from the people closest to them is authentic and representative and generally true.

Principle of Socialization: Other things being equal, socialization will be more *effective* to the degree that the person being socialized (a) depends on the socializing agent, (b) trusts the socializing agent, and (c) has an opportunity to act out or practice new norms and roles with peers.

Trust Principle: Other things being equal, people withdraw from roles/relationships if practical, and tend to use formal and informal rules to minimize their obligations and reduce room for ambiguity if withdrawal is not practical, (1) as a direct function of perceived vulnerability in the setting and (2) as an inverse function of degree of trust in the people in that setting.

Commitment Availability Principle: Other things being equal, the intensity of a person's commitment to a social unit, and one's inclination to make sacrifices for collective purposes, (1) increase to the degree that one's sense of self and identity are acknowledged and valued in the setting, and (2) decrease to the extent that one's sense of self and identity are unrecognized, unappreciated, or demeaned in the setting.

Quiz

Check your answers in the back of the book. If you get any wrong, consider reviewing chapter 13 before continuing.

1. What is the most fundamental difference between dramaturgical analysis and mainstream (Chicago or Iowa) symbolic interactionism?
2. Symbolic interactionists of the Iowa school believe that outcomes in social situations are rather predictable. What makes outcomes relatively predictable, in their view?
3. Define:
   a. Identity
   b. Role
4. What does the Trust Principle suggest a person will tend to do when he or she feels trust is lacking in a role she or he occupies or in a relationship where she or he interacts?

Application Exercise

Describe an event in which it seems to you that either impression management or alter-casting was used. Assess how things turned out in this situation.

14

Exchange Theory on
What People Get from Others

EXCHANGE THEORY WAS RATHER SLOW TO TAKE SHAPE as a self-identified perspective distinct from the other theoretical paradigms. Like symbolic interaction, exchange theory was born of an effort to bring people as decision makers into sociological theory. Exchange was initially thought of as a generic concern of equal interest to everyone, with a few of the theorists who were already working within each of sociology's other theoretical perspectives taking some special interest in exchange phenomena. But over time, those interested in exchange began talking more to one another and formulating strategies for trying to understand this aspect of social reality. As they did this, there began to emerge a perspective that is somewhat distinct and deserves separate recognition and review.

Exchange Metatheory: Motives and Calculations

As introduced earlier, the basic premise of exchange theory is that every person is, on some level, oriented to making choices based on calculations about risks and benefits. The Benefit Maximization Axiom places appreciation of motives at the heart of any exchange theoretical understanding of human decision making.

Benefit Maximization Axiom: People tend to make benefit-maximizing decisions based on their priorities.

While the Benefit Maximization Axiom is an important metatheoretical tool, it is less informative than may seem at first glance, for it leaves challenging questions unanswered. Important orienting questions for exchange theory include: What do people value, and why? What kinds of decisions are most often motivated by cost-benefit calculations, and what kinds of decisions are typically governed by other considerations, such as altruistic concern for others or commitment to rules even when the rules work against one's self-interest? What structural arrangements can be understood as emerging to facilitate, moderate, or control individual exchanges, and what is the birthing process through which such structural arrangements take shape and are institutionalized? It is in answering these orienting questions that the boundary conditions for exchange theory will be established and practical utility and pertinence of exchange theory relative to other theoretical perspectives will be determined.

Thinking of Exchange in Narrow Terms

When most Americans use the word *exchange,* a financial sale or purchase is often the first thing that comes to mind. Would you rather buy a soda for one price or a cup of coffee for twice as much, or would you perhaps rather have free water from a drinking fountain and save your money? Would you prefer to spend a lot of money on a great sound system and eat peanut butter for a year, or eat what you want while you listen to the radio? Or would you perhaps rather put your money in the bank, or invest it in the stock market? Would you rather go to a movie or buy a book? Which movie or book? Would you rather study for a test or go to a party or spend extra time at work? In a sense, these are all utilitarian economic questions. They suggest at least the possibility of rational calculation by weighing costs and benefits, with the determination of benefits influenced by some combination of personal taste and immediate need.

Thinking of Exchange in Broad Terms

From the start, those sociologists who were most informed by utilitarian economics had a special interest in economic exchange. But it is important to stop and think about the fact that many noncommercial transactions can be viewed as exchanges, and early sociologists understood this fact. When you say hello to someone and anticipate an acknowledgment in return, there is a kind of exchange going on. At least most exchange theorists view it that way. Think about how you feel when you say hello to someone, but that person fails to acknowledge you. Do you say hello the next time you see that person? That may depend on whether, deep down, you really consider this an exchange. If you offer your positive recognition as a gift in the truest sense of the term, freely given without regard to how it will be received or whether it will be reciprocated, the lack of acknowledgment should not matter. But if you offer your positive recognition to other people in the expectation of and with the hope of receiving a certain amount of positive recognition in return, you may think twice about acknowledging the person next time.

When thought of as an exchange, recognizing others without being recognized in return can be seen as a bad trade, especially if it involves a loss of face. In a way, this kind of experience can result in a person's social capital being reduced (recalling the concept of social capital from chapter 12). And to what beneficial end for you? To no beneficial end at all for you if your investment failed to yield the expected returns of (a) enjoying the social acceptance of those you hope accept you and (b) experiencing the upward value in your social capital that is implicit when others indicate (especially when the right people indicate, and especially when they indicate in public) that you are a person who is worth acknowledging. All this is as an exchange theorist might view it. Exchange theorists' axiomatic assumptions lead them to believe that people are generally motivated to act because of the cost-benefit calculations they make.

The more we think conceptually about exchange, the more interesting it becomes. When a person gives a friend a birthday card and gets some good feeling from seeing pleasant surprise register on the friend's face, is this an exchange? Or should it considered an act of exchange done only in the expectation of reciprocity?[1] Does a norm of reciprocity imply a kind of long-term exchange relationship, with social exchange as the mechanism people use to sustain their relationships?

Can it be thought of as an exchange when you give directions to a stranger in anticipation that someone else will return the favor to you the next time you find yourself a stranger in a strange place? Most exchange theorists would regard this as a clear example of the ubiquitous phenomenon of "generalized exchange" or freely giving to others (including people you may not even know) without an expectation that those particular individuals will be around to respond in kind when you need it, but with the conviction that someone else (quite possibly a complete stranger) will reply in kind at the moment you are in need of similar assistance.[2] Indeed, many people conceive of every transmission as an exchange. Part of the challenge of exchange theory, and a reason exchange theorists enjoy interacting with one another so much, is the fun people have in discussing what really does or does not constitute an exchange. Discussion on these matters is unresolved at this point. But one thing exchange theorists do agree on is that the individual act of a single exchange can be viewed as the most rudimentary and fundamental building block of all social organization.

Symbolic Exchange

From the start, both George Herbert Mead and Émile Durkheim conceived of human interaction in terms of symbolic exchange. For Mead, interaction is based on exchange of gestures that are packed with meaning. He specifically wrote about symbolic interaction as an exchange of gestures. And for Durkheim, awareness of the exchange dimension of interaction bordered on mystical. Do you recall Durkheim's preoccupation, really almost an obsession, with societal integration? And what integrates modern industrial society more than anything else? According to Durkheim in his early work, the answer is division of labor grounded in the complex networks of economic exchanges people rely on in order to acquire all the goods and services they cannot provide for themselves. And how many of sociology's other founding figures were economists who initially focused on exchange aspects of social life and then branched out to sociology as they sought answers to their questions? We can start with Marx, Weber, Pareto, and Veblen.

Durkheim's later work describes how exchange integrates society in ways that go beyond provision of goods and services by symbolically validating the significance of relationships and by heralding the importance of those relationships. According to Durkheim, the primary purpose of the most important ritual behaviors is to allow people to acknowledge and celebrate the connections linking them. This view receives its clearest expression in Durkheim's last great work, *The Elementary Forms of Religious Life*, published in 1912.[3]

It was through reading *The Elementary Forms of Religious Life* that the British and French anthropological communities became aware of Durkheim's functional theorizing and began to apply his ideas. Durkheim's *Elementary Forms* and the anthropological works that followed, written by people such as Siegfried Nadel (who profoundly influenced role theory, exchange theory, and network theory in sociology with his short conceptual book *The Theory of Social Structure*),[4] focused explicitly on rituals affirming membership and celebrating the distinctiveness of groups. Of all the rituals studied by the early structural functionalists, exchange rituals gained the most attention because they gave clues about alliances and affiliations that had hitherto gone unobserved or had been underappreciated.

Among the first of the anthropological works to follow Durkheim's conceptual lead was Bronislaw Malinowski's 1922 study of the Trobriand Islands, *Argonauts of the Western Pacific*.[5] A key facet of Malinowski's study was his report on a decidedly noneconomic exchange of armlets and necklaces known as the *kula ring*. The Trobriand Islands consist of a circular archipelago. In a kula ring, there is an exchange of armlets moving in one direction within the circular island chain, and exchange of necklaces moving in the other direction. The armlets and necklaces are made of local materials, so on the surface the exchange is of limited material value. This is not a barter of something one has excess of for something one cannot find on one's own. Instead, kula exchange is understood as a giving of a gift that is actually an opportunity to revive and reaffirm a prior relationship (whether it be a relationship of equals or a subordinate-superordinate relationship). It may interest readers to know that some of the implications of this exchange were worked out in a book (*The Gift*, 1925) written by one of the lone members of Durkheim's cadre of young protégés to survive World War I, Durkheim's own nephew, Marcel Mauss.[6] Mauss helped carry Durkheim's theoretical orientation into anthropology, influencing overlapping but distinct structural functionalist and exchange perspectives in the process. This exchange orientation was later recaptured by Robert K. Merton and others for reexport back to sociology. It is also worth noting that this exchange orientation validates the symbolic interactionist view that relationships must be actively reaffirmed and reinvigorated in order to be sustained. A relationship that is not actively sustained on a symbolic level will be muted and will atrophy.

Reaffirmation Axiom: **Social ties are reaffirmed and strengthened by events suggesting mutual recognition and acceptance.**

Exchange theorists, over and over again in setting after setting, have discovered that exchange rituals are a common instrument people use for symbolically affirming relationships and keeping them alive. Sociological treatments of symbolic exchange focus on gift giving as a strategy for cementing friendships and affirming alliances in everyday life. A perfect illustration is found in Christmas and Hanukkah gift-giving practices. In the 1920s, when the research for *Middletown* was conducted, Americans were giving many more gifts to neighbors than they do now. Perhaps Americans were more generous a century ago. But exchange theorists offer another explanation for the change in gift-giving practices. The prevailing pattern a century ago was to give simple, inexpensive, homemade gifts such as Christmas cookies. Such gifts have mainly symbolic value, specifically announcing that people have time for one another and might reasonably call on one another for help.

In *Middletown*, gift recipients typically included people living up and down the road who might do things such as give you a ride to work if you, for example, had a flat tire; they also included a broad swath of extended family living anywhere nearby. That was, after all, the 1920s, when car batteries were less reliable, when car tires frequently went flat, and when bosses were far more insistent that people start the workday precisely on time. It was also an age when people installed the electrical wiring in their homes themselves, fixed their own roof leaks, and even built their own garages and barns on weekends (in "barn raisings") with the help of family, friends, and neighbors. Exchange theorists do not think Americans gave more gifts in the 1920s because they were inherently disposed to be more generous in those days. Exchange theorists think Americans gave more gifts because their pattern of life was different. They had a habit of relying on a larger number of others for help under a wider range of circumstances. They more frequently relied on others, and consequently needed to symbolically affirm more relationships.[7] We can reasonably infer, as a corollary from the Reaffirmation Axiom, that the size of a person's network for symbolic exchange will vary in direct proportion to that person's expectation of having to rely on the cooperation and support of others in the future.

Rational Choice and Game Theory

Most versions of exchange theory rely on a rational choice model of behavior. Exchange decisions are often made on the basis of simple cost-benefit calculations such as those described by George Homans in *Social Behavior: Its Elementary Forms*.[8] Rational choice theorists have made steady strides in trying to develop and test their explanations. One of the interesting applications, which illustrates the versatility of rational choice analysis, is the discovery that there seems to be a balance between what religious congregations demand from parishioners and what they offer to parishioners. This idea was first suggested by Peter Berger in his book *The Sacred Canopy*,[9] and it was more systematically developed by economist Larry Iannaccone.[10] Some congregations ask a great deal (mandatory tithing, for example) and offer a great deal (for instance, help finding jobs for congregants who are unemployed). Other congregations ask comparatively little and in return offer comparatively little by way of tangible benefits (in the here and now, as distinct from guidance in finding one's way to an afterlife). Congregations that ask little but give a great deal of material support go bankrupt, and those that ask a great deal and give little in return tend not to survive because, as Iannaccone hypothesizes, people find what they might conceive of as a better deal elsewhere. The congregations that survive are those that either (a) ask comparatively little but basically leave people to find their material safety net elsewhere or (b) give a great deal of tangible support to people when they need it but ask for a good deal in return.

As Homans aptly points out, drawing from both utilitarian economics and behavioral psychology, that rational choice is essentially a calculation of expected costs and probable benefits that might be expected from one possible courses of action relative to possible alternative courses of action.[11] In doing what we are doing right now, we are accepting expected costs in the anticipation of expected benefits. We are simultaneously forgoing the benefits we think we could get by doing something else. To borrow a useful concept from economics, we are forgoing *opportunity costs.*

Even when we are continuing in an old pattern of action, there are still rational calculations to be made. The last bite of food we took may have satisfied our hunger (*satiation* in psychological terms), so being able to have another bite of food may lose its appeal for a few hours (the *law of diminishing returns* in economic terms). This presents people at a restaurant with the classical situation for rationally calculating the point at which to stop eating (the point of *marginal utility* in economic terms). You are out with someone on a date and stop at a restaurant on the way home from a movie. You stop because you are hungry and want a slice of pie. The pie is good, and the cost is little enough that you are glad you stopped at the restaurant. You conclude that you made an accurate rational choice decision because it seems to you that satisfying your hunger was worth the money you had to spend. Then the waiter comes and asks you if you would like another slice of pie. You figure that another piece of pie would be the same price, because the menu hasn't changed. The first slice of pie satiated your appetite sufficiently so that you are no longer very hungry. Do you really want another piece?

The pie example is interesting because it can be used to make Homan's concerns come to life. If hunger was the whole reason for stopping, why not go to the grocery store for a half gallon of milk, a package of celery, and a canister of peanut butter to take home? This probably would have been cheaper than stopping at the restaurant for pie, and the peanut butter approach might have the added benefit of allowing for leftovers to be stored in preparation for the eventuality of hunger tomorrow. Or by going to the restaurant, were you actually doing more than satisfying hunger? Might it be that you were also "buying time" to talk with your date without the prying eyes of family members or roommates around? Just what is it that makes this restaurant stop worth the cost? And whoever made up the rule that a movie followed by a stop at a restaurant makes for a good date? Why not go on a date to the coin-operated laundry with dirty clothes and talk while the clothes are being washed and dried? That would be a practical and economically rational place to spend an evening together. But, as Homans points out, the reason why people want what they want is sociological rather than economic. And how individuals project costs and weigh probabilities is subject to a complex mix of considerations.

When rational calculation is assumed, outcomes can be predicted and the consequences of various changes in scenario can be worked out using game theory, but this can accurately be done only so long as players are willing and able to make a wide range of assumptions about the people whose behavior is being modeled. The utility of game theory is strictly limited to situations in which the number of pertinent variables is limited and relationships among variables are reasonably well known, as explained by John Harsanyi and Reinhard Selten in their 1977 book, *A General Theory of Equilibrium in Games and Social Situations.*[12]

For rational choice theory, one of the most vexing issues is that of *externalized costs* (a concept originally borrowed from economics employed in a more scientific way, with more attention to explanation of variance, in sociological analysis). Externalized costs are side effects the actor is allowed to ignore—expenses that can be ignored in the cost-benefit calculations of some actors because they are absorbed by someone else. Examples might include a government building a new and better transportation corridor so that industry can transport products at a lower coast, or depleting valuable resources that are not replaced.

If the state provides roads and water delivery systems for a factory that does not pay taxes for a period of time, the cost of transport and utility infrastructure is to some degree paid for by the society at large. This portion of the cost of production is externalized in the sense that the producer is freed from paying the full and true cost of operating. In this instance the costs of production are socialized (which gives some penetrating new meaning to the term *socialism*). Or if a student takes friends home to eat dinner from Mom's fridge, the meal is free to the student only if the cost is externalized to Mom (who is typically quite happy to oblige).

Fixed costs are also important to calculate. When a fishing company borrows money to purchase a large fishing trawler, the loan must be repaid with interest whether the ship sails or not. If the ship sails, the crew needs to be paid whether the ship puts out all its fishing nets or only half its nets. The costs of operation are largely fixed. So to improve cost-benefit ratios, shipowners need to have their ships stay at sea as long as possible, keep as many miles of net out as possible, to catch as many marketable fish as possible. The more financially overextended a business is, the closer it is to losing collateral if it does not do everything it can to maximize revenue stream. Therefore, the more incentive the business has for externalizing costs whenever possible by, for example, extracting everything it can from the environment today without worrying about sustaining the fisheries for the future if business survivability is tenuous in the present.

Externalization of costs to others (including future generations) and absorption of risk by others (including workers willing to risk dangerous conditions because they have few options and have bills to pay) each tend to increase to the degree that income is scarce relative to outflow. For instance, when indigenous men fishing in small boats use explosives to catch more fish, but in so doing destroy coral reefs and reduce their future catch, you know costs are being externalized. And when factory trawlers deplete fish stocks by laying out miles of net, you know costs are being externalized. Knowledge of economic conditions can help us understand such scenarios. Another example is when greenhouse workers in poor countries accept exposure to pesticides because they need a job to feed their children, but they do not realize that the traces of pesticide they bring home at night can find their way back to their children in dozens of ways, such as washing children's clothes in the same water as the parent's work clothes. The more viable options one has, the less compelled one feels to take on such risks.

Balancing Power in Exchange through Pricing

Richard Emerson outlines a dramatically different approach to the study of exchange in a groundbreaking 1962 paper, "Power-Dependence Relations."[13] Emerson starts by describing simple exchange relations in terms of dependence and power. The more a person needs what she gets from an exchange, and the fewer alternatives she has for satisfying her needs elsewhere, then the more dependent she is on continuation of the relationship and the more power her exchange partners will have to extract compliance as a condition for continuing in the exchange relationship.

This seems straightforward enough. But Emerson develops these points and reaches conclusions that are anything but obvious, and these have been elaborated on by other scholars over the years.[14] First, conceiving of exchange in terms of shifting patterns of power and dependence leads to the conclusion that all participants in voluntary exchange are to some degree dependent on continuation of the relationship, even if only in a tiny way, because (exchange theorists conceive of it) every party continuing the exchange relationship does get something useful out of that exchange relationship. It also suggests that any change in the terms of exchange rearranges patterns of dependence. So when a more-powerful exchange partner forces a more-dependent exchange partner to pay more dearly for continuation of the relationship, the more-powerful exchange partner suddenly becomes somewhat more dependent than he had been, and consequently somewhat less powerful, at the same time that the person who started out more dependent and less powerful in the relationship now becomes more powerful (although perhaps somewhat poorer) than he had been. Hence, the relationship moves toward balance in power and dependence. For example, a popular person in high school may not tolerate an unpopular student hanging around unless that less-popular individual is obsequious and does things for Mr. or Ms. Popular. But if the less-popular student feeds some craving the popular person has with obsequious behavior, then Mr. or Ms. Popular becomes more dependent on the less-popular individual than the popular person had been previously. If that happens, the less-popular individual might then demand something she wants, such as insider recognition, as an implicit condition of her continued participation in this exchange. (But all bets are off if the more-powerful person becomes satiated by obsequious behavior.) The fundamental point is that greater balance is brought to a relationship simply by changing the pricing structure. If costs go up for the person who started off as less powerful, or if costs go down for the person who started off as more powerful (by virtue of their giving less), then power and dependency move in the direction of balance.

Pivotal for Emerson is the notion that power imbalance will lead to some kind of change, with the result that the relationship will become more balanced over time, unless there are limits set on the demands exchange partners can place on each other. Such limits can be based on friendship ties, communal solidarity, custom, norm formation, administrative rule, or law.

Power Imbalance Axiom: Social settings tend to (a) change over time in the direction of greater symmetry of power and dependence and (b) develop formal and informal limits on exploitation to the extent that nonsymmetrical relation-ships defy balance.

One obvious kind of change would be to have the more-dependent person contribute more in the future than she did in the past, essentially paying more to sustain the relationship, or to have the more-powerful person contribute less in the future while continuing to get just as much as she did in the past. Social structural changes can also take place to bring greater balance to exchange relationships. But in relationships defying balance, exchange theorists make the axiomatic assumption that the development of structural mechanisms or normative rules will constrain people from unsustainably high levels of exploita-tion. This marks a clear boundary demarcation between exchange metatheory and those versions of conflict metatheory inspired by Marx. Both perspectives acknowledge that inequality is an inherent feature of social life in all nonutopian societies, and that inequality always has potential for giving rise to conflict. But this is a point at which the perspectives diverge. Marx tended to believe that people in power, because they are unable to restrain their exploitive tendencies, will eventually exploit others to the point that the fabric of society is destroyed in convulsive change. This is, after all, the basis of Marx's *dialectical* view of human history. But Emerson made his own observations and concluded that exploited people are often willing to tolerate exploitation for generations when they believe they are protected (by rules or norms) from things getting much worse.

Structurally Balancing Power in Exchange

Emerson's real genius was in realizing that there can be social structural al-terations beyond changes in individual pricing and that these can go a long way toward rectifying a power imbalance.[15] Coalitions can form, as when farmers establish a cooperative to sell their grain collectively. Greater division of labor can allow people to leave jobs characterized by labor oversupply and low wages, in favor of jobs characterized by labor undersupply and high wages.

Other kinds of structural change can stabilize an imbalanced relationship by preventing the more-powerful (less-dependent) person from exploiting a power imbalance to his or her advantage. It often happens that norms can develop to limit the exploitation of a power imbalance. These can be norms particular to a specific relationship or they can be professional norms applying to whole catego-ries of relationships. Hierarchical regulatory agencies and administrative controls within organizations can also set boundaries preventing some forms of exploita-tion. This is why teachers cannot legitimately demand babysitting services or lawn mowing from their students. A teacher who offers extra credit in exchange for babysitting services might find that some students are interested, but few school administrators would regard this as a legitimate practice. Babysitting for money or even out of kindness, yes, but not for course credit or favorable grading.

The babysitting example is interesting because it introduces the concept of regulatory authority within an exchange theoretical rubric. We have also discussed regulatory control in our review of structural functionalism and conflict theory. Drawing those ideas together, and especially within Emerson's framework, suggests a useful principle.

Principle of Regulation: **Other things being equal, the extension of regulatory control over new spheres of activity (1) is a positive function of (a) the significance of costs resulting from unregulated activity, (b) the potential for taxing activity relative to the cost of regulating it, and (c) the degree to which the existence of a regulatory vacuum compromises the legitimacy of existing institutions, and (2) is a negative function of intensity of disagreement over (d) the moral/political appropriateness of any regulation and (e) the proper jurisdictional boundaries of potential regulatory agencies.**

Why, one might ask, are we at this moment in time suddenly seeing much tighter regulation of smoking? Many states and localities now have regulations against smoking in public places. A good theoretical principle allows us to develop a compelling explanation, one that comports with the facts, as to why regulations differ from place to place, and why they might change over time in any given place.

By thinking conceptually about simple exchange, Emerson was able to deduce conditions for the development of more complex social arrangements. He even put his ideas to the test in remote tribal areas of northern Pakistan (long before that region came under focus following September 11, 2001), applying exchange theory to the study of chieftain patterns. Of all the exchange perspectives developed, Emerson's scheme may ultimately offer the most promise. Even with Emerson's work, however, we are left with Homans's most pressing questions unanswered: Why do people value what they value? And how can we understand why the externalization of some costs is allowed, while the externalization of other costs is not allowed?

Extensions to Network Theory

The exchange framework extends naturally to a body of literature sociologists refer to as *network theory*, which explores the nature of interconnections linking people. The way in which we are interconnected with others determines the range of choices open to us and the range of resources we have for exploiting opportunities.

Mark Granovetter ignited excitement about network theory (already a part of the intellectual scene through the work of people like Nadel), defying conventional wisdom by offering a fresh new network explanation for the success of upper-middle-class people. In addition to all their other advantages, members of the upper middle class tend to maintain a comparatively wide range of comparatively shallow friendships. This network pattern tends to generate more job prospects and business opportunities than the network pattern that is more common among working-class people, who typically have a more narrow range of somewhat closer friendships. Close friendship networks tend to be small, homogeneous, closed, and therefore not very useful when people are trying to identify a wider range of potential opportunities. This follows from the fact that whatever information or help one member of the homogeneous circle can provide is likely to only replicate rather than add to whatever information and help every other member of the same social circle can provide. In contrast, someone with a heterogeneous range of shallow acquaintances is likely to hear of a wider assortment of opportunities. Each person in the network is likely to have information that adds to rather than merely replicates information available from others in the network.[16]

The link between network theory and exchange theory developed around norm formation. There is a tendency to develop normative rules that constrain terms of exchange within networks.[17] These rules often take the form of understandings that limit the kinds of compliance more-powerful parties extract from weaker parties. The will of people to subordinate themselves to rules is closely tied to the degree of dependence on the group and feelings of solidarity with the group.[18]

Recap

Among sociology's four main explanatory perspectives, exchange theory was the last to take shape, and it is the one to be most formally systematized. The concept of dependence and the assumption that people act in ways designed to minimize dependence are central tenets of exchange theory. But exchange theorists have gone far beyond an examination of individual exchange decisions to offer revealing insights about the emergence of system properties to limit and channel exchange. These include the appearance of coalitions, the formation of norms, the extension of regulatory controls, and changes in complexity of social networks. More than theorists of any other of sociology's main perspectives, exchange theorists have striven for a level of conceptual clarity that keeps them talking together (not past one another) with energy focused on explaining the appearance of the different kinds of social structural arrangements that are at the heart of sociology's subject matter.

Some Terms to Know

Externalized Costs: Side effects an actor is allowed to ignore, including expenses absorbed by others and depletion of resources without their replacement.

Dependence: The felt need to continue a relationship, which increases as a function of desire for whatever the person gets out of the relationship and which diminishes with the availability of alternative sources of the same thing or suitable substitutes for it.

Review of Axioms and Principle

Reaffirmation Axiom: Social ties are reaffirmed and strengthened by events suggesting mutual recognition and acceptance.

Power Imbalance Axiom: Social settings tend to (a) change over time in the direction of greater symmetry of power and dependence and (b) develop formal and informal limits on exploitation to the extent that nonsymmetrical relationships defy balance.

Principle of Regulation: Other things being equal, the extension of regulatory control over new spheres of activity (1) is a positive function of (a) the significance of costs resulting from unregulated activity, (b) the potential for taxing activity relative to the cost of regulating it, and (c) the degree to which the existence of a regulatory vacuum compromises the legitimacy of existing institutions, and (2) is a negative function of intensity of disagreement over (d) the moral/political appropriateness of any regulation and (e) the proper jurisdictional boundaries of potential regulatory agencies.

Quiz

Check your answers in the back of the book. If you get any wrong, consider reviewing chapter 14 before continuing.

1. True or false? Gift-giving patterns tend to change as people's needs to rely on one another change.
2. True or false? Changes in social structure can sometimes be explained in terms of people's efforts to escape unequal power in exchange relationships.

Application Exercise

Think of the three people outside your family who are on the top of your list for receiving birthday cards from you in the next year. Then write out the criteria you have used to decide what names go the list. Write down any theoretical insights you feel you gain by thinking about the criteria you have used.

PART V

TAKING STOCK OF
SOCIOLOGICAL THEORY: A RECAP

THIS BOOK IS NOT ENCYCLOPEDIC. Material covered has been trimmed to a bare minimum and explained clearly. Anyone who might be tested on sociological theory or the history of the discipline really should know everything covered in this book. Nevertheless, the various details are never as important as the recurrent themes.

There are five recurrent themes of this book. First, it means something particular when we say sociology is a science. It means (a) we want to improve our descriptions of the interpersonal attachments, shared beliefs, and systemic ways people are indirectly linked; (b) we want to be able to explain variation, which can either mean explaining differences between cases or change within a single case over time; (c) we want to understand the consequences of different patterns of attachments, shared beliefs, and systemic interconnection; (d) we want to be honest and explicit about the axiomatic assumptions we are making when we try to model sociological processes; (e) we want to be as accurate as possible in articulating our best current approximation of explanatory principles that can allow us to understand and make predictions about variability in outcomes in the social world; (f) we want to subject our provisional principles to repeated testing under different circumstances in order to define limiting conditions and otherwise refine our axioms and improve our principles; and (g) we aim for theoretical understanding revealing enough to help guide us as we work for better organizational, community, and societal outcomes.

Second, sociology is a coherent discipline with a coherent history. Sociological theory makes sense and is fundamentally understandable in its rough outline; hence the title of this book, *Making Sense of Social Theory*. Durkheim, Weber, Marx, and Mead raised questions that make fundamental sense for sociologists to investigate, and successive generations of sociologists have pressed forward with these questions.

The third theme of the book is that the various theoretical perspectives that have developed in our discipline are mutually informing rather than mutually exclusive. While each of the perspectives has a different focus, all have fundamental points of synergy. This means they help us to understand different pieces of the same broad tapestry. Sociological awareness is incomplete when it disregards any of the perspectives covered in this book. Richer, deeper, fuller understanding with more immediate application comes from drawing on multiple perspectives for intellectual inspiration and theoretical insight. Privileging a single perspective to the exclusion of all the others is equivalent to wearing blinders.

Fourth, sociologists know something. In fact we know a lot. And much of what we know can be communicated in a few useful axioms and a few robust and powerful explanatory principles. These axioms and principles can no doubt be reworked and improved on. But for now, the wording used in this book serves as a reasonable approximation for some important sociological insights. Readers will not walk away from this book empty-handed. The axioms and principles that have been summarized here can serve as a useful analytical tool kit.

The fifth and final theme of this book is that sociological theory is intellectually alive. We deal with key questions that cry out for treatment. Sociology is a vibrant discipline arriving at useful insights about important topics.

Part V consists of three minichapters. Chapter 15 revisits the important distinction between metatheory and theory through the prism of the axioms and principles presented in this book. Chapter 16 reviews the lessons of *Making Sense of Social Theory* in more philosophical terms, considering the intellectual coherence of the discipline. Chapter 17 provides some helpful hits about writing for impact in a social science discipline.

15

From Metatheory to Theory in Sociology: A Compendium of Axioms and Principles

M AKING SENSE OF SOCIAL THEORY is a textbook in the sense that it provides a broad overview of theoretical thinking in sociology, and to a certain extent, to sociology's sister disciplines in the social sciences. But the book is also an exercise in form of theory construction befitting a genuine science. *Making Sense of Social Theory* presents many of the key theoretical premises of the social sciences in the form of axioms and principles. These are written clearly enough to be accessible to students and to be readily understood by analysts and researchers. They are robust enough to be applied in a wide range of settings. And they are powerful in the sense that they can help us understand so much that their utility is readily apparent.

Genuine science is always evolving, so these axioms and principles are offered as a version other people will continue to add to and improve on in the future. Readers of *Making Sense of Social Theory* are invited to do so. Any steps taken to improve on or extend beyond the axioms and principles presented in *Making Sense of Social Theory* will be understood as steps taken in the best tradition of science. Science is a collaborative and community effort in which improvements are taken one step at a time and every improvement is welcome. In the spirit of Alpha Kappa Delta, sociology's national honor society, the goal is always to identify more clear, more robust, more powerful insights others can use in pursuit of a world made better by the application of social science understanding.

The Metatheoretical Perspectives
Examined through Axiomatic Assumptions

Axioms are assumptions theorists sometimes find it useful to make, even if these assumptions are not universally true. When we are engaged in social science analysis, being specific about certain key assumptions helps us to adopt a particular perspective in order that we might be able to more carefully search for things that are plausible to expect and, if present, important not to overlook. Each of sociology's main perspectives can be understood in metatheoretical terms by considering the axioms introduced at various points in this book.

Twelve axiomatic assumptions have been introduced in association with four main perspectives. Three axioms are associated with exchange theory. Four are associated with symbolic interaction. Three are associated with structural functionalism. And two are associated with conflict theory. However, none of the axioms should be thought of as exclusive to one group of social scientists or another. Most social scientists employ all twelve of these axioms at various points. When an axiom is explicitly used, it helps the user maintain a particular perspective. It encourages him or her to ask a distinctive set of orienting questions. Thus, using different axioms allows each researcher to look at a topic from significantly different points of view and perhaps observe more in the process.

Exchange Metatheory

Of the twelve axiomatic assumptions presented in *Making Sense of Social Theory*, three are associated primarily with exchange theory. The most basic of the exchange assumptions is the Benefit Maximization Axiom, suggesting that people tend to do what is best for themselves. When keeping this axiom in mind, we are alert to rational self-interest however it might express itself.

Benefit Maximization Axiom: **People tend to make benefit-maximizing decisions based on their priorities.**

Most people immediately recognize that the Benefit Maximization Axiom reminds us of something worth remembering. Human behavior often appears to be self-serving. In this respect, rational calculation is often a prime motivator of human behavior. Although any social scientist might find it useful to employ this assumption in various instances, this assumption is at the heart of most applications of exchange theory.

When exchange theorists turn their attention beyond examining individual exchanges as discrete activities, they try to understand how widespread patterns of transformative change can be developed over time. When attention turns to patterns of exchange and the evolving character of the social structural arrangements in which exchanges unfold, an additional assumption is often added. This can be expressed as the Power Imbalance Axiom.

Power Imbalance Axiom: Social settings tend to (a) change over time in the direction of greater symmetry of power and dependence and (b) develop formal and informal limits on exploitation to the extent that nonsymmetrical relationships defy balance.

Any social scientist may find an assumption like this helpful, but exchange theorists put this axiom to what is, in theoretical terms, very good use by allowing us to understand conditions for structural change in enduring relationships in which exchange regularly takes place. This turns out to be quite critical from an exchange perspective. The emergence of enduring and highly structured exchange arrangements provides us with a way of accounting for the continuation of exchange even at times or under conditions when the Benefit Maximization Axiom might suggest that exchange should come to a stop. It turns out, then, that the Power Imbalance Axiom suggests a possible point of linkage at which to integrate exchange theory with conflict theory and also with structural functionalism.

The Reaffirmation Axiom stipulates that many nonutilitarian interactions can be conceptualized and can perhaps be best understood as exchanges to forestall social ties from weakening. The introduction of this axiom transforms exchange into a concept that extends beyond the trade of things having material value. Indeed, simply allowing people to exchange mutual recognition is an important way of solidifying feelings of attachment.

Reaffirmation Axiom: Social ties are reaffirmed and strengthened by events suggesting mutual recognition and acceptance.

What we have called the Reaffirmation Axiom is a critical theoretical premise. When invoked, it enables us to look at a wide range of phenomena with the analytical clarity that comes to us from our experience in commercial exchanges. Moreover, this axiom suggests a way of connecting exchange theory with other perspectives, particularly symbolic interaction but also structural functionalism and general conflict theory.

Symbolic Interactionist Metatheory

Of the twelve axiomatic assumptions presented in this book, four are associated primarily with symbolic interactionism. The most basic of the interactionist assumptions is the Definition of Situation Axiom, suggesting that human behavior needs to be understood from the point of view of the actor herself or himself.

Definition of Situation Axiom: **People respond to situations according to what they believe to be true about those situations, rather than what is actually true.**

Most people immediately understand why the Definition of Situation Axiom is central to a symbolic interactionist way of understanding the world. The idea that each person's understanding of a situation motivates her or his responses rests at the heart of symbolic interactionist analysis. It is certainly an implicit element in virtually all sociological thinking.

Symbolic interactionists do try to identify factors influencing definition of situation. In this, they generally make one or the other of two companion assumptions, and sometimes both assumptions at the same time. One of these assumptions is that we adopt attitudes and viewpoints about the world outside ourselves based on our own immediate experiences and our interaction with others (Social Location Axiom). The companion assumption is that we come to see ourselves as "objects" having distinct individual qualities and salient memberships, also based on our own immediate experiences and our interaction with others (Self/Identity Axiom).

Social Location Axiom: **People tend to think that what they have personally encountered or heard from the people closest to them is authentic and representative and generally true.**

Self/Identity Axiom: **The individual qualities we feel we have (self) and memberships we regard as salient (identity) reflect how other people have responded to us in the past and seem to respond to us in the present.**

The Social Location Axiom and the Self/Identity Axiom help us better understand people as actors reacting to the world in which they live. At times symbolic interactionists reflect on the ways that actors reacting to the world can also change the social world in ways that extend beyond their own face-to-face encounters. When the focus shifts to lasting structural and cultural change, another assumption is often added, that people modify old identities and commitments in those ways that prove useful in a changing environment.

Selective Retention Axiom: **We selectively retain old beliefs and practices and we actively redefine old identities and commitments in ways that optimally balance our sense of belonging with our ability to successfully adjust to changing conditions.**

The Selective Retention Axiom does not always figure prominently in symbolic interactionist analysis, but it is important for providing a clear axiomatic link between symbolic interactionism and the other frameworks, particularly structural functionalism but also exchange and general conflict theory.

Conflict Metatheory

Of the twelve axiomatic assumptions presented in this book, two are associated primarily with conflict theory. These two basic conflict assumptions stipulate that social structural arrangements can be understood as (a) fundamentally exploitive, and (b) resistant to change.

Structured Inequality Axiom: **The social structural arrangements that survive tend to be those that protect the interests of more-powerful people at the expense of less-powerful people.**

Intransigence Axiom: **The powerful do not loosen the grip of exploitation without being pressed to do so.**

There are many different versions of conflict theory. But the most common versions, informed by Marx, are grounded in these two assumptions. These assumptions are quite important because they more or less necessitate that the holder adopt an oppositional stance toward those in power. If one believes that people in power are compelled to exploit and that people in power are unable to ever willingly reduce their oppressive grip on others, then it follows rather logically that, at all times in all places, rulers should be opposed.

Structural Functional Metatheory

Of the twelve axiomatic assumptions presented in this book, three are associated primarily with structural functionalism. The most basic of the structural-functional assumptions is the Form Follows Function Axiom, suggesting that social/organizational/institutional change is a natural outcome of a systemic drive for improvement.

Form Follows Function Axiom: **Form follows function in the sense that widespread patterns of structural change emerge as systemic responses to meet new needs or correct for poor performance in the face of old needs.**

Most people immediately understand why the Form Follows Function Axiom is central to a structural functional way of understanding the world. The idea that social systems change to meet challenges is at the heart of structural functional analysis. But from a structural functional point of view it is important to understand how and why systems come to have different characteristics, and at the same time, what stabilizes a system from constant change that might be chaotic and destabilizing. Shared values and institutional history or traditions each play this role in structural-functional analyses.

Values Axiom: As a set of values becomes more deeply embedded and more uniformly held by people in a society, common social roles and widely institutionalized systems of rules are progressively modified in ways that manifest and maximize adherence to core values.

Founder Effects Axiom: Those interests and concerns of earlier figures that became active parts of institutional memory or are deeply embedded in institutionalized practice shape the activities of others for a long time to come.

An interesting feature of these two assumptions is that, unless used carefully, they can both be taken to imply systemic tendencies toward stability (or rigidity) rather than change (or adaptation). This is a key reason many social scientists turned away from structural functional analysis. When improperly used, a structural functional framework too often appears to apologize for a status quo that in many ways cries out for change. But if structural functionalism appears to have a bias toward support of the status quo, this bias would seem to be rooted in the way some people apply the perspective rather than being necessarily inherent to the perspective itself. The very idea of structural functionalism is that change is necessary to improve adaptation to shifting conditions. The basic orientation is that structural change can be functional, and we need to be able to understand how functional change occurs in order to try to prevent functional change from being blocked by antiprogressive elements and special interest groups.

Axioms and Metatheory

As has been often repeated, axioms are assumptions theorists find it useful to make in certain instances, even if the axioms are not universally true. There is good analytical justification for doing so. Making an assumption in a particular case can help us ask probing questions that can lead to more penetrating investigation yielding fresh insight. That is, assumptions remind us of the kinds of things we definitely want to be alert to. This heightened state of alertness enables us to see things we might otherwise miss.

At the same time, the act of formalizing our assumptions tends to keep us honest in our scientific inquiries. Having explicitly worded axioms invites vigilant review of those assumptions. Do the assumptions really make sense in the kind of environment and for the types of phenomena under study? This important theory-building question is more likely to be asked, and reflection about it is likely to be more thoughtful (leading to improvement in our thinking over time), when our assumptions are made explicit in the form of axiomatic statements.

Part of the particular value of axioms is that they provide a way of powerfully encapsulating a particular framework or intellectual approach we want to use in our analyses. Introducing a number of different axioms can help us to look at subject matter from a variety of perspectives and helps keep us honest as we try to develop strenuous tests of our theories in order to get closer to the truth.

Ultimately, to get closer to the truth it is important to move past adherence to our own favored assumptions. This suggests the necessity of moving beyond metatheory to theory by trying to articulate theoretical principles. Good principles move toward deeper scientific understanding than we can arrive at by simply using axiomatic assumptions. Indeed, good theoretical principles often make it possible to bridge or integrate different metatheoretical perspectives by arriving at a more comprehensive understanding of phenomena under study.

Sociological Insights Expressed as Social Science Principles

One of the contributions of this book has been the articulation of twenty-one theoretical principles that are either explicit or implied in pivotal works written by exchange theorists, symbolic interactionists, conflict theorists, and structural functionalists. True to the scientific orientation expressed throughout the book, these principles deal with matters of central importance in the social sciences. They are central rather than peripheral. In fact, they define the heart of our cumulative social science awareness and understanding, both in theoretical terms and in terms of our practical ability to engineer a better world with better outcomes.

Many of the principles in this book are complicated and need to be read carefully to be understood. Complexity is difficult to avoid because each principle deals with something important and is meant to capture a range of insight that has different facets. But despite their inherent complexity, each principle is written with sufficient precision that it should be understandable in more or less the same way by every careful reader. Each principle, true to the qualities of good theory, is robust. That is, each principle is generic enough that its wording will allow careful readers to envision different settings and circumstances where application of the principle can yield predictions about outcomes to be expected under a range of real-world conditions. And each principle is powerful in the sense that it explains a great deal about some aspect of the social world that is highly consequential.

This is not so say, however, that the principles presented in *Making Sense of Social Theory* are perfect and represent an end state in sociological understanding. Modification of any of these principles, where based on careful examination of valid data about the social world, would illustrate the fifth and final step in the scientific method. Enhancing social science understanding by improving on our theoretical principles is, after all, our primary goal as scientists. This book does not end the quest for an ever-improving set of principles. Rather, the goal of the book is to propel every reader farther along on that quest.

These principles mark sociology's development beyond metatheoretical assumptions into what is more clearly the realm of explanatory science. The theoretical breadth and coherence of the discipline become most clearly apparent if we step beyond studying individual theorists (part III of the book) and step beyond the study of established theoretical perspectives (part IV of the book), in order to realize a scientific vision (explained in parts I and II of the book).

It is clear that the theoretical principles reviewed in the passages that follow really do stretch beyond any single metatheoretical perspective. Instead, each principle finds a way of bridging metatheoretical divisions by explaining variation in phenomena of central importance to more than one perspective. Each principle captures a truth that is testable in its own right and transcends constraint by axiomatic assumptions. The principles captured and conveyed in *Making Sense of Social Theory* encapsulate much of what social scientists have learned about seven key issues. These issues are social formation of the person, a person's reaction to discrete situations, redefinition of social/organizational/ institutional roles, changes in organizational structure, broad societal patterns of change, systemic conflict, and widely shared beliefs.

Social Formation of the Person

Every sociological inquiry, even those sociological studies focusing on macro-societal patterns, treat individual people as relevant to an adequate social science understanding of the way events transpire. Consequently, in order to develop a comprehensive understanding of the discipline, it is necessary to incorporate our most powerful insights about factors influencing what individual people believe and how individuals orient to their social environments. We might refer to this as the *social formation of the person.*

In taking stock of the current state of disciplinary knowledge about the formation of the person, it is important to note that social scientists have a relatively well-developed (by no means perfect, but relatively well-developed) understanding of (a) conditions that optimize learning from others (socialization), (b) conditions in which others exert the greatest noncoercive influence over us (that is, get us to do what they want without "forcing" us to), and (c) the way a person's orientation to the social world is influenced by sense of self and identity.

Principle of Socialization: **Other things being equal, socialization will be more effective to the degree that the person being socialized (a) depends on the socializing agent, (b) trusts the socializing agent, and (c) has an opportunity to act out or practice new norms and roles with peers.**

Principle of Social Control: Other things being equal, the degree of social control a group or community exerts over its members (1) increases as a positive function of group/community integration (how interconnected members' activities are and how tightly bound members are by a common set of beliefs), and (2) diminishes to the degree that members have offsetting ties to other groups or communities.

Commitment Availability Principle: Other things being equal, the intensity of a person's commitment to a social unit, and one's inclination to make sacrifices for collective purposes, (1) increase to the degree that one's sense of self and identity are acknowledged and valued in the setting, and (2) decrease to the extent that one's sense of self and identity are unrecognized, unappreciated, or demeaned in the setting.

These three principles are each integral parts of good social science understanding in its present state. They are among the most widely relied on of sociology's discoveries because they are clear, robust, and powerful.

The Person's Reaction to Discrete Situations

In addition to understanding social forces and experiences acting on individuals as a person enters an arena of engagement with others, it is important to understand how individuals will react to discrete situations. While our axioms (such as the Definition of Situation Axiom) are certainly helpful in this respect, we can also add two predictive principles. These principles delineate the things people weigh in making calculations, and the reactions people have after miscalculating.

Principle of Rational Choice: Other things being equal, the likelihood of following a particular course of action (1) increases as a function of (a) the value of the desired outcome and (b) the probability of success in achieving that outcome, and (2) decreases as a function of (c) the projected cost of the activity, (d) fear of ultimately being held responsible for externalized costs, and (e) availability of alternatives having attractive cost-benefit ratios.

Anger Principle: Other things being equal, anger increases in magnitude (a) to the degree that actual outcomes fall short of expected outcomes and (b) opportunities forgone seem to exceed the benefits that have been actualized.

These two principles are each integral parts of good social science understanding in its present state. Here, however, the "other things being equal" proviso is especially important to remember. The Principle of Rational Choice is certainly governed by some boundary conditions. That is, the principle seems to apply in certain kinds of situations but not others. These boundary conditions will be specified in time. And the Anger Principle is probably too simple to have as much explanatory power as we would like. These two principles are, however, good starting points. In admitting their imperfection we are doing two important things. First, we are practicing one of the most basic premises of good science, which is to treat current theoretical insight as provisional. Second, we are welcoming every person engaged in social science inquiry to try suggesting new and potentially improved versions of the axioms and principles presented in this book.

Redefinition of Social/Organizational/Institutional Roles

Social scientists have successfully made the link between individual responses to discrete situations and the transformation of roles and relationships. While more social science progress is still to be made on this topic, important first steps are already in place. The trust or distrust that emerges out of discrete encounters has important ramifications for whether people will either stay in a role or relationship or depart from it, and for the time that someone remains in a role or relationship, whether she/he will try to make it more expansive or narrow (Trust Principle). The way in which roles and relationships are redefined is, of course, also contingent on and characteristic of the organizational or institutional environment (Principle of Role Redefinition).

Trust Principle: Other things being equal, people withdraw from roles/relationships if practical, and tend to use formal and informal rules to minimize their obligations and reduce room for ambiguity if withdrawal is not practical, (1) as a direct function of perceived vulnerability in the setting and (2) as an inverse function of degree of trust in the people in that setting.

Principle of Role Redefinition: Other things being equal, the latitude people have to redefine a role relationship is (1) a positive function of the degree to which (a) role occupants listen to and understand one another's points of view, (b) role occupants agree about the kind of change they would like to see, (c) the role relationship is shielded from direct observation by others, and (d) there is peer support for change, and (2) is an inverse function of the levels of (e) anticipatory socialization for current definitions and (f) validation for adhering to current definitions.

These two principles are vital for helping us understand the role individuals play in reshaping their own corners of the social universe. They point to phenomena that are ubiquitous and necessary to understand if we are to make coherent links among our understandings of micro-, meso-, and macrolevels of social activity.

Changes in Organizational Structure

While most of the founding figures of the social sciences tended to view themselves as students of either the "micro" world of face-to-face interaction or the "macro" world of broad societal trends, it would be reasonable to argue that sociology's most common applications, and many of its most tangible applications, are in the mesolevel world of organizational structure and culture. Sociologists know a great deal about the world of organization, management, and administration. We have, among other things, a sound theoretical understanding of the conditions under which market, hierarchical, or network designs for organization are likely to be most successful (Uncertainty Principle of Hierarchy and Innovation/Complexity Principle of Networking).

Uncertainty Principle of Hierarchy: Other things being equal, the rationality of a market solution in comparison with a hierarchical solution to an organizational challenge is (1) a positive function of the cost effectiveness of the market solution and (2) an inverse function of risks of uncertainty that come with the market solution.

Innovation/Complexity Principle of Networking: Other things being equal, the tendency to adopt network/strategic alliance solutions to organizational challenges is a positive function of (a) the complexity of activity and (b) the necessity to maintain ongoing creativity and innovation in order to remain competitive.

And within hierarchically structured organizations, we have considerable insight about conditions for success (Principle of Organizational Efficiency/Effectiveness) and the conditions under which subunits are likely to act with greater or lesser autonomy relative to the mission of the broader organization (Principle of Systemic Coupling).

Principle of Organizational Efficiency/Effectiveness: Long-term organizational efficiency/effectiveness is a positive function of (a) success in maintaining uniform mission awareness and accurate institutional history, (b) depth of commitment to minimizing repetition of past mistakes and taking other steps to improve performance, (c) organizational capacity for assessing challenges and instituting change without interrupting normal operations, and (d) adequacy of alignment of training, information, resources, and operational authority with the tasks people are called on to perform in their roles.

Principle of Systemic Coupling: Other things being equal, the ability of a system of organization to maintain mission focus (and avoid mission creep) is a positive function of the extent to which (a) a stable and shared awareness of common ends can be maintained, (b) lines of communication remain open and honest, (c) subordinate units remain resource dependent on higher-level units, (d) resource allocation is aligned well with mission involvement, and (e) people at different locations within the system of organization have a sense of common fate.

Taken together, these four principles have highly practical value in applied sociology. They encapsulate a social science understanding about core economic and political activity in a society. They help explain why activity tends to be organized in different ways at different times. And they offer us ways to understand when organizations are most likely to be successful, and conversely, most likely to have their goal-oriented focus subverted.

Broad Societal Patterns of Change

Most of the founding figures of the social sciences were preoccupied with understanding sweeping patterns of change in society: urbanization, industrialization, democratization, homogenization, and the rise of state power. Hence, it should be of no surprise that our body of theoretical insight contains revealing statements about broad patterns of change. These broad patterns include societal differentiation and homogenization (Principle of Evolution) and redeployment of labor and other economic resources (Principle of Supply and Demand), which are widely shared across disciplines and are insights arrived at deep in our social science past.

Principle of Evolution: Other things being equal, the rate at which social units differentiate from one another is (1) a direct function of their isolation and (2) an inverse function of their size.

Principle of Supply and Demand: Other things being equal, the level of incentive potential suppliers have to provide something and consumers have to find substitutes (1) are positive functions of demand and price, and are (2) inverse functions of supply and aggregate elasticity.

There have also been more recent theoretical developments helping to explain broad patterns of change. Of particular interest have been (1) the extension of regulatory authority, usually in the form of growth of government (Principle of Regulation), and (2) propensity for social systems to minimize incoherence (Principle of Structural Strain).

Principle of Regulation: Other things being equal, the extension of regulatory control over new spheres of activity (1) is a positive function of (a) the significance of costs resulting from unregulated activity, (b) the potential for taxing activity relative to the cost of regulating it, and (c) the degree to which the existence of a regulatory vacuum compromises the legitimacy of existing institutions, and (2) is a negative function of intensity of disagreement over (d) the moral/political appropriateness of any regulation and (e) the proper jurisdictional boundaries of potential regulatory agencies.

Principle of Structural Strain: Other things being equal, the pressure for change aimed at greater internal coherence within a system of organization grows as a function of degree of (a) incompatibility among the various demands people face as role occupants and (b) inconsistency between expressed values and common patterns of behavior, with change of behavior in the direction of greater consistency with core social values when there is general agreement about the value that seems most relevant, and with values changing in the direction of greater alignment with behavior when there is disagreement about which values apply.

These four principles are sweeping in their coverage and help us explain a great deal about broad patterns of organizational phenomena in the societies in which we live. They speak to our capacity as social scientists to make analytical sense of the broad complexities of the world.

Systemic Conflict

Perhaps no single topic has commanded as much sociological attention as conflict when studied on a societal level. One important variety of social science research on conflict addresses the development of deep fissures between groups (Principle of Intergroup Conflict and Principle of Violent Conflict).

Principle of Intergroup Conflict: Other things being equal, the degree to which intergroup antagonism is likely to manifest itself in organized conflict is a function of (a) how much homogeneity there is within groups and how much inequality there is separating groups, (b) how much historical or symbolic unity there is within each group and how little historical or symbolic unity there is between groups, (c) how much mobility and communication there is within groups and how little there is between groups, and (d) how often resource competition coincides with differences in group membership.

Principle of Violent Conflict: Other things being equal, the likelihood of a conflict turning violent is inversely related to (a) frequency of conflict is and (b) how thoroughly regulated conflict is.

Another important variant of conflict research is concerned with the relationship between governments and the people. Do ordinary people have input? And does the government protect their interests? Some of what we have learned can be captured in two powerful principles: the Diversity of Voice in Governance Principle and the Principle of Legitimate Authority.

Diversity of Voice in Governance Principle: Other things being equal, the diversity of voices heard in the public arena is a function of (a) the breadth of distribution of control over economic activity, (b) the organizational density of social life, (c) the level and breadth of distribution of human capital, and (d) the number and openness of channels of public communication.

Principle of Legitimate Authority: Other things being equal, the degree of legitimacy enjoyed by a government is a positive function of (a) the reliability with which the rights or ordinary citizens are protected and services are provided, (b) enforcement of laws is viewed as fair, and (c) ideology and information are skillfully used to deflect blame in the direction of internal opposition or external enemies.

These four principles capture some of our most valued and widely used social science insights. Importantly, these principles illustrate the way in which scientific progress can be made even if axiomatic assumptions are wrong. It is clear that the Structured Inequality Axiom and the Intransigence of Power Axiom, which are clearly detectable in Marx's work, are wrong in the sense that they do not apply to all cases. But in making those axiomatic assumptions, Marx was able to work out the lessons we have labeled as the Principle of Intergroup Conflict. Principles of this kind can be used to help the discipline move beyond deadlocked debates between competing camps of metatheorists, each of which insists on the accuracy of its own mutually exclusive descriptions of "reality" (for example, the pluralist and power elite theorists). The Diversity of Voice in Governance Principle and the Principle of Legitimate Authority are good cases in point.

Widely Shared Beliefs

A review of theoretical progress in sociology would not be complete without considering insights sociologists have advanced about shared beliefs. Among other things, social scientists know that shared beliefs do oscillate somewhat with economic conditions (Principle of Cyclical Change in Beliefs) as well as with certain categories of what are collectively dramatic events (as suggested by the Conflict/Cohesion Principle).

Principle of Cyclical Change in Beliefs: Other things being equal, (a) the more social constraint there is, then the more slowly that innovation and problem solving occur, which generates pressure for greater tolerance of individuality, but (b) the more tolerance there is of individual action, then the greater the number of new problems people create, which generates greater insistence on conformity.

Conflict/Cohesion Principle: Other things being equal, cohesion within groups or other social entities increases as a function of the degree of conflict between those entities.

While this statement of sociological understanding about shared beliefs is obviously not complete, it is a start. In real science, theoretical starting points are clearly stated, and forward progress from those starting points is eagerly anticipated.

Recap

This short chapter is a compendium of formal statements of theoretical axioms and principles. Presenting axioms and principles in this way should convey a sense of the breadth and coherence of sociology's social science project. In order to use these axioms and principles, one needs to read them carefully and thoughtfully because their content is tightly packed and complicated. Used carefully and thoughtfully, these axioms and principles constitute a body of theory that is robust and powerful, as good scientific theory should be. But the compendium also suggests a body of theory that is open to testing and improvement, as good scientific theory should be.

The material reviewed in this chapter illustrates the second step of the scientific method, specifying theoretical insights that can be used to explain variation or change in the social world we live in and study. To fit with the intent of *Making Sense of Social Theory*, these sociological axioms principles should be thought of as a starting point for research designed to test and improve on theory, rather than as a revelation of ultimate social science truth. Indeed, modifying our principles, when informed by careful examination of data about the social world, is exactly what the fifth and final step in the scientific method is all about. The goal of social science is to work toward enhanced understanding of processes responsible for variation and change in the world around us. Science is a collective enterprise. Everyone reading *Making Sense of Social Theory* is invited to participate in this enterprise.

This brings us to a wonderfully empowering and liberating paradox. Having been explicit about twelve key axioms and twenty-one powerful principles, *Making Sense of Social Theory* has achieved three different ends simultaneously. (1) This book has made an immense storehouse of sociological discovery readily available to every reader in a way that facilitates quick recall and confirmation.

(2) *Making Sense of Social Theory* provided a skeletal structure of the discipline in its intellectual outlines, and cultivated analytical skills readers can use to reinterpret works referenced here or interpret additional works and locate those works within an intellectual map of the discipline. (3) Finally, while every reader has reasonably been expected to "memorize" the axioms and principles as written, the philosophy and approach to science on which this book is predicated invites innovative thinking—articulation of alternative viewpoints is not anathema in science; it is a vital and integral part of science. Theorists do their jobs by encouraging alterative viewpoints, so long as those views are expressed clearly enough that they will be understood in more or less the same way by most careful readers, and can be tested by creative researchers. Then, when competing theoretical ideals have been clearly articulated, leave it to a culture of evidence to sort out which theoretical ideals are most robust and powerful. When this method is followed, the different theorists having clearly articulated competing ideas have all done their jobs and the "winner" is always science. In this heartfelt spirit, I welcome readers as colleagues in the scientific enterprise.

16

Sociology as a Coherent Discipline: Unifying Themes

A SIDE FROM LEARNING A LOT OF SPECIFIC DETAILS and amassing a useful analytical tool kit, the reader should take three general lessons from this book. First, theory is both the beginning and the end of the scientific process. Second, despite the fact that the discipline of sociology is broad and expansive (seeming to "deal with everything"), sociology is nevertheless a coherent field. Readers of this book should have acquired an integrated overview of the discipline; this overview is something every sociologically trained person should have. Third, when considered together, sociology's various theoretical perspectives offer a richer framework for analysis than do any of the perspectives taken in isolation.

Theory in Science

Theory gains its scientific significance from intimate connection with research. The scientific method begins with theory. It starts with conceptualization allowing for formulation of a research question. This is followed by the identification of axioms that help us model what may be happening and the articulation of explanatory principles to be tested. The data collection aspects of science that people normally think of when they hear the word "research" really begin only when a theoretically grounded and purposeful test has been designed. Unless a research protocol is theoretically well grounded and purposeful, its science value is compromised. Good science begins with theory. And the less mature the science, the more crucial it is that practitioners really understand the rightful connection between theory and research in science, in order to prevent the process from driving for years down a dead end.

Just as it begins with theory, the scientific method ends with theory. Whenever research activity begins to reach a conclusion, the scientific method involves revisiting our body of theory for the purpose of trying to learn lessons that translate into more robust and powerful theoretical understanding. The ultimate objective is to revisit the axioms and principles we started with and either add to or modify them, or learn something useful about the way they operate and the conditions under which they apply. The point is that scientists are not very satisfied by conducting years of research that leaves our state of theoretical understanding unchanged. Science is exploratory and not just confirmatory.

Once all this is understood, it should leave readers with the realization that sociology is a science, that sociologists are practitioners of a science, and that theoretical activity should be the starting point and the culminating activity of each research investigation. We are in the business of developing better explanations for how cases change over time and how differences emerge between cases. Designing data collection strategies and executing those strategies is research activity. But deciding what explanations to test and how to revise those explanations after data have been collected and carefully examined are theoretical activities. As long as developing better explanatory frameworks is at the center of the scientific enterprise, theory activity will both necessarily launch and necessarily conclude the endeavor.

Science is defined by a culture of evidence. Data become evidence when they are marshaled in ways that help us challenge and stretch our understandings. Data become evidence when they are used in a meaningful test. As long as it is our explanation that is being tested, the quality of our effort will be determined first and foremost by the clarity of our expression of theoretical ideas and the robustness and power of the theoretical insights as they are formally expressed.

A Concise Understanding of the History of the Discipline

Everyone studying a subject should have an understanding of the basic outline of that discipline's history. Readers of this book should now understand the basic outline of sociology's history, and should be able to speak and write intelligibly about the evolution of sociology as a discipline.

The nineteenth century, the time when the social sciences really came into being, was a period of convulsive change. Both western Europe and the United States were overwhelmingly rural and agricultural in 1801 but by 1899 had already begun to urbanize and industrialize at a rapid pace. Though the United States led the world in its move toward democracy, almost all other governments were autocratic or just beginning to be meaningfully democratic in 1801. Yet by 1899 most governments were under substantial pressure to democratize or make the promise of democracy more meaningful. Throughout the nineteenth century, democratization was viewed with suspicion by vested interests everywhere, and this too changed in some noticeable degree by 1899.

At the same time, the scientific revolution offered hope for a better life. The natural and biological sciences had improved transportation, magnified productive capacity, and begun to combat disease. This gave cause for optimism, and many people began to imagine that it would be possible to develop social sciences to inform better public policy and more effective public programs. The social sciences, it was hoped, could yield the insight necessary to build better societies—more peaceful and more prosperous societies that would allow greater freedom of opportunity for personal growth and improvement. Brazil even emblazoned a motto of the scientific age on its flag at the time of its founding. (Perhaps this gives us a small clue how it came to pass that Brazil was the first country to elect a sociology professor as president.)

In that environment, a few dozen people working on the borders of other disciplines outlined the parameters of what was to become sociology. Some of the most important of these people were Émile Durkheim and William I. Thomas working on the borders of anthropology, George Herbert Mead and Charles Horton Cooley working on the borders of psychology, and Max Weber, Karl Marx, Vilfredo Pareto, and Thorstein Veblen working on the borders of economics. They generated a pool of insights that were to become the intellectual foundation for all the sociological work to follow. They focused our attention on the importance of community transition and organization/disorganization. They alerted us to the importance of defining situation and self-concept. They understood that people organized their lives around roles, with those roles in some sense shaped by values. And they recognized that economic life, around which human activities often revolve, could be most adequately understood within the context of an encompassing sociological framework.

Besides fixing the parameters of the new discipline, with its focus on social attachments, shared beliefs, and institutional or systemic linkages, the earliest pioneers in sociology gave us an *epistemology* of science (that is, a way of arriving at better understanding by validating, identifying the limits of, and improving on our knowledge claims). This is most evident with Durkheim, who used the language of science and showed us how the scientific method could be followed in sociology as long as we kept our focus on social facts, that is, characteristics true of groups or collective units and not simply of individuals. But it was also true of people who may have been less comfortable with the language of science. Marx was one such person: his contribution to economics is of arguable significance but he made a stunningly important set of sociological discoveries by identifying conditions leading to polarization and conflict. He pointed out that intergroup antagonism is most likely to develop when there are big differences between groups, a lot of competition for scarce resources, and few avenues for mobility, and when opposing groups are internally homogeneous, have a lot of internal communication, and are characterized by high levels of symbolic unification.

Then came intellectual giants of a different sort: great synthesizers such as Talcott Parsons and, to a somewhat lesser extent, George Homans. Parsons became the standard-bearer for structural functionalism when he synthesized insights from Durkheim, Weber, and Pareto to show us how long-term societal trends, such as democratization and the spread of universal education, could be understood as structural responses to meet societal needs. And Homans became the first standard-bearer for exchange theory when he translated the basic principles of behavioral psychology and utilitarian economics into a formulation that could be broadly applied to all aspects of social life.

By the mid-twentieth century, as different theoretical paradigms began to form and there were many more sociologists to apply them, there was an explosion of work that bore fruit. To name just a few topics that were covered: studies of core self-concept, role strain, reference groups, equilibrium processes within organizations, and the changing contours of class and class conflict in contemporary society. All of these added to our understanding of the questions that have remained integral to sociological investigation since the time of the discipline's founders.

Making Sense of Social Theory offers a way of mapping the intellectual terrain of sociology as a discipline and provides a holistic view of the history of sociology. The conceptual mapping developed in *Making Sense of Social Theory* should make it possible to locate any work somewhere meaningful on an evolutionary tree of sociological ideas.

Mutual Compatibility of Perspectives

Sociology students often leave their first sociology classes feeling that sociological theory is a combat zone in which one perspective should be victorious and all others should be vanquished. This impression is wrong, and it would be an intellectually wasteful, self-limiting, and stifling view of the discipline. Theory is insight, and insight is a terrible thing to waste, which is what happens when a perspective is dismissed before one discovers how it can be used.

Ninety years ago, natural scientists did not ask whether the theory of electricity was to be preferred to the theory of magnetism or vice versa. They asked what we had to know before we could link those then-distinct theoretical frameworks for understanding different parts of our observable reality into a more integrated, consistent, informative understanding of the physical universe (electromagnetism). Then they set about doing the research that led to a theoretical breakthrough. This did not happen by accident, however. The explanatory goal and our preliminary (but insufficient) theoretical efforts at explanation were always clearly in mind. So when pertinent research was completed, that research effort was not wasted. Research in a theoretical activity squanders investigative resources and stunts scientific momentum.

Likewise, sociological theory is most informative when we take advantage of the richness of all our perspectives rather than privilege one by discounting the others. The key is to understand how those different perspectives can actually do link up at synergy points, so that they mutually inform each other.

Although the mid-twentieth century was characterized by a certain degree of insularity, with people who were interested in developing one theoretical perspective tending to ignore or discount the others, any antipathy between perspectives was counterproductive to social science progress. Conditions are now right to make significant theoretical progress.

Sociologists uniformly embrace the view that we cannot understand the real world shaping our lives without taking into account class and stratification (the focus of conflict theory) and values and organizational and institutional patterns (the focus of structural functionalism). Nor can we understand society without recognizing that people do sometimes have agency and use it (a focus of symbolic interactionism). Nor can we understand the role of agency without considering goal-maximizing behavior (a focus of exchange theory) or our ability to reconsider interpretations and adjust behavior (another focus of symbolic interactionism). Universal acceptance of these simple points makes sociology a multiple-paradigm discipline in which each paradigm brings value.

Whatever insights we do feel we are able to articulate, we must always be open to the possibility that we are wrong (the fundamental tenet of science). The postmodernist admonition that we always need to ask ourselves what special interests current beliefs may be supporting in a veiled way is a kind of healthy skepticism science should never sacrifice.

Conclusion

As promised from the beginning, *Making Sense of Social Theory* is anything but encyclopedic. The purpose is to introduce theory in a way that relays a good general understanding and presents an accurate overview of useful material. This book is not meant as an ending but rather as a beginning. It is my hope that this book will help readers feel more comfortable than ever discussing theory in ways that are explicit about social science insight, progress, and relevance when applied to real events.

17

Writing for Impact in the Social Sciences: Some Practical Remarks for Students

WRITING FOR REAL IMPACT IN A SCIENCE requires paying careful attention to theoretical principles while following the scientific method. This last, brief chapter distills some pieces of advice readers may find useful. In the process, the chapter draws together main themes of the book.

The First Step in the Scientific Method

The first step in the scientific method is to pose a research question. If one's goals include having social scientific impact, the choice of research question is crucial. For scholarly inquiry to have impact on a discipline, it needs to address a question that broadly engages the interests of other professionals in the same field.

The key to a good question is that it either (a) inquires into the causes of variation or change in social attachments, shared beliefs, or systemic linkages found in the social word, or (b) asks about something else people care about that may be a consequence of the kinds of social attachments, shared beliefs, or systemic linkages found in the social word. In either case, most good research questions place a conceptual focus on better understanding causes of difference or change. More accurately describing the state of something is definitely important science activity, but doing so is the empirical rather than the theoretical side of science. The theoretical side of science is to ask why and how something got to be as it is. Explanation is key, and staying focused on explanation is facilitated by having a research question that makes clear what kind of difference or change we seek more explanatory understanding of.

There is no end to the questions one might ask. But *Making Sense of Social Theory* identifies several broad umbrella questions that have succeeded in engaging the sustained interest of members of the social science community. The list is not exhaustive, but it is useful. A person contributing to examination of some particular aspect or illustration of any one of these broad umbrella questions would be understood by most other social scientists as doing something worthwhile. But remember, of course, that most people would write their own more specific version of one of these umbrella questions.

a. What social processes or mechanisms influence how the benefits of society are distributed, and how do those processes or mechanisms work?
b. What are the processes through which control over organizational or institutional power is gained and exercised, and for what purposes is that organizational or institutional power exercised?
c. Why do different groups and organizations vary in structural characteristics and culture attributes, and how do group or organizational structure and culture change?
d. How does feedback work in groups and organizations? What organizational features and dynamics influence the validity and effectiveness of feedback mechanisms?
e. What do different people come to value most, and why?
f. When and how are different senses of self and identity activated and energized, and when or how are they deactivated and de-energized?
g. How are expectations of different kinds transmitted to people, reinforced among people, or transformed?

If one were exploring any one of these questions, it would of course be normal to customize them somewhat. That is, a research question one person asks will usually be more specific, suggesting something about the setting or data set to be studied, and perhaps something about more narrowly defined points to be explored. For example, one person's specific version of the fifth question (e) on the list might be, "How do peers influence what college students set as priorities?" The more specific version of the question is useful for keeping research focused and manageable, as well as for accurately communicating the topic of the research to a wider audience.

The question could be made much more specific. Is the focus on all college students or on a particular category of college students, such as commuter students who do not live on campus? Is the focus on all priorities, or one specific priority, such as how much emphasis to place on studying? Will the research focus on all peers or a particular category of peers, such as peers of the same gender, or fellow students taking the same classes at the same time? In writing a research question, the researcher has considerable latitude. Keeping the focus of the question on an explanation of certain things in particular settings under identified circumstances tends to ensure that findings, even null findings (and sometimes especially null findings), will have theoretical importance. What if a researcher were to find, for example, that the peers with whom a student is enrolled in classes, and who might consequently be thought of as having the direct experience most relevant to the question of study priorities, ultimately have little influence on a person's priority-setting decisions, but that other kinds of peers do have influence? A finding like this could have broad import by helping shape how we think about peer influence as a process.

Science moves ahead when people look at similar processes at work in different settings and then use points of convergence and divergence to better understand underlying processes in order to build robust and powerful theories. The findings of one researcher looking at the role of peers when college students decide how much to study can be taken up by the scientific community for fruitful comparison or contrast with findings of a researcher looking at driving decisions made by people with declining eyesight. With data from different settings in hand, both the points of similarity and the points of contrast inform theory-building efforts taking place within the scientific community. When deciding which studies to consider alongside each other for comparison or contrast purposes, it is necessary to envision an umbrella question (like questions a–g above) that the more specific research questions each inform. For if you are writing for impact in a science, you want people with a wide range of empirical interests reading your work because of its broader importance. You want people to appreciate the fact that what you write about one setting or data set or type of phenomena can inform their work, even when their work centers on a different setting or data set or type of phenomena. The way people can recognize this is to see that your research addresses a dynamic, issue, or phenomenon that is pervasive in the social world.

This merits brief explanation. If you, for instance, want to study reinforcement of expectations among soldiers in an army platoon, you will want to read what you can about reinforcement of expectations in corporations, hospitals, schools, and gangs. Even if reinforcement occurs differently in different kinds of settings, as one might expect, there is a lot to learn from contrast.

By the same token, if you are writing about an army platoon and you are writing for impact, you do not want your audience restricted to military sociologists. You also want people who study corporations, hospitals, schools, and gangs to read your work. The question is, why should they? And the answer is that in framing a theoretically interesting question, for example when looking at reinforcement of expectations in one setting, you should be revealing insights of potential interest to people posing the same or comparable questions in all kinds of other settings. The broad applicability of your work is more likely to be apparent to others if you yourself see your research question as having generic interest. Settling on a question that engages interest in the discipline is a crucial first step in writing for impact. A question can be much more specific than the umbrella questions outlined above, yet can clearly point to an explanatory dynamic that may yield understanding that is pertinent to and potentially generalizable to other settings.

The Second Step in the Scientific Method

The second step in the scientific method is to articulate at least one axiom, or more often a principle, that might help us to explain the kind of variation or change stipulated in the research question. The axioms and principles developed in this book and reviewed in chapter 15 can be an enormous aid in this respect. Whether you use axioms and principles in the form they appear in this book or modify their wording in an effort to develop and test your own version, having clearly written and plausible theoretical premises that are broadly applicable to many settings makes studying them worthwhile.

The Third Step in the Scientific Method

The third step in the scientific method is to articulate hypotheses. Research hypotheses usually take the form of testable predictions that (other things being equal) should be true if the axiom or principle being tested is correct, and should be false if the axiom or principle being tested is either generally incorrect or fails to apply in the kind of settings from which our data is drawn. Having specifically worded axioms and/or principles to begin with allows us to make specific predictions. We arrive at research hypotheses when we predict that outcomes that should be observable in certain settings and under specified circumstances, if our axioms and principles really apply to such phenomena in those kinds of settings and under the specified circumstances.

Linking research hypotheses to theoretical axioms and/or principles is easy and is an essential step in good research. But this research step is often sidestepped. Spinning hypotheses is undisciplined inquiry unless those hypotheses are connected in a clear and transparent way to theoretical premises we want to test—"a hypothesis doth not a theory make." It is important to always recognize that a study is, at least in scientific terms, more appropriately understood as a test of theoretical principles and processes than as a description of a particular setting. Studying a setting or a data set, in science, is a means to an end rather than an end it itself. Science cares about progressive improvement in our body of explanatory principles.

A component of good science practice is a process for arriving at research hypotheses. This process provides a lot of guidance and direction. Simply ask one question: What is an outcome or pattern (a) that would be clearly measurable, (b) that we should expect to see if our axioms and/or principles (from the second step of the research method) apply, and (c) that we should expect not to see if those axioms and principles do fail to apply in this setting and under these circumstances? A researcher who can answer each component part of this question has arrived at a good research hypothesis.

The Fourth Step in the Scientific Method

The fourth step in the scientific method is to test research hypotheses. One of the essential and indispensable characteristics of scientific research is that it should be possible for a research hypothesis to be disconfirmed.

The Final Step in the Scientific Method

For a social science professional, research usually involves making a contribution that goes beyond description, to enhance our understanding of the ways change occurs and/or differences develop. Writing successfully in a science is contingent on arriving at a professional's awareness of the goal of research.

The tough question at the end of the process is this: what has been contributed to the advancement of science? Following the lessons of this book, this tough question should only have one of three possible answers, and each of them is a good answer from the standpoint of writing for impact in the social sciences. Members of the scientific community like all three of these answers. Whichever of these three outcomes is the end result of a research project is *the theoretical significance of the project.*

One possible outcome is that you find exactly want you expect to find. Science rejoices in this kind of result. With the addition of one more piece of confirmatory research, the scientific community gains more confidence in the axioms or principles tested. If the research is a replication (same setting or data set, research conducted in the same way), the replication validates and supports our confidence in past findings. This has real value in a science, and that value is more easily conveyed to others by referring to the research question and the axiom(s) and/or principle(s) tested. But social science research is rarely precise replication. If, as is common, the research setting or data set or specific research design differs at all from past work, then confirmation of a research hypothesis also enhances the claim that the theoretical axiom(s) or principles(s) are robust. That is, we place more value on theoretical insights and have more confidence in them when we find that our insights are more robust in the sense that they seem to apply in more settings or under a wider range of circumstances.

The second of three outcomes that are possible when the scientific method is followed carefully is rejecting the research hypothesis and going on to suggest ways of changing our axioms or principles so that they comport more closely with observable reality. This is, of course, what is most characteristically meant by scientific progress. For the research to be considered science, rejection of the research hypothesis must be a real possibility. When rejecting the research hypothesis is the outcome of a research project, researchers should always ask themselves if the data gives clues about ways our axiom(s) or principle(s) could be rewritten to better comport with what we have observed. Science rejoices in this kind of result, too. What we mean by scientific progress is, after all, increasing the correspondence between our theoretical precepts and what we can observe of the real world. Rejecting a research hypothesis is, therefore, in no way a disappointment or a defeat. In a sense, it is precisely what scientists try to do. It is when scientists find that the explanations they had been using are not in accord with observable reality that scientists really get enthused, because this means there is a theoretical breakthrough waiting to be discovered. And having formally articulated the axiom(s) or principle(s) being tested makes it far easier to offer alternatives and to clearly communicate the difference between the theoretical understanding we had when we posed the research hypothesis and the revised theoretical understanding we offer after having considered the theoretical implications of rejecting the research hypothesis. When communicating with a wider audience, we want to be as specific as possible about the way our current theoretical understanding differs from, and what it adds to, the conventional disciplinary wisdom prior to completion of your research: conventional wisdom that was captured by our axioms and principles and made manifest by the research hypothesis which has now been rejected.

There is a third possible outcome when the scientific method is followed carefully. The third, as discussed, is that we confirm prior theoretical understandings, often substantiating the robustness of our axioms and principles in the process. The second is that we modify our axioms or principles, offering an alternative version that comports better with observable data. But there is a third option, and this involves contributing to a more accurate specification of limiting conditions. This happens when a researcher rejects a research hypothesis but has no idea how to improve on axiom(s) or principle(s) except to say that they did not apply. Again, science rejoices in this kind of result. It suggests that the theoretical premises, if accurate at all, definitely apply to a more narrow range of phenomena or settings than had been previously thought. Thus, this kind of result helps establish the *boundary conditions* for theoretical premises by helping set more clear parameters on the range of events the axiom(s) or principle(s) can inform us about. Helping determine a more accurate set of boundary conditions for a theory is one of the important ways researchers make valuable contributions to science.

By the time a research process is complete, the question that other scientists will ask is, what have you contributed to the advancement of science? This tough question does indeed have a good answer for anyone following the scientific method in his or her work. Working in ways that are consistent with the lessons of this book should make it easy for a person to make a valid claim about what any careful investigative effort contributes of theoretical significance to the current state of social science understanding. Research incorporating theory as discussed here will have an easier time producing works that contributes to the advancement of the social sciences. Importantly, researchers incorporating theory as discussed in *Making Sense of Social Theory* should also have an easier time describing the theoretical and scientific merits of their work. Following the scientific path suggested by this book means (a) starting with a research question that excites wide disciplinary interest, (b) offering clearly articulated theoretical insights (c) as the foundation for testable research hypotheses, (d) being careful in research design and data collection, and then (e) reflecting on what the data have to tell us in our quest for robust and powerful theoretical explanation of differences or change. The three possible outcomes are validating an initial theoretical approach, offering modifications to an initial theoretical approach, or setting tighter boundary conditions on an initial theoretical approach. Each of these possible outcomes constitutes a meaningful contribution to scientific discourse.

Avoiding Some Common Mistakes

Good research papers begin with short abstracts of about four sentences in length. The purpose of an abstract is to let readers know what setting or data will be examined in the paper and to identify the key theoretical premise tested in the paper. The final version of an abstract, after research is complete, needs to state the research finding (acceptance or rejection of the key research hypothesis) and should briefly indicate the theoretical significance of the finding (replicates, suggests robustness, suggests grounds for modifying an established theoretical premise, or helps establish boundary conditions for an established theoretical premise). An abstract that fails to do these things, and/or that distracts readers with other things, does not provide a good start when one is trying to write for social science impact.

When writing for impact in science, it is essential to try to locate your inquiry along a frontier of knowledge where (1) the things you and everyone else believe to be true collide with (2) what the people in your discipline are unable to explain or perhaps need more confirmation about. Locating your inquiry along a discipline's frontier of knowledge is usually accomplished in a literature review. (a) A literature review is not an annotated bibliography. That is, it is *not* a sequential listing of things that have been read, with an attempt at a brief but accurate summary of the works covered. When writing a "literature review" it is consequently unwise to follow the typical "book review" approach focusing on the intent of the author of the work being reviewed and straining for accurate summary. (b) By the time the final version of a scientific paper is being prepared, the author's treatment of the literature should have moved past simple summary of others and on to thematic development, borrowing selectively as dictated by the purpose of the research, which in science is to improve on and move beyond rather than restrict ourselves to summary repetition of what was done in the past. A literature review should always locate the researcher's work along a frontier of scientific inquiry. What is already known? Relative to earlier work, what does this paper seek to add? A literature review should make the answer to these questions apparent.

Many authors of research papers write with the assumption that readers already know things about the project. That is not a good assumption to make when writing for impact in a science. Authors who write as if readers already have knowledge of the specific project are not writing for the professional audience at large. Part of the art of writing for impact in the sciences is to learn to write with strangers in mind; you are writing for experts, but experts who do not know you.

The professional research paper is not a novel and should not provide a linear review of every misstep taken. The art of writing a novel is one of having readers reexperience the author's own discovery process. But in a social science research paper the key empirical findings and interpretive contributions are what matter. If digressions are included at all, they should be located in endnotes. Editing a strong paper typically involves a good deal of pruning to cut back sprawling paper content that will distract readers or even confuse them about your main point. When writing for impact in the sciences, it is important to get past the diary approach of wanting to report on all the dead ends that were eventually bypassed, because doing so runs the risk of obscuring what was done, what was discovered, and what the author has concluded are the important lessons to derive from the study. In sociology, the disciplinary convention is to use footnotes to insert material that may support but do not directly develop the main line of argumentation.

In science, good research is theoretically grounded. This means theory should help us generate verifiable predictions that should be true if our theoretical premises are accurate. The purpose of the theory section of a paper is to develop explanations and clarify why testing those explanations might be theoretically useful in helping advance the way people in the discipline understand the world around them. No matter what methodology is used, social science research writing projects should, at least on a conceptual level, raise the question of generalizability.

It is common to desperately want to find whatever we may have initially predicted in our research hypotheses. When confirmation of the research hypothesis is the outcome, the theoretical model used to make the prediction is validated, but by considering the precise nature of the findings we may be able to add to our understanding in important ways. To realize this, it helps to ask a particular set of questions: How fast does the process work? Are there threshold effects? Do identifiable factors speed up or slow down the process? It is also important to remember that when unexpected findings emerge, professionals with a scientific orientation have something genuinely exciting to report. Data that are inconsistent with well-reasoned theoretical predictions should raise questions about the accuracy of the theory, and this opens the door for making a significant social science contribution by rethinking and revising axioms and principles, and/or by identifying boundary areas between places and phenomena where the premises tested do an do not apply. The fundamental lesson is very important. Whatever the findings, when testing axioms and principles that have proved useful to others in the past, both confirming and disconfirming evidence are meaningfully interpretable. At the risk of being repetitive, we recall that when the scientific method is followed carefully in sociology, we can interpret and gain meaningful insight from carefully gathered data, whether the results confirm or disconfirm the initial research hypothesis.

Ethics are important. Sociology's ethics code prohibits sociologists from tricking, threatening, embarrassing, or compelling people into participation as research subjects. Sociologists are also careful not to reveal identities or divulge confidences. We try very hard not to make people feel bad in any way. And we never knowingly expose people to risk of harm or ridicule.

Writing is usually judged according to the conventions of the profession, even on stylistic matters. Thus it is best to adhere to the style and conventions normally used in the discipline. One should, for example, always use the citation and referencing style most appropriate for the audience. In sociology, the *American Sociological Review* can be looked to for one of the discipline's set of style standards. There are, of course, many good publishing outlines (different book-publishing companies and different journals) in sociology, and the citation and referencing styles they employ are not all the same. Also, citation and references format and other style standards do change over time. In fact, small changes are introduced rather frequently. This means it may be necessary to carefully examine recent issues of a particular journal or recent books from a particular publishing house if questions are raised about the most current style standards for a particular publication.

People writing for professional impact need to pay a lot of attention to "harmonizing" different parts of the paper. For example, make sure that the names and labels used for variables in the beginning of the paper are still being used for the same variables at the end of the paper. Inconsistencies in language should be corrected and any logical gaps in the analysis should be filled during frequent bouts of editing and rewriting. Writing for impact requires a lot of editing and rewriting. Make sure it is clear how interpretive claims are supported by data.

Editing takes time and often feels anticlimactic, but it is necessary to do it when writing for impact.

Recap

Making Sense of Social Theory offers a theoretical tool kit of twelve axioms and twenty-one principles that can be used for better understanding the social world. Translated into axioms and principles, sociology's theoretical knowledge is relatively clear, robust, and powerful. As a body of work, it is far reaching and captures greater coherence of understanding and approach than people sometimes attribute to the social sciences. *Making Sense of Social Theory* lays out clear steps every social science researcher can take in order to be directly engaged in disciplinary discussion and, potentially, contribute in meaningful ways to improvement in and advancement of social science understanding. It is apparent that appreciating this path to social science development provides a method for bridging divides between different metatheoretical perspectives within sociology as a single discipline and even the theoretical divides between different social science disciplines. While narrowness of focus is necessary when conducting research, unnecessary isolation of theoretical insight is artificial and counterproductive. Theory construction strategies involving formalization of axioms and principles is a reliable technique for making progress toward clearer, more robust, more powerful theory, and for doing so by taking incremental steps with each research project.

Following the approaches outlined in this book, you will know that as a person with social science training, you have a great deal of useful social science insight at your disposal. And when you have new experiences or complete research endeavors, you will be not only more conscious about what you are learning, but also better able to express the distinctive quality of your own analysis and your contribution to disciplinary advancement and to science.

Postscript

IT IS CENTRAL TO THE VITALITY OF SOCIOLOGY as a science that people entering the field need to be open to the possibility of fruitful knowledge growth through theoretically grounded inquiry. This book is not alone in pressing that claim. But in comparison with other theory books, this one more clearly and consistently makes the case that theory should be understood with reference to its role in the research process. It is by strengthening the connection between theoretical effort and research activity that sociology will make the fastest progress as a science, that sociological insights will be made most accessible to practitioners, that gaps between the theoretical perspectives will be reduced, and that the mutually informative nature of all the social sciences will be most fully realized.

Invitation to Further Dialogue

S CIENCE BEGINS AND ENDS WITH THEORY. I welcome exchange of ideas with others interested in discussing ways of improving the accuracy, clarity, and power of sociology's axioms and principles. Readers are invited to e-mail me at cpowers@scu .edu or to write to Charles Powers, Department of Sociology, Santa Clara University, Santa Clara, CA 95053-0261

Notes

Part I

1. Jonathan Turner, *The Structure of Sociological Theory*, 7th ed. (Belmont, CA: Wadsworth, 2002).

Chapter 1

1. Robert K. Merton, *Social Theory and Social Structure* (Glencoe, IL: Free Press, 1968).

2. Georg Simmel, *Conflict and the Web of Group Affiliations* (1908; repr., New York: Free Press, 1968).

3. Peter Blau and Otis Duncan, *The American Occupational Structure* (New York: Wiley, 1967).

4. Keith Basso, *Portraits of "THE WHITEMAN": Linguistic Play and Cultural Symbols among the Western Apache* (New York: Cambridge University Press, 1979).

5. Dora Cost and Matthew Kahn, *Heroes and Cowards: The Social Face of War* (Princeton, NJ: Princeton University Press, 2009).

Chapter 2

1. William I. Thomas, *The Unadjusted Girl* (Boston: Little, Brown, 1923).

2. Edwin Lemert, *Social Pathology* (New York: McGraw-Hill, 1951).

3. George Homans, *Social Behavior: Its Elementary Forms*, 2nd ed. (New York: Harcourt, Brace, Jovanovich, 1974), 43.

4. Homans, *Social Behavior*, 37.

Chapter 3

1. George Homans, *The Human Group* (New York: Harcourt Brace, 1950).

2. Georg Simmel, *Conflict and the Web of Group Affiliations* (1908; repr., New York: Free Press, 1955).

3. Guillermina Jasso, "A New Unified Theory of Sociobehavioral Process," *European Review of Sociology* 24, no. 4 (Sept. 2008): 411–34.

4. Vilfredo Pareto, *The Transformation of Democracy* (1921; repr., New Brunswick, NJ: Transaction, 1984).

5. Max Weber, *The Methodology of the Social Sciences* (New York: Free Press, 1949).

6. Jean-François Lyotard, *The Postmodern Condition* (Minneapolis: University of Minnesota Press, 1984).

7. Harold Garfinkel, *Studies in Ethnomethodology* (Englewood Cliffs, NJ: Prentice Hall, 1967).

8. Jack Whalen and Geoff Raymond, "Conversational Analysis," in *The Encyclopedia of Sociology*, 2nd ed., ed. Edgar Borgatta and Rhonda Montgomery. (New York: Macmillan, 2000), 431–41.

Chapter 4

1. Steven Johnson, *The Ghost Map* (New York: Riverhead Books, 2006).

2. William I. Thomas and Florian Znaniecki, *The Polish Peasant in Europe and America* (Urbana: University of Illinois Press, 1918).

3. Louis Wirth, *The Ghetto* (Chicago: University of Chicago Press, 1928); Robert Park and Herbert Miller, *Old World Traits Transplanted* (New York: Harper & Row, 1921). William I. Thomas authored major portions of this work, but he is not mentioned as a coauthor. At the time the book was being readied for publication, Thomas had some bad press relating to events in his personal life. Thomas did not want his association with the book to slow its release. People in the sociological community understood this at the time.

4. Ivan Light, *Ethnic Enterprise in America* (Berkeley: University of California Press, 1972).

5. W. E. B. Du Bois, *The Philadelphia Negro* (1899; repr., New York: Schocken, 1967).

6. Nels Anderson, *The Hobo: The Sociology of the Homeless Man* (Chicago: University of Chicago Press, 1923).

7. Paul Cressey, *The Taxi-Dance Hall* (Chicago: University of Chicago Press, 1932).

8. Alfred Lindesmith, *Addiction and Opiates* (Chicago: Aldine, 1968).

9. Robert Park, Ernest Burgess, and Roderick McKenzie, *The City* (Chicago: University of Chicago Press, 1925).

Chapter 5

1. Paul Davidson Reynolds, *A Primer in Theory Construction* (Boston: Pearson, 2007). This is an Allyn and Bacon Classics release of a book originally published in 1971 by Bobbs-Merrill.

2. Thomas Kuhn, *The Structure of Scientific Revolutions* (Chicago: University of Chicago Press, 1962).

3. For an excellent collection of papers, each attempting formal theory construction from a different theoretical perspective, see the *Humboldt Journal of Social Relations* 7 (Fall/Winter 1980) special issue on theory edited by Jonathan Turner.

4. Robert Dubin, *Theory Building*, rev. ed. (New York: Free Press, 1978).

5. Kathy Charmaz, *Constructing Grounded Theory* (Thousand Oaks, CA: Sage, 2006).

Chapter 6

1. Adam Smith, *The Wealth of Nations* (1776; repr., New York: Irwin, 1963).

2. Charles Powers, "Bridging the Conceptual Gap between Economics and Sociology," *Journal of Socio-Economics* 25, no. 2 (June 1996): 225–43.

3. Jerald Hage and Charles Powers, *Post-Industrial Lives* (Thousand Oaks, CA: Sage, 1992).

4. Herbert Spencer, *Herbert Spencer: Structure, Function, and Evolution*, ed. Stanislav Andreski (London: Michael Joseph, 1971).

5. Thorstein Veblen, *The Theory of the Leisure Class* (1899; repr., New York: New American Library, 1953).

6. Vilfredo Pareto, *The Transformation of Democracy* (New Brunswick, NJ: Transaction, 1984).

7. Oliver Williamson, *Markets and Hierarchies* (New York: Free Press, 1975).

8. Manuel Castells, *The Rise of the Network Society* (Malden, MA: Blackwell, 1996).

9. Herbert Hans, *The Urban Villagers* (Glencoe, IL: Free Press, 1962).

10. Ronald Coase, "The Nature of the Firm," *Economica*, no. 4 (November 1937): 386–405.

Chapter 7

1. Auguste Comte, *The Positive Philosophy of Auguste Comte* (1854; repr., London: Bell and Sons, 1896).

2. Émile Durkheim, *Rules of Sociological Method* (1895; repr., New York: Free Press, 1982), chap. 1.

3. Erving Goffman, *Asylums* (New York: Doubleday, 1961).

4. Émile Durkheim, *The Division of Labor in Society* (1893; repr., New York: Free Press, 1964).

5. Émile Durkheim, *The Elementary Forms of Religious Life* (1912; repr., New York: Free Press, 1951).

6. William Goode, *The Celebration of Heroes: Prestige and Social Control* (Berkeley: University of California Press, 1978).

7. Émile Durkheim, *Suicide* (1897; repr., New York: Free Press, 1951).

8. Bronislaw Malinowski, *Argonauts of the Western Pacific* (New York: Dutton, 1922).

Chapter 8

1. Friedrich Engels, *The Origin of the Family, Private Property, and the State* (1844; repr., New York: International, 1972).
2. Karl Marx, *Capital* (1867; repr., New York: International, 1967).
3. Richard Appelbaum, "Marx's Theory of the Falling Rate of Profit: Toward a Dialectical Analysis of Structural Social Change," *American Sociological Review* 43, no. 1 (February 1978): 67–80.
4. Karl Marx and Friedrich Engels, *The Communist Manifesto* (1848; repr., Northbrook, IL: AMH, 1955).

Chapter 9

1. Richard Mulcahy, *The Economics of Heinrich Pesch* (New York: Holt, 1952).
2. Stephen Kalberg, *Max Weber's Comparative-Historical Sociology* (Chicago: University of Chicago Press, 1994).
3. Max Weber, *From Max Weber*, ed. Hans Gerth and C. Wright Mills (New York: Oxford University Press, 1946).
4. Tony Waters, *Bureaucratizing the Good Samaritan: The Limitations of Humanitarian Relief Operations* (Boulder, CO: Westview, 2001).
5. Max Weber, *The Protestant Ethic and the Spirit of Capitalism* (1904–1905; repr., New York: Scribner, 1930).
6. Randall Collins, "Weber's Last Theory of Capitalism: A Systemization," *American Sociological Review* 46, no. 6 (December 1980): 925–42.

Chapter 10

1. Charles Horton Cooley, *Human Nature and the Social Order* (New York: Scribner, 1902).
2. Peter Burke and Jan Stets, *Identity Theory: Overview and Future Directions* (New York: Oxford University Press, 2009).
3. George Herbert Mead, *Mind, Self, and Society* (Chicago: University of Chicago Press, 1934).
4. Arlie Hochschild, *The Second Shift: Families and the Revolution at Home* (New York: Viking, 1989).

Chapter 11

1. Vilfredo Pareto, *The Transformation of Democracy* (New Brunswick, NJ: Transaction, 1984).
2. Barbara Heyl, "The Harvard 'Pareto Circle,'" *Journal of the History of the Behavioral Sciences* 4, no. 4 (October 1968): 316–34.

3. Talcott Parsons, *The Social System* (New York: Free Press, 1951).

4. Robert K. Merton, *Social Theory and Social Structure* (Glencoe, IL: Free Press, 1968).

5. Talcott Parsons, *The Structure of Social Action* (New York: McGraw-Hill, 1937).

6. Talcott Parsons, *Societies: Evolutionary and Comparative Perspectives* (Englewood Cliffs, NJ: Prentice Hall, 1966).

7. Talcott Parsons and Gerald Platt, *The American University* (Cambridge, MA: Harvard University Press, 1973).

8. Gunnar Myrdal, *An American Dilemma* (New York: Harper & Row, 1944).

9. Philip Selznick, *TVA and the Grass Roots* (Berkeley: University of California Press, 1949).

Chapter 12

1. Robert Lynd and Helen Merrell Lynd, *Middletown in Transition* (New York: Harcourt Brace, 1937).

2. C. Wright Mills, *The Power Elite* (New York: Oxford University Press, 1956).

3. William Domhoff, *The Bohemian Grove and Other Retreats* (New York: Harper & Row, 1974).

4. Floyd Hunter, *Community Power Structure* (Chapel Hill: University of North Carolina Press, 1953).

5. Robert Dahl, *Who Governs?* (New Haven, CT: Yale University Press, 1961).

6. Karl Marx and Friedrich Engels, *The Communist Manifesto* (1848; repr., Northbrook, IL: AMH, 1955).

7. Erik Wright, *Class, Crisis, and the State* (London: New Left, 1978).

8. Pierre Bourdieu and Jean-Claude Passeron, *Reproduction in Education, Society, and Culture* (Beverly Hills, CA: Sage, 1977).

9. Nicos Poulantzas, *State, Power, and Socialism* (London: New Left, 1979).

10. Melvin Gurtov and Ray Maghroori, *The Roots of Failure: United States Foreign Policy in the Third World* (Westport, CT: Greenwood, 1984).

11. Theda Skocpol, *States and Social Revolutions* (New York: Cambridge University Press, 1979).

12. Lewis Coser, *The Functions of Social Conflict* (New York: Free Press, 1956).

13. Ralf Dahrendorf, *Class and Class Conflict in Industrial Society* (Stanford, CA: Stanford University Press, 1959).

14. Theodore Caplow, *Two Against One: Coalitions in Triads* (Englewood Cliffs, NJ: Prentice Hall, 1986).

15. Andre Gunder Frank, *Capitalism and Underdevelopment in Latin America* (New York: Monthly Review Press, 1967).

16. Immanuel Wallerstein, *The Modern World System*, 2 vols. (New York: Academic, 1974, 1980).

17. Fernando Cardoso, *Charting a New Course: The Politics of Globalization and Social Transformation* (Lanham, MD: Rowman & Littlefield, 2001).

18. Randall Collins, *The Credential Society* (New York: Academic, 1978).

Chapter 13

1. George Herbert Mead, *Mind, Self, and Society* (Chicago: University of Chicago Press, 1934).

2. Jerald Hage and Charles Powers, *Post-Industrial Lives* (Thousand Oaks, CA: Sage, 1992).

3. Tamotsu Shibutani, *The Derelicts of Company K* (Berkeley: University of California Press, 1978).

4. Herbert Blumer, *Symbolic Interactionism* (Englewood Cliffs, NJ: Prentice Hall, 1969).

5. Hage and Powers, *Post-Industrial Lives*, 132.

6. Mead, *Mind, Self, and Society*.

7. Manford Kuhn and Thomas McPhartland, "An Empirical Investigation of Self Attitudes," *American Sociological Review* 19, no. 1 (February 1954): 68–76.

8. Peter Burke and Jan Stets, *Identity Theory: Overview and Future Directions* (New York: Oxford University Press, 2009).

9. David Heise, *Understanding Events* (New York: Cambridge University Press, 1979).

10. Erving Goffman, *The Presentation of Self in Everyday Life* (New York: Doubleday, 1959).

11. Eugene Weinstein and Paul Deutschberger, "Some Dimensions of Alter-casting," *Sociometry* 26 (1963): 454–66.

12. Peter Berger and Thomas Luchmann, *The Social Construction of Reality* (New York: Doubleday, 1967).

13. Louis Zurcher, *Social Roles* (Beverly Hills, CA: Sage, 1983).

14. Ralph Turner, "Role Change," *Annual Review of Sociology* 16 (1990): 87–110.

15. William Goode, "A Theory of Role Strain," *American Sociological Review* 25 (1960): 483–96.

16. Arlie Hochschild, *The Time Bind: When Work Becomes Home and Home Becomes Work* (New York: Holt, 1997).

17. Hage and Powers, *Post-Industrial Lives*, 211–15.

Chapter 14

1. Alvin Gouldner, "The Norm of Reciprocity: A Preliminary Statement," *American Sociological Review* 25, no. 4 (April 1960): 161–77.

2. Linda Molm, Jessica Collett, and David Schaefer, "Building Solidarity through Generalized Exchange: A Theory of Reciprocity," *American Journal of Sociology* 113, no. 1 (July 2007): 205–42.

3. Émile Durkheim, *The Elementary Forms of Religious Life* (1912; repr., New York: Free Press, 1954).

4. Siegfried F. Nadel, *The Theory of Social Structure* (London: Cohen and West, 1956).

5. Bronislaw Malinowski, *Argonauts of the Western Pacific* (1922; repr., New York: Dutton, 1950).

6. Marcel Mauss, *The Gift* (1925; repr., New York: Norton, 1967).

7. Theodore Caplow, "Christmas Gifts and Kin Networks," *American Sociological Review* 47, no. 3 (June 1982): 383–92.

8. George Homans, *Social Behavior: Its Elementary Forms*, 2nd ed. (New York: Harcourt, Brace, Jovanovich, 1974).

9. Peter Berger, *The Sacred Canopy: Elements of a Sociological Theory of Religion*, 2nd ed. (New York: Random House, 1990).

10. Larry Iannaccone, "Why Strict Churches Are Strong," *American Journal of Sociology* 99, no. 5 (March 1994): 1180–1211.

11. Homans, *Social Behavior*.

12. John Harsanyi and Reinhard Selten, *A General Theory of Equilibrium in Games and Social Situations* (Cambridge: Cambridge University Press, 1977).

13. Richard Emerson, "Power-Dependence Relations," *American Sociological Review* 27, no. 1 (February 1962): 31–41.

14. Linda Molm and Karen Cook, "Social Exchange Networks," in *Sociological Perspectives on Social Psychology*, ed. K. Cook, G. Fine, and J. House (Boston: Allyn & Bacon, 1995).

15. Charles Powers, "Clarification and Extension of Emerson and Cook's Exchange Theory," *Sociological Theory* 3, no. 2 (Fall 1985): 58–65.

16. Mark Granovetter, "The Strength of Weak Ties," *American Journal of Sociology* 78, no. 6 (May 1973): 1360–89.

17. See David Willer and Bo Anderson, eds., *Networks, Exchange, and Coercion* (New York: Elsevier, 1981).

18. Michael Hechter, *Principles of Group Solidarity* (Berkeley: University of California Press, 1987).

Quiz Answers

Chapter 1

1. science
2. d
3. b
4. d
5. a, b, and c, but not d
6. c

Chapter 2

1. a
2. d
3. d
4. b
5. b

Chapter 3

1. Focus on differences or changes to be explained; advance a principle that might explain that difference or change; identify one or more research hypotheses that could be used to test the principle; test the research

hypotheses using real-world information; use results in order to rethink and improve on the original theoretical explanation.

2. Simmel's *Conflict/Cohesion Principle:* Other things being equal, cohesion within groups or other social entities increases as a function of the degree of conflict between those entities.

3. b
4. c
5. b

Chapter 4

1. a reign of terror similar to that experienced during the French Revolution
2. a–ii; b–iii; c–i
3. The Selective Retention Axiom tells us that people retain traditional beliefs and practices in the modified form that helps them best adjust to changing conditions.

Chapter 5

1. Theory construction is formal when key elements are written out and are written clearly enough that different readers will arrive at essentially the same understanding of what is written.
2. Formal theory construction need not take many words, but it should present the research question, identify and define the most important concepts used, stipulate any axiomatic assumptions key to the work, and identify any predictive principle(s) to be tested.

Chapter 6

1. The characteristics of a perfect market are that (1) people must be engaged in exchange that we can at least loosely conceptualize as having "buyers" and "sellers" or traders engaging in discrete transactions (that is, where who you trade with today is not determined by who you traded with last week); (2) there must be freedom of choice, so that each buyer/seller/trader can decide whom, if anyone, it makes the most rational sense to trade with at this given point in time; (3) there must be many potential exchange partners, so that freedom of choice is real; and (4) "barriers" to entry and exit must be minimal.

2. *Principle of Evolution:* Other things being equal, the rate at which social units differentiate from one another is (1) a direct function of their isolation and (2) an inverse function of their size. *Globalization reduces cultural heterogeneity.*

3. *Uncertainty Principle of Hierarchy:* Other things being equal, the greater the risk of uncertainty implicit in market solutions, the more cost effective market solutions need to be in order to make them rational in comparison with hierarchy as a mode of organization. *Thus, uncertainty raises the value of hierarchical organizing strategies.*

Chapter 7

1. Auguste Comte
2. Harriet Martineau
3. a. Growing interdependence because of specialized division of labor
    b. Legal institutions that regulate ever-wider realms of interaction
    c. Occupational subgroup formation

Chapter 8

1. *Marx's Principle of Intergroup Conflict:* Other things being equal, the degree to which intergroup antagonism is likely to manifest itself in organized conflict is a function of (a) how much homogeneity there is within groups and how much inequality there is separating groups, (b) how much historical or symbolic unity there is within each group and how little historical or symbolic unity there is between groups, (c) how much mobility and communication there is within groups and how little there is between groups, and (d) how often resource competition coincides with differences in group membership.

2. Marx's axiomatic assumptions left him convinced that societal arrangements through which people are exploited cannot really be reformed but must instead be destroyed. This view restricted his theoretical horizons to trying to understand how revolutionaries could be mobilized rather than trying to understand how social structural arrangements could be reformed.

3. For Marx, class is defined as a person's position within the wage-labor system that structures social relationships of production in capitalist industrial societies.

Chapter 9

1. b
2. traditional, charismatic, and rational-legal
3. hierarchical chain of command, functional division of labor, hiring based on training rather than nepotism, decisions made according to a system of codified and uniformly applied rules, and records as property of office rather than of officeholders
4. *Weber's Values Axiom:* As a system of values becomes more deeply embedded and more uniformly held by people in a society, common social roles and widely institutionalized systems of rules are progressively modified in ways that manifest and maximize adherence to core values.

Chapter 10

1. How do people manage to adjust to one another effectively?
2. a–ii; b–i
3. *Self-concept* is our sense of our own qualities as individual people. *Identity* refers to group memberships that are inescapably important, usually because they matter so much to others that they dictate how the world responds to us.
4. The process of symbolic interaction people work through as they adjust to others involves:
   a. reading gestures
   b. role taking
   c. taking stock of the self
   d. imaginative rehearsal
   e. adjusted response

Chapter 11

1. Structure changes when functional problems magnify. And the structural forms that evolve help meet system needs.
2. Evolutionary patterns of structural change:

   role upgrading
   structural differentiation
   inclusion
   value generalization

3. Structural functionalists believe that structural change should be expected either (a) as a solution-oriented response to new or changing problems, or (b) as a response to structural strain, when there is a lack of alignment between different aspects of systems structure.

Chapter 12

1. If the axioms in chapter 12 are correct, established power should not be expected to be capable of genuinely reforming itself in the interest of alleviating inequality. This is why people who share the assumptions common to conflict theory tend to have a combative orientation toward centers of power. When established power does work to reduce inequality, it tends to be interpreted as a part of a broad strategy for perpetuating exploitation. For example, providing people with extended unemployment benefits during an economic downturn could be easily interpreted, from a conflict perspective, as a crafty effort to maintain the legitimacy of the system that caused the problem.
2. When the level of concentration of economic control and human capital is greatest (see the *Pluralism Principle*).
3. three

Chapter 13

1. Chicago and Iowa are both about coconstructed change. Impression management and alter-casting, on which dramaturgical analysis focuses, are both about a relatively static and fictional image that is projected from a single source rather than cocrafted.
2. Symbolic interactionists of the Iowa school believe that outcomes in social situations are rather predictable because the core self-concepts of people in a situation incline them to interpret and react in particular ways, and this channels outcomes in a certain direction.
3. a. "Identity" refers to group memberships that are inescapably important, usually because they matter so much to others that they dictate how the world responds to us.
   b. "Roles" are rights, obligations, and dignities normally expected of anyone in that particular social position.
4. To the degree that trust is lacking, people will try to escape roles or relationships if they can. If escape is impractical, people will try to precisely define expectations to remove ambiguity.

Chapter 14

1. true
2. true

Index

About the Author

Charles H. Powers is a professor of sociology at Santa Clara University, where he has taught since 1986. His former full-time teaching positions were at Talladega College and at Indiana University. In addition to sociology, Powers has taught business administration and gerontology, and has lectured for executive development programs. His other book publications are *Vilfredo Pareto* (author), *The Transformation of Democracy* (editor), *Post-Industrial Lives* (coauthor), and *The Emergence of Sociological Theory* (coauthor). Powers has also served as coeditor of *Sociological Perspectives*, the scholarly journal of the Pacific Sociological Association. He has a special interest in the study of social change and in the analysis of organizational cultures that foster innovation.